# LOVE YOUR ENEMIES

# LOVE YOUR ENEMIES

## *Discipleship, Pacifism, and Just War Theory*

LISA SOWLE CAHILL

FORTRESS PRESS MINNEAPOLIS

LOVE YOUR ENEMIES
Discipleship, Pacifism, and Just War Theory



Cover design: Peggy Lauritsen Design Group

---

Library of Congress Cataloging-in-Publication Data

Cahill, Lisa Sowle.
Love your enemies : discipleship, pacifism, and just war theory / Lisa Sowle Cahill.
p. cm.
Includes bibliographical references and index.
ISBN 0-8006-2700-8 (alk. paper) :
1. Peace—Religious aspects—Christianity—History of doctrines.
2. War—Religious aspects—Christianity—History of doctrines.
3. War—Religious aspects—Christianity—History of doctrines.
4. Just war doctrine—History. 5. Christian ethics—Catholic authors. I. Title.
BT736.4.C34 1994
261.8'73—dc20 93-35461
CIP

---

The paper used in this publication meets the minimum requirements of American National Standard for Information Sciences—Permanence of Paper for Printed Library Materials, ANSI Z329.48-1984. ∞™

---

Manufactured in the U.S.A. AF 1-2700

4 5 6 7 8 9 10

To my parents:
*Donald E. Sowle*
*Gretchen MacRae Sowle*

# CONTENTS

stance. He also demonstrated that the major figures in the larger Christian tradition constitute an inclusive community of discourse in which Protestants and Catholics alike could find a home.

Himself an heir of the Reformed tradition—Calvin, Jonathan Edwards, and his own mentor H. Richard Niebuhr—Gustafson exhibited a deep admiration not only for Aquinas, but also for the theologically and socially radical stances embraced by Menno Simons and John Howard Yoder. The expectation that a student of Christian ethics would take the Bible seriously, and the full awareness of the hermeneutical and moral challenges that seriousness would present, underlay every class Gustafson taught. This book is another installment in my ongoing attempt to live up to that expectation.

This project is in many ways a daunting one. Its interdisciplinary and historical scope is as problematic as it is necessary in this era of specialization. I have forayed into every historical period since the New Testament, and into biblical scholarship as well. Whatever my own limitations, I have felt that a genuine appreciation of the range of Christian responses to war and peace demands that biblical and historical sources be brought together with contemporary questions. I hope this study will allow readers access to the thought of major figures whose remarks on war and biblical interpretation I have gathered or excavated from diverse sources and quoted directly, often at length.

Because my own interests are theological, I have relied heavily for historical context on the research of other scholars, for instance, James Turner Johnson. His work is prominent among the fine studies already available that examine Christian teaching about war and peace (particularly the development of just war theory) in relation to the social, political, and economic factors that stimulated and shaped it. In several sections of this book I rely on reasonable scholarly consensus in historical and biblical studies, and on the basis of this discern patterns of interpretation within and among the writings of major Christian thinkers as they address pacifism or the just war.

This book stresses the interplay of theological understandings of war-and-peace questions, including nonresistance, nonviolence, coercion, self-defense, just war, and holy war. A formative influence in such theological understandings both in the tradition and today is biblical materials, which call to conversion and discipleship as part of their portrayal of the mission and meaning of Jesus, which begin to indicate both parenetically and prescriptively what discipleship should look like in the life of the Christian individual and community, and which open the clear but disconcerting possibility that converted discipleship presumes the inbreaking of a kingdom in which it is no longer possible to conduct "business as usual." The major motive of this study is to complicate and refine both the historical and the normative sensibilities of the contemporary Christian ethicist who approaches these difficult questions with a view to eventual resolution. Most of all, I want to achieve greater clarity about how the eschatological reign of God and social responsibility meet in Christian discipleship.

I am immensely grateful to the editors and editorial board of *Interpretation: A Journal of Bible and Theology* for giving me a chance to begin to write seriously outside my usual areas of sexual and medical ethics. (It is hard for female Catholic moral theologians to break out of a certain mold.) On behalf of the journal, editors Paul Achtemeier and Jack Dean Kingsbury invited me (thanks to a vote of confidence from board member Charles M. Swezey) to write three essays. The first, "Nonresistance, Defense, Violence, and the Kingdom" (38/4 [1984]: 380–97) is the backbone of the present book. Portions of the others, "The Ethical Implications of the Sermon on the Mount" (41/2 [1987]: 144–56) and "New Testament Ethics: Communities of Social Change" (44/4 [1990]: 383–95) form parts of Chapters 2 and 10. A sabbatical granted to me by Boston College during the 1989–90 academic year allowed me to make the headway I needed on a field of research that seemed sometimes to me so vast as to be untraversible. I owe an exceptional debt to Richard B. Miller, who read my draft manuscript for Fortress Press with extraordinary care, and offered a lengthy and detailed roster of suggestions. An author's dream critic, he refrained from the kind of complaint that is as vague as to the specific remedy as it is devastating to one's thesis, and instead referred to exact page numbers in the many books that he has read and I had not.

Several other fellow theologians gave advice and attentive readings to my work in progress. My colleague at Boston College, Pheme Perkins, has replied generously to impositions on her time, attention, and library and contributed her own invaluable expertise in New Testament ethics. My good friend Anthony Saldarini, also a Boston College New Testament professor, has likewise given counsel out of his own work on sociological approaches to the Bible. Others who have read large and small pieces of this book or the articles preceding it are Charles Carlston, James F. Childress, Patricia De Leeuw, James T. Johnson, John Langan, Stephen Mott, and David Hollenbach. I could not have hoped for more expert critics. My editors at Fortress Press, Marshall Johnson and David Lott, have helped me shape my manuscript into final form, and copy editor Sheryl Strauss has been an asset to my style and precision.

My husband Larry has always been particularly helpful: his repeated "*When* are you going to get it done?" kept in perspective the fact that I had better bring my eight or nine years of intermittent research to closure sometime before the ideas I set out to write about had grown in enough directions to be useless in focusing my concentration on a unified thesis—or before other people had done so much more research that mine would be utterly superfluous to the discussion now proceeding.

In hope that neither of those eventualities has yet come to pass, I submit the present work as a stimulant to further reflection on how the teaching and example of Jesus—his injunction "Love your enemies"—could have given rise both to pacifism and to just war thinking.

I dedicate this study to my parents. My father, Donald E. Sowle, sought sincerely to embody his Roman Catholic faith as he successfully pursued an officer's career in the United States Air Force. My mother, Gretchen MacRae Sowle, who died in 1993, took satisfaction in the fact that she had a child who wrote books. She liked to attach the covers to the side of her refrigerator with magnets.

# 1 PACIFISM OR JUST WAR THINKING?

## *Setting the Stage for the Contemporary Question*

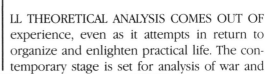

ALL THEORETICAL ANALYSIS COMES OUT OF experience, even as it attempts in return to organize and enlighten practical life. The contemporary stage is set for analysis of war and peace by the two world wars of this century, the Cold War and its nuclear threat, and the continuing prospects of terrorism, revolution, and the armed confrontation of nation-states around the globe. What has Christian social ethics to say to these modern versions of an age-old problem? This question can be answered satisfactorily only on the basis of a historically, theologically, and biblically informed approach, as recent pastoral and policy efforts of the churches have made clear.

Such efforts have attempted to marshal at the practical level the fruits of various traditional understandings of just war theory and Christian pacifism. While church statements have sometimes had a significant impact on the public discussion of war, however, no clear and consistent theological resolution of the issues between the just war and pacifist interpretations of Christian teaching has been achieved. Many Christians and their leaders seem caught on the horns of a "both/and" approach, in which some credence is given both to resort to war and to the renunciation of violence. Does this settle or avoid the theological issues? Are just war thinking and pacifism distinct but complementary answers to the same question? Are they mutually exclusive? Or do common Christian understandings of their meaning and relation require more nuance before such questions can be successfully engaged?

Although one thesis of this book is that "just war" and "pacifism" can each have more than one meaning, they are both generally agreed to arise out of a common concern to avoid violence. Both respond to conflict situations in which some great good can be protected (or evil avoided) only by resorting to violence as a means. Just war theory allows violence under certain conditions but attempts to limit it, both by constricting the valid causes for going to war (for example, defense of the common good, proportionality, last resort, declaration by a legitimate authority, hope of success) and by restraining actions of war (by criteria such as noncombatant immunity and proportionality of specific measures).[1]

Pacifism is more difficult to define in relation to ethics, in that it does not begin so much as an ethical reply to the violence question (as it is often interpreted to do, especially by just war theorists) but as a practical embodiment of a religious conversion experience—as a way of life rather than a theory. Christian pacifism is essentially a commitment to embody communally and historically the kingdom of God so fully that mercy, forgiveness, and compassion preclude the very contemplation of causing physical harm to another person.[2] Pacifists generally are opposed not only to war, but to any form of direct physical violence, although they may make exceptions to this bias by permitting police action. The moral rule that absolutely excludes resort to arms is a secondary consequence of the pacifist conviction, not its focus or zenith. One reason for the Christian tradition's continuing fascination with the just war-pacifist dialectic is that it embodies the ancient and profound problem of reconciling Christian discipleship with public responsibility.

In the 1980s, two mainline ecclesial bodies published much-discussed educational and pastoral documents on war and peacemaking: the Roman Catholic Bishops' *The Challenge of Peace: God's Promise and Our Response*,[3] and the Methodist Bishops' *In Defense of Creation: The Nuclear Crisis and a Just Peace*.[4] Each attempts to give a Christian response to the nuclear arms race, particularly the U.S. policy of nuclear deterrence, from a Christian perspective. Neither episcopal body speaks only to church members. Both address the broader social and political situation, seeking a hearing from policymakers, voters, and citizens in general. Each document appeals to the ideal of peace, couched in biblical terms, and commends pacifism as a way of life, but each also accepts just war theory, using it in fact to bolster a critique of the arms race. Thus the two statements exemplify in different but similar ways the difficulty of interpreting the implications for public or social accountability of the New Testament mandate to love one's enemy as well as one's neighbor. Although the tentative thawing of East-West relations in the late '80s and early '90s seems to have reduced the immediate prospects of a nuclear conflagration, and the superpowers have begun to address the economic disproportion of their massive military expenditures, the threat of

1. See Richard B. Miller, *Interpretations of Conflict: Ethics, Pacifism, and the Just-War Tradition* (Chicago: Univ. of Chicago Press, 1991), 12–15, for a review of just war criteria.

2. This book is essentially about Christian pacifism (and just war thinking), its origin, characteristics, and practical implications. I do not intend to argue, however, that Christianity is necessary to ground all pacifism, or to deny that non-Christian and non-theistic forms of pacifism do exist.

3. Issued by the National Conference of Catholic Bishops in May 1983. Available from the United States Catholic Conference, 1312 Massachusetts Ave. NW, Washington, D.C. 20005.

4. Issued by the United Methodist Council of Bishops in 1986. Available from Graded Press, 201 Eighth Ave. South, P.O. Box 801, Nashville, Tenn. 37202.

war is a perennial moral problem for the citizen and the Christian. For that matter, the threatened use of nuclear weapons around the globe is still hardly negligible.

The authors of the Catholic pastoral letter explicitly offer that "we want it to make a contribution to the wider public debate in our country" about war and peace, and they express awareness that their teaching may even have "consequences . . . not only for the United States but for other nations as well."[5] The broad range of the bishops' intended audience is not surprising, given the "natural law" tradition out of which they speak. This tradition, rooted in Thomas Aquinas's synthesis of Aristotle with Christian—especially Augustinian—thought, is premised on a commitment to an objective moral order, knowable by reason, that yields universal moral laws by which all human persons and communities should abide. This is evident in the human rights language employed in modern papal social teaching, a vocabulary that appears in the peace pastoral also. Catholic natural law ethics is specifically not a "religious" ethics in any way that intentionally marks off Catholic Christian behavior from that of other intelligent and good-willed persons. Scriptural warrants, therefore, are not used to point out a distinctive way of Christian moral living, but are used to support the validity of moral obligations regarded as binding on everyone.

Traditionally, Catholic ethics has been vulnerable to the criticism that the life of committed discipleship has not been taken seriously enough. Is the life of the Christian community reducible to the life of the morally serious pagan? Are "reasonable" moral decisions really enough to define the flavor of a life converted by the cross and resurrection of Christ? Certainly the prospect of Christian use of violence, even in self-defense, makes these questions about the nature of discipleship very pointed. Although certain ambiguous or qualifying biblical texts can be cited (for example, Luke 3:14; Matt. 8:5-13; Rom. 13:1-4; 1 Tim 2:1-2; 1 Pet. 2:13-17), nothing is more clear in the moral message of Jesus than his exhortations to and example of forgiveness, mercy, and meekness in the face of abuse or assault. A central portion of the Sermon on the Mount (Matt. 5:38-48) traditionally has been deemed the "hard sayings" for precisely this reason.

The Roman Catholic pastoral letter endorses the Christian "presumption against war," but also asserts that "every nation has a right and a duty to defend itself against aggression."[6] The letter restates the classic just war criteria (just cause, competent authority, comparative justice, right intention, last resort, probability of success, proportionality, noncombatant immunity[7]) and uses these to explicate the limits to be placed even on justified war. Because it would violate the principles of proportion and noncombatant immunity,

5. *Challenge of Peace*, Summary, ii.
6. Ibid., iii.
7. Ibid., ¶¶85–110, 28-34.

the bishops give a "definitive and decisive" negative answer to nuclear war.[8] They seem to back off slightly when they subsequently express "profound skepticism" about "any use of nuclear weapons," though they make it clear that any use that would "violate the principle of discrimination [between combatants and noncombatants] merits unequivocal condemnation."[9] A focus of the letter is the problem of nuclear deterrence, which the bishops conclude is justified as an interim measure only under strictly limited conditions, particularly that of progress toward bilateral disarmament.[10]

Despite central attention to just war theory, the letter also upholds the value of gospel-based pacifism and of nonviolent means of resisting injustice.

> While the just-war teaching has clearly been in possession for the past 1,500 years of Catholic thought, the "new moment" in which we find ourselves sees the just-war teaching and non-violence as distinct but interdependent methods of evaluating warfare. Both find their roots in the Christian theological tradition; each contributes to the full moral vision we need in pursuit of a human peace.[11]

The last two of the four parts of the letter are devoted to a positive view of peacemaking and of Christian education toward that goal. The fourth part concludes, "Finally, we reaffirm our desire to participate in a common public effort with all men and women of good will who seek to reverse the arms race and secure the peace of the world."[12] It is clear that in the basic perspective of the Catholic bishops, the practical political goals endorsed by Christian teaching are the same goals that should be apparent to the reasonable citizen. Yet to some degree, this presupposition is tenuous, as is the letter's proposal that just war theory and pacifism are complementary. Gospel-based nonviolence and the notion that nations have a right to self-defense seem to have very different, if not opposite, implications for practical moral and political behavior.

The bishops are not unaware of this dilemma. They acknowledge that love of neighbor is a presumption which "binds all Christians," and that love of enemy is the "key test" of neighborly love. Nonetheless, they adopt as "historically and theologically the clearest answer" to the problem of love and violence the position of Augustine that war can be "a tragic remedy for sin in the life of political societies." War can even be understood as a demand of the command of love if used "to restrain evil and protect the innocent." Explaining this response, the letter notes that "Augustine was impressed by the fact and the consequences of sin in history—the 'not yet' dimension of the kingdom."[13]

8. Ibid., ¶138, 43.
9. Ibid., ¶193, 61.
10. Ibid., ¶¶188–191, 59–60.
11. Ibid., ¶¶120–121, 37.
12. Ibid., ¶328, 98.
13. Ibid., ¶¶80–81, 26.

A good deal of attention is devoted in the pastoral to the "eschatological peace" of the kingdom of God.[14] Clearly, a major problem for any Christian theory of just war is the degree to which, first, discipleship entails peacemaking and nonviolence or even nonresistance; and, second, genuine discipleship is a temporal possibility. If true peace is possible only in the kingdom, and if the kingdom is to be fulfilled eschatologically by God's action, what does that mean for Christian life in the world now? Conversely, if Jesus calls his disciples to a converted life, how can the Christian justify any use of violence, even against enemies or in self-defense? Christian just war theory often goes hand-in-hand with an insistence that since the kingdom is not yet fully present, Christian behavior cannot be expected to conform fully to it. Instead, even Christians should deal realistically with the threats to human welfare that sin presents. The authors of *The Challenge of Peace* attempt not to slide into this refuge too quickly. "Jesus proclaimed the reign of God in his words and made it present in his actions. . . . The call to conversion was at the same time an invitation to enter God's reign." The Sermon on the Mount, for example, describes "a new reality" and calls for a way of life marked by forgiveness, love, and mercy. Moreover, because of Jesus' own actions and the gift of his spirit, the words of Jesus cannot remain "an impossible, abstract ideal."[15]

Nonetheless, a section on "Kingdom and History" moves toward a "sober and realistic" view of political life by citing a tension between the reign of God and "its concrete realization in history." Appealing to a familiar characterization of the biblical kingdom symbol, the bishops use the phrase "already but not yet": "we already live in the grace of the kingdom, but it is not yet the completed kingdom."[16] A key statement of the pastoral letter draws together the stress on the futurity of the kingdom, which makes possible just war theory, with the emphasis on natural justice and social order, which makes possible the tradition of "natural law" ethics and its tendency to universalize moral obligation. "In the kingdom of God, peace and justice will be fully realized. *Justice is always the foundation of peace.* In history, efforts to pursue both peace and justice are at times in tension, and the struggle for justice may threaten certain forms of peace."[17]

To make justice prior to peace is, evidently, to make peace provisional in relation to the use of coercion, violent if necessary, in order to create the just or properly balanced human relationships that are the conditions of peace as harmony. Whether any genuine or profound harmony can be established coercively is a further question, not addressed in the pastoral but certainly posed by its critics and by those of just war thinking in general. The Roman Catholic bishops settle forthrightly for a paradox: "we must continue to articulate our belief that love is possible and the only real hope for all human

14. Ibid., ¶27, 9.
15. Ibid., ¶¶44–48, 14–15.
16. Ibid., ¶¶56–58, 18.
17. Ibid., ¶60, 19. My italics.

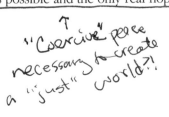

relations, and yet accept that force, even deadly force, is sometimes justified and that nations must provide for their defense."[18] Finally, to the extent that they portray pacifism as aiming at defense of the common good and of human rights,[19] they tend to assimilate pacifism to the natural law just war model, and to overlook the roots of pacifism in a transformative conversion.

The Methodist bishops, emerging from a tradition more solidly based in biblical commitments, are willing to allow a more salient role for the church as witness to a way of social life that may not seem reasonable by cultural standards. To begin with, they offer a "*No*, a clear and unconditioned *No*, to nuclear war and to any use of nuclear weapons."[20] They believe this answer to be demanded by just war theory as well as by depictions of peace as *shalom* in both the Hebrew Scriptures and the New Testament. Moreover, and more importantly, the witnessing role of the church has a much higher profile than it did in the Catholic document.

> The Church of Jesus Christ, in the power and unity of the Holy Spirit, is called to serve as an alternative community to an alienated and fractured world: a loving and peaceable international company of disciples transcending all governments, races, and ideologies, reaching out to all "enemies," ministering to all the victims of poverty and oppression.[21]

The bishops cite the examples of John Wesley, who, although not a pacifist, regarded war as the ultimate example of human depravity, and of prominent Methodist pacifists, as well as of the philosophies of nonviolence of leaders, including Mahatma Gandhi and Martin Luther King, Jr. Although not officially pacifist, the United Methodist Church has adopted a "Social Principles" statement that defines a much more urgent stand against war than Roman Catholicism:

> We believe war is incompatible with the teachings and example of Christ. We therefore reject war as an instrument of national foreign policy and insist that the first moral duty of all nations is to resolve by peaceful means every dispute that arises between or among them."[22]

The witness of the church against war does not imply sectarianism, but a hope for social change through example and education. "Peacemaking is inescapably political. It means changing the policies and perhaps some of the leaders and structures of government."[23] The church is to be the advocate in the political arena for the ideal of *shalom* yielded by the Scriptures.

18. Ibid., ¶78, 25.
19. Ibid., ¶74, 24.
20. *In Defense of Creation*, 13.
21. Ibid., 37.
22. Ibid., 40, quoting the "Social Principles" statement.
23. Ibid., 88.

Yet, although the Methodists give even more attention than the Catholics to the role of the church as peacemaker, they too are loathe to abandon the just war tradition. "We seek to keep the just-war tradition alive, even as we seek to keep the pacifist tradition alive, each serving as a partial but vital testimony to the requirements of justice and peace."[24] In a sense, the tension and paradox of which the earlier document spoke become even more pointed in the Methodist analysis, because the latter has expressed much more confidence in the demand and possibility of kingdom life in history. However, in practice, the theory of the just war is deployed much less extensively and prominently by the Methodist group, and the negative assessments of the nuclear crisis are clear and comprehensive. It can no doubt truly be said of both documents that the gospel commitment to nonviolence has informed the use of just war criteria, so that acceptance of nuclear deterrence as an inevitable ongoing policy was in both cases rejected, even though such a policy enjoyed widespread cultural support. But the Methodist writers—with a more extensive tradition of scriptural foundations and a less extensive tradition of political influence—have tended to make the biblical witness a more prominent factor, and reasonable public discourse a less prominent factor, in their discussion than have the Roman Catholics.

These two letters illustrate a persistent difficulty in Christian thinking about war and peace, and indeed, about all social ethics. What do social responsiblity and love of neighbor mean for the committed Christian individual or community, especially if direction is taken from the New Testament? Some early Christian writers, Reformation thinkers such as Menno Simons, the "historic peace churches," and modern pacifist authors such as H. Richard Niebuhr (at points), Stanley Hauerwas, John Howard Yoder, Dorothy Day, James Douglass, and Gordon Zahn have replied that discipleship permits no compromise with the violence that a sinful world employs to achieve historical ends. These authors are not necessarily sectarian, yet they hold that social change is contingent upon and secondary to fidelity in the life to which Jesus calls.

Others, including just war theory under some version of political "realism," see the kingdom as more distant and the obligation to intervene in present injustice as more pressing. Such authors include Augustine, Aquinas, Luther, Calvin, Reinhold Niebuhr, and some modern Roman Catholic authors such as John Courtney Murray, David Hollenbach, and Bryan Hehir. These thinkers do not necessarily abandon attempts to live in the kingdom as inaugurated in history, but they do see the demands of love as entailing measures that would not be required were the kingdom present in its fullness. These measures can include political coercion, violence, even killing.

The latter is certainly the dominant position in Christian analyses of war and peace today. The Roman Catholic and Methodist bishops' pastoral letters fall into this category. Both manifest the peculiar tension it involves and

24. Ibid., 33.

demonstrate that different emphases within it are possible. Is either the pacifist or the just war perspective adequate, or is one more adequate than the other? Is it possible to give current reflection on these problems more depth by viewing historical precedents, particularly in light of their presuppositions about social life and Christian community, their appeals to Scripture, and their internal coherence? How can concrete moral discipleship be faithful to the gospel's eschatological edge, while coming to terms with demanding and conflictual human relationships? Issues of war, nonviolence, and pacifism as a positive way of life are test cases for these questions.

## THE SCRIPTURES AND THE CHURCH

As authors such as Norman Perrin, Richard Hiers, J. L. Houlden, Wayne Meeks, and Wolfgang Schrage clearly indicate,[25] the Scriptures offer an impetus toward community formation, or rather a living source of reexperience and renewal of the impetus that was provided by the life, death, and resurrection of Jesus. But they do not offer a blueprint for the practical shape of that community, including its moral identity. The fact that the New Testament does include many specific moral directives implies that such are a necessary part of Christian existence. The specific shape of Christian ethics, however, must be defined in subsequent communities as it was in the earliest one, in interaction with concrete human experience and historically available sources of insight. Indeed, these are not somehow outside or in addition to the Christian religious experience, but are formative of the meaning of that experience in any age.

Of course, there has never been any such thing as a theology or ethics that is not rooted in practice. What distinguishes the present theological situation is that this inevitable fact is lifted up consciously and critically as an object of deliberation. In *Biblical Hermeneutics,*[26] J. Severino Croatto notes that each new reading of a text, including the Bible, is a "production of meaning." Although meanings are indefinite in number, a new reading is not entirely free-flowing, but should be linked both to the structure, language, and possibilities of the text itself and to the practices and events that occasion the reading. It is the present practice that is finally determinative of the reading given. Although any reading may claim to appropriate the text—that is, to give the definitive and final reading—this never happens, because of the text's polysemy. Each new reading creates in a sense a new text, against which other readings arise, shaping a tradition of interpretation. Successive readings result in an "*accumulation* of meaning," yielding an ever more rich resource for interpretation.[27] Each new interpretation or "text" occasions new practices,

25. These authors and others will be discussed in more detail in chap. 2.

26. J. Severino Croatto, *Biblical Hermeneutics: Toward a Theory of Reading as the Production of Meaning* (Maryknoll, N.Y.: Orbis, 1987).

27. Ibid., 35.

in a "progressive, enriching movement of the hermeneutic continuum."[28] The Christian tradition of interpreting biblical texts, images, and themes that are relevant to the basic shape of Christian moral discourse, and to particular choices about nonresistance, peacemaking, and using violence, constitutes such an interpretative tradition of accumulated meaning.

## PROGRAMMATIC QUESTIONS

The succeeding chapters of this book will examine the ways in which several influential Christian figures have examined the biblical text on love, peacemaking, and social responsibility. Each chapter will do so from the standpoint of a social, political, and ecclesial practice that shapes the questions asked and the response derived. Not to be neglected is the fact that the cultural praxis from which each reading proceeds includes not only important practical questions about the use of force itself, but also various philosophical or pagan attempts to deal reflectively with what human social life and moral agency in general mean. All Christian biblical interpreters also implicitly or explicitly borrow meaning from earlier interpretations that help mediate the text they understand themselves to be reading. We will approach the figures or groups within this study in such terms as fidelity to the biblical text; use of other readings of it; sensitivity to social and political practice, and to the appropriate Christian (biblical) response to it; and internal consistency in the reading each attempts. For some authors, such as Augustine, we will also explore the ways in which their readings have become important reinterpreted "texts" for later figures in the tradition, shaping the meaning that the latter give both to the biblical accounts and to their own situations. The overarching question of this project is how these figures in the tradition can or should serve as texts for a contemporary understanding of the biblical message (or messages) regarding war and peace, and also regarding discipleship as "already" manifesting the presence of a kingdom that is "not yet" completed.

Despite religious and theological commitments that often differ radically in many other aspects, one common point of loyalty among Christian just war theorists and pacifists is the foundational importance of the Scriptures, especially those texts that seem either to justify or to preclude the resort of nations or Christian persons to violent force. Today we are more aware of the eschatological horizon of New Testament and early Christian thought than were premodern authors. Yet, kingdom symbolism is integral to the New Testament presentation of the gospel, and draws on the promised land and messianic traditions of the Hebrew Scriptures. Thus the eschatological problem has always been a part of Christian thought. A good portion of biblical scholarship since Bultmann has tended to emphasize the *presence* of the

28. Ibid., 65.

kingdom, to make Jesus' apocalyptic message more palatable to modern ears.[29] But mainstream ethical writing about war and peace, both traditional and recent, has defended some form of just war theory, and hence has emphasized the *futurity* of the kingdom—and has used this emphasis to put at various distances the ethical obligations Jesus' gospel preaching implies.

There is another major problem that is more an explicit focus in modern times than previously, but that has nonetheless always been a vital determinant of Christian positions on war and peace. That is how the biblical collection is to be taken as normative, or as canon, an authority for the church. This problem involves at least four distinct questions. (1) How are discrepancies within the Bible to be dealt with if it is the whole that is authoritative? (2) What interpretation is to be given to particular texts that seem to cut against obvious moral commitments? (3) How should the Bible be related to the person's or the community's non-Christian sources of self-understanding or self-definition, such as politics, philosophy, and cultural ethos? (4) Exactly what does discipleship mean as historical practice now? This last returns us to eschatology as that element in a Christian religious world view that not only derives from Scripture, but which also reflects in turn on the way in which scriptural texts and the canon as a whole are to be understood as a norm for practical decision-making. These four subquestions may be addressed in turn.

The rise of historical criticism has led to increased interest in and knowledge about the sociocultural setting in which biblical texts were produced. Thus the first question is today frequently answered with reference to different communal settings and concerns. The conclusion may then be drawn that biblical literature or specific instructions that arise from settings closer to contemporary ones are more authoritative than those whose origins are more dissimilar. Following also from this historical-critical approach is a tendency to answer the second question by relativizing "nonsensical" texts to their original settings. This raises obvious difficulties. Often, contemporary cultural assumptions determine the way in which a given text is used or rejected. A moral exhortation or viewpoint might be argued to be normative "for us," either because it is closer to the original meaning of Jesus or a biblical author or community, or because it is a later and therefore supposedly more "developed" theological response to a more primitive stratum. The evaluative move often originates in a preconviction about the normativeness of, for instance, the submission of women, use of violence, homosexuality, military service, or the universality or particularity of the Christian moral mission. Although the genesis of a text may indeed be relevant to its continuing interpretation and authority, it is crucial to give well-developed religious and theological reasons why a certain point of origin and not others is privileged.

29. Richard H. Hiers, Jr., "Pivotal Reactions to the Eschatological Interpretations: Rudolf Bultmann and C. H. Dodd," in *The Kingdom of God in 20th-Century Interpretation,* ed. Wendell Willis, (Peabody, Mass.: Hendrickson Publishers, 1987), 24.

Traditional authors differ from modern ones in that they tend to assume that all texts can be harmonized, and that the intention of God as inspirer of revelation, the meaning of a text in its context in the Bible, and the normative meaning for subsequent theology are the same. The biblical author's intention was not always separated clearly as an object of study from the intention of God or from the integral meaning of a text considered as such. Nonetheless, theologians in the tradition have been as active in interpreting the Scriptures in terms of levels of authority for ethics as have modern ones. Authors from the patristic period onward rely on theories of the multiple senses of Scripture in order to differentiate among texts that, in their prima facie sense, should be taken as normative for the moral life and those that should not. Premodern authors employ allegory, levels of interpretation, and ingenious constructions of what a biblical author may have had in mind in order to achieve a convergence between the biblical witness and common sense, or the moral ideals that they otherwise accepted. Augustine and others interpret the Bible to conform to the doctrine of the church as it was or as they understood it to be.[30]

In response to the third question, both traditional and modern authors have commonly isolated at least a practical "canon within the canon" as a keystone for interpreting other texts. In so doing, they necessarily have been informed by extrabiblical factors, though these are not necessarily admitted through the front door. The attention of Croatto and others to the importance of praxis in giving direction to a hermeneutical program leads us to see that certain biblical materials may become more important and illuminating than others at different times or in relation to different problems. Because of the extent, complexity, and multivocity of the canon, it hardly seems possible—or even desirable—to incorporate the entirety in reaching a position on every concrete moral issue.

Because the total life situation and praxis of the interpreter mesh many intellectual, moral, aesthetic, and religious strands within a distinctive cultural milieu, the interpretive process will inevitably depend on influences that are not specifically Christian. In the case of war and peace, these will include philosophical analyses of the values of human life and of justice and peace; the rights and duties of the nation-state and the proper handling of conflict situations; the political and economic histories and present situations of those analyzing the problem of violence; as well as the insights, injunctions, and general value perspectives of those religious and moral traditions that shape the world views of the analysts. The question is not whether this intermeshing ought to happen, but how the process can and should be controlled to achieve a balance that is on the whole faithful to the central gospel message: that we are to lay hold of the gift of the kingdom by trust in the love and mercy of

30. G. W. H. Lampe, ed., *The West from the Fathers to the Reformation,* vol. 2 of *The Cambridge History of the Bible* (Cambridge: Cambridge Univ. Press, 1969), 179.

the Father of Jesus Christ, and imitate the divine generosity in our actions toward others.

Finally, the recurrent eschatological question is perhaps the most crucial one for the use of the Bible in ethics. Eschatology provides a guiding view of how the Christian community lives and relates to the larger social reality. It sets the present life against a horizon of transcendent values and a transcendent destiny that not only relativize the present, but transform one's vision of how one's circumstances should be engaged now, in light of a higher and more comprehensive standard of evaluation. The task of Christian ethics, and especially social ethics, is to construct the practical working relationship between the community and disciples for whom the kingdom is already initiated and the enveloping community or social context whose life will not be entirely transformed until the consummation of the kingdom by God's final judgment and saving action. As we have seen already, the issues of war and peace test both eschatology and ethics. If the kingdom is really to be present in the lives of believers, then how can they participate in violence and killing? But if the world is not yet consummately transformed, and if one's fellow human beings are in any sense one's neighbors, then how can a Christian refuse to take the means necessary to protect the neighbor from evil?

Authors who are most insistent on the inbreaking presence of the kingdom—such as Tertullian, Origen, Menno Simons, George Fox, John Howard Yoder, Dorothy Day, and Thomas Merton—tend to be pacifists in their dedication to kingdom faithfulness. Authors who defend the just war—including Augustine, Aquinas, Luther, Calvin, and the Methodist and Roman Catholic bishops—do not deny the New Testament mandate to disciples to live a transformed life, but they give that mandate less practical force through a process of translation that gives great weight to the social context and more freedom to the biblical and ethical interpeter. That interpreter then develops more complex lines of relationship between the New Testament's depiction of kingdom life and the community's embodiment of it in history.

Many just war authors incorporate into their positions some particular qualification intended to safeguard the importance of the nonviolent ideal. Augustine and Luther, for example, give up the Christian individual's right to self-defense even while maintaining it for a Christian nation. Erasmus and sometimes H. Richard Niebuhr hold the nation itself to Christian values, such as a commitment to peacemaking or mercy toward the vanquished. In their pastoral letter, the Catholic bishops acknowledge that the pacifist stance is an integral component of the Christian perspective on war and peace, even while reserving the practical application of it to a minority within the religious tradition. The Methodist bishops similarly exhort the religious majority to obedience to the ideal of peace, but at the same time grant that the nation and the citizen have a moral right to defense. Only a very few in the tradition—the Crusaders, Thomas Müntzer, and William Gouge, for instance—have seen violence as in some situations an unambiguous good that is wholly consistent with and even demanded by their religious faith.

For those who have carried the Christian moral tradition, then, the question is not *whether*, all things considered, Jesus represents and calls us to peacemaking (positively) and nonviolence (negatively). That much is established, even in just war thinking from Ambrose and Augustine onward. The question is *how* the mandate to live in love, peace, and forgiveness is to function in the practical moral life. Is it an absolute principle or even rule, binding in a clear and specific way each and every decision a Christian may face in which violent action is a possible outcome? Is it an ideal, which encourages us onward, but to whose distance in this life we must be resigned? Or is nonviolence the integral counterpart of a communal faith experience emerging from Jesus' kingdom preaching, announcing that God rules even now among us, as well as his unequivocal association of discipleship with mercy, forgiveness, and long-suffering? If so, how can present Christian communities live analogously to biblical ones in view of social pressures toward use of violence for valid political ends? This is the overriding challenge both to Christian pacifism and to Christian just war thought.

The present study will confirm the fairly familiar thesis (following James Childress) that Christian just war theory is akin to pacifism at least in the fact that it begins from a presumption against violence. At its best, just war theory isolates war as a boundary situation and disputes the assumption of nation-states that their right to resort to mass violence is a given. Yet we shall also note that merely to phrase the prohibition against war as a "presumption" is already to contemplate the inevitability of exceptions, provision for which it is exactly the job of the just war theory to make. Just war theory in general is a rule-based approach to the problem of violence; and critics of pacifism sometimes interpret it similarly as holding (and, indeed, focused primarily upon) an absolute rule prohibiting the taking of human life. However, we shall question whether moral rules are at the heart of Christian pacifism at all. An alternative interpretation would begin with the radical community of discipleship that gospel preaching of the kingdom creates—and then ask after a way of life consistent with incorporation into Christ.

As well as pursuing the possibility that pacifism is primarily a description of a particular but integrated aspect of Christian living in community, I shall also suggest that there are at least two distinct forms of Christian pacifism. Consistent with the thesis that pacifism is not primarily a rule-based enterprise, its forms will be distinguished, not according to the types of killing or coercion they might or might not disallow, but according to the core understanding of the Christian moral life upon which they are premised. Pacifists who see discipleship above all in terms of obedience advocate a life of faithful witness to the nonviolent, and in some respects even nonresistant, example of Jesus. Pacifists who see discipleship in terms of a love of neighbor reflecting love of God advocate a life of compassion and service, of which violent force would be a contradiction. At the same time, the ability to see the potential foe as a fellow human being, to be able to extend to him or her the inclusivity of the gospel love command, and to be able to regard even the enemy as the object of mercy and forgiveness, have been important to pacifism in most of its historical manifestations. Conversely, to view the enemy not only as a stranger, but as an infidel and the embodiment of an evil threatening the cohesion of one's own, delimited social sphere is to justify violence readily in repelling that threat.

Just war thinking may also be said to assume two forms. In its Augustinian strand, it tries to retain the biblical love command as a functional moral guide even when killing is undertaken. Some authors, like Augustine himself, go beyond claiming that a violent act can be an act of love toward an innocent victim, and try to include even the killed aggressor within love's scope and motive. This strand also tends to see the relation between love and homicide or love and justice as a paradox, perhaps in recognition of the difficulty of describing an act of killing as an act of love in its direct outcome. In its Thomistic version, Christian just war thinking removes killing from the purview of Christian love, avoiding the resort to paradox, and places it on the footing of natural order, natural justice, and the common good. In the natural law approach, criteria for discriminating among types of killing and their moral evaluations can be more carefully elucidated; however, the ideal of kingdom discipleship becomes more distant.

Finally, without claiming to offer a final resolution to the Christian problem of violence and peace, we shall use some recent work in biblical ethics to suggest an alternative way to relate kingdom discipleship to social responsibility. This alternative will not concentrate on action-specifying norms, but on the formation of communities that are analogous to the biblical communities in terms of their challenge to standard patterns of social living. In so doing, it will build on the historical and biblical insight that the kingdom bears on moral agency not first and foremost in terms of moral prescriptions but by the creation of inclusive community.

# 2 | THE KINGDOM COME?

## *Perspectives on New Testament Discipleship, Eschatology, and Social Responsibility*

HISTORICAL-CRITICAL STUDY OF THE CREATIVE roles played by the early churches and evangelists in authoring the Gospels has cast doubt on almost every traditional Christian assumption about the identity and career of Jesus. Yet scholars can still agree, as G. R. Beasley-Murray shows, that at least on one point the Gospels give unanimous and authentic historical testimony. The kingdom of God "pervades the entire proclamation of Jesus," and, moreover, "appears largely to have determined the course of his ministry."[1] The biblical symbol "kingdom of God" is thus an obvious starting point for ethical reflection on discipleship.

### KINGDOM OF GOD

James D. G. Dunn notes that the territorial connotations of "kingdom" should be qualified by the recognition that "reign of God" or "rule of God" better captures the dynamism of the Aramaic "kingdom of God" as "equivalent to God himself in the exercise of his sovereignty."[2] To recognize the reality of God's rule is also to receive an urgent summons to decision, to repentance, and to a full reorientation of life through Jesus. As Jesus' parables illustrate, to live in the kingdom is to replace trust in power and wealth with an attitude of dependence on God, and to break religious and social boundaries by including the poor, the outcast, the sinner, and even the enemy within the community's fellowship.

To recognize the importance of the kingdom concept as characteristic of Jesus' preaching does not, however, settle the issue of what relevance it can or should have to the life of discipleship today. Although the terminology

1. G. R. Beasley-Murray, *Jesus and the Kingdom of God* (Grand Rapids: Eerdmans, 1986), x.
2. James D. G. Dunn, *Jesus' Call to Discipleship* (Cambridge: Cambridge Univ. Press, 1992), 10.

of "kingdom present," "future," and "already/not yet" that is the vehicle for much discussion about practical discipleship and the use of force is a twentieth-century innovation, the problem it captures is as old as the gospel. This problem has received varied resolutions, even within the New Testament. The issue is essentially that of eschatology: What impact does the nearness of God's reign as proclaimed by Jesus (Mark 1:15) have on our lives now? And, in the matter of ethics, how does the way we behave toward others, both inside and outside our religious community, manifest that proclamation?

The liberal Protestant Social Gospel movement of the late nineteenth century (as exemplified by Albert Ritschl and Walter Rauschenbusch) placed Jesus' teaching to love the neighbor in the context of an ethical mandate to transform unjust social relationships. The kingdom of God is present, in this view, in the lives of individuals and groups who achieve social reform by following and extending Jesus' example of brotherly love. The optimism of Christian social liberalism was shattered by the First World War. Even before that, however, the development of historical-critical research on the Bible encouraged Johannes Weiss[3] and Albert Schweitzer[4] to criticize the equation of the biblical kingdom of God with programs of social change. Wendell Willis sees these two authors as marking a major modern shift in twentieth century interpretation of the kingdom, "by their discovery of the eschatological Jesus, preacher of the apocalyptic kingdom of God."[5] Although their views are certainly not identical, Weiss and Schweitzer agreed that Jesus expected that the kingdom was to be established by an apocalyptic act of God, probably after Jesus' own death. Though imminent, it was not a reality in his own ministry; Jesus called his hearers to repent and to love one another in preparation for the coming judgment. His message to his contemporaries was therefore not intended "for us," nor are we in a comparable situation of "interim" expectation. Richard Hiers demonstrates the immensity of the problem that this historical reinterpretation created for biblical theology and for Christian ethics:

> The central problem was that Jesus had apparently expected the kingdom of God to come in the near future. If he had been mistaken about that, how could he and his first-century message be relied on in the twentieth? Moreover, what could the kingdom of God mean to people today who do not share the eschatological world-view?[6]

3. Johannes Weiss, *Jesus' Proclamation of the Kingdom of God* (Philadelphia: Fortress, 1971; originally published 1892).

4. Albert Schweitzer, *The Mystery of the Kingdom of God* (New York: Schocken, 1914); and *The Quest for the Historical Jesus* (New York: Macmillan, 1968; originally published 1910).

5. Wendell Willis, "The Discovery of the Eschatological Kingdom: Johannes Weiss and Albert Schweitzer," in *The Kingdom of God in Twentieth-Century Interpretation,* ed. Wendell Willis (Peabody, Mass.: Hendrickson Publishers, 1987), 1.

6. Richard H. Hiers, Jr., "Pivotal Reactions to the Eschatological Interpretations: Rudolf Bultmann and C. H. Dodd," in ibid., 31.

Rudolph Bultmann[7] and C. H. Dodd[8] tried to reply to this dilemma by emphasizing the presence of the kingdom of God in Jesus' own ministry, and by extension in the lives of those who are converted. Jesus' message is not limited to his first-century audience but is for all times. However, both downplayed the future aspect of the kingdom so much as to virtually eliminate it. Bultmann did not deny that there was a future element to Jesus' own preaching, but he derived from it an essence of timeless relevance, a call to decision and conversion that can be extracted from Jesus' mythological (including eschatological) concepts.[9] Dodd adopted the solution of "realized eschatology"; that is, that the kingdom of God and its blessings were already present in Jesus' own ministry and continue to remain present in the life of faith. Dodd then offers interpretations of futuristic sayings in the Synoptics that are consistent with his realized eschatology; for instance, he interprets some sayings to refer to future participation of those presently not included in the kingdom.[10]

Dodd has had an immense influence on biblical scholarship in this century, a general task of which has been the reconciliation of the eschatological or apocalyptic aspects of Jesus' teaching with his message that the kingdom in some sense begins now. Jesus both proclaims that the kingdom is beginning and holds out the prospect of future judgment and completion of the kingdom by a decisive act of God. For ethics, this "already/not yet" approach can ground both a present moral seriousness and a reliance on, hope in, and fear of God as the one by whom the kingdom is to be established.

However, it is important to note that the earlier critical discussions of the ethical significance of the kingdom did not turn on the question of a gospel perfectionism versus a sociopolitical realism, a question that has become more important in recent discussions of war and peace. The issue at the turn of the century and shortly thereafter seemed rather to be the credibility to the modern religious sensibility of any supernatural meaning that might be attached to the notion of the kingdom. The Social Gospel movement, in turning Jesus' kingdom preaching into a present and achievable moral requirement, did not hinge so much on insisting on adherence to absolute moral ideals, such as nonresistance, as it did on translating Jesus' message about God into terms that could credibly be enacted in present human relationships.

When Weiss and Schweitzer recovered the apocalyptic element, they did so out of dissatisfaction with a prevailing tendency to equate the teaching of

7. Rudolf Bultmann, *Theology of the New Testament,* 2 vols. (New York: Scribner's, 1954–55); *New Testament and Mythology* (Philadelphia: Fortress, 1984); *Jesus and the Word* (New York: Scribner's, 1958); *Existence and Faith* (New York: Meridian, 1960).

8. C. H. Dodd, *The Gospel in the New Testament* (London: National Sunday School Union, 1926); *The Parables of the Kingdom* (New York: Scribner's, 1961); *The Founder of Christianity* (New York: Macmillan, 1970).

9. Hiers, "Pivotal Reactions," 25.

10. Ibid., 18–19.

the historical Jesus simplistically with contemporary moral notions, rather than primarily out of realism about what can and cannot be accomplished morally by Christians in society. Their interpretation of the content of Jesus' apocalyptic expectation tended to discount attempts to reappropriate it in any supernatural or transcendent terms; they focused instead on showing that it was a historically limited and even mistaken version of Israelite apocalyptic thinking. Similarly, Dodd and Bultmann were not interested primarily in presenting the Christian churches with a call to radical moral renewal as part of eschatological witnessing required now, but rather with combating any notion that the kingdom of heaven is of the future in the sense of constituting a supernatural realm to which entrance is gained by the righteous only after death.

The issue of the presence/distance of the kingdom has continued to interest biblical scholars, and some of these same religious questions still shape the way they interpret the evidence. One concern is the credibility of a supernatural religion; but gaining in visibility in recent years, and of special importance to exegetes concerned with ethics, is the connection between eschatology and the transformation of present social life. The kingdom as present is generally emphasized in the service of both these concerns. But some authors, like Beasley-Murray, are intent on holding onto the futurity of the kingdom, even while stressing the difference that its initiation makes for community now, in order to retain the transcendence of Christianity as well as its ethical substance, and to avoid simply reducing religion to ethics.

According to the late Norman Perrin, the futurity of the kingdom in the New Testament is largely the product of "early Christian apocalyptic" and did not originate with the teaching of Jesus himself.[11] Perrin illustrates possible theological consequences of using historical critical work to discredit the future, eschatological, and transcendent referent of Jesus' kingdom language that is so important to Beasley-Murray. In Perrin's view, "kingdom of God" is, borrowing a phrase from Philip Wheelwright, a "tensive symbol," having a set of meanings that can never be exhausted by any one referent.[12] In the teaching of Jesus, the symbol of the kingdom of God evokes the myth of God acting as king on behalf of God's people, a myth that had and continues to have meaning for a religious people in cultural continuity with ancient Israel.[13]

Perrin does not totally do away with futurity in the kingdom teaching of Jesus, precisely because Jesus himself evidently expected a future consummation (as in Mark 14:62). Rather, he relates the tension between present and future, captured in the Lord's Prayer, primarily to the individual's present

11. Norman Perrin, "The Theology of the New Testament," *Journal of Religion* 64 (October 1984): 421.

12. Norman Perrin, *Jesus and the Language of the Kingdom: Symbol and Metaphor in New Testament Interpretation* (Philadelphia: Fortress, 1976), 30. Citing Philip Wheelwright, *Metaphor and Reality* (Bloomington: Indiana Univ. Press, 1972), 130.

13. Perrin, *Jesus and the Language of the Kingdom,* 40, 197.

experience, and he makes Christian moral obligation much more central to his interpretation of the significance of Jesus' kingdom preaching than Beasley-Murray does. Jesus teaches his hearers "to pray for the consummation of that which has begun within their experience,"[14] and for a continuing "eschatological fellowship with one another and with Jesus."[15] The key to both is a willingness to forgive as God forgives; forgiveness is the link between eschatology and ethics.[16]

In his monumental study of the presence and futurity of the kingdom in the teaching and ministry of Jesus, Beasley-Murray draws comprehensively on Gospel materials to demonstrate that the present and future aspects of kingdom must both be seen against the eschatological horizon of a divine intervention in history, and that the two aspects are together integral to the mission of Jesus and hence to the continuing life of the community. Beasley-Murray's fundamental thesis is that the kingdom of God is the "saving sovereignty" of the divine will. Jesus is the mediator of this sovereignty, "in its initiation in his ministry, in its powerful 'coming' in the cross and resurrection, and in its consummation at the parousia."[17] This debate about whether the life of discipleship ought to and can reflect eschatological harmony and righteousness is of immense importance for any consideration of violence as an option for a Christian. The Christian just war tradition has been built on the premise that the present world so entangles the disciple in conflict and "brokenness" that gospel fidelity requires compromise action. Christian pacifism is premised instead on the accessibility of kingdom life now and the reality of a community in which the kingdom already begins.

A paradigmatic text for understanding the kingdom as already effectively present in history is Mark's summary of the content of Jesus' message: "The time is fulfilled, and the kingdom of God is at hand, repent, and believe in the gospel" (Mark 1:15 RSV). Beasley-Murray reads the text to mean: "*If the time before the kingdom is finished, the time of the kingdom is begun.*"[18] He cites several other scholars to support an emergent consensus in his favor.[19]

14. Ibid., 193.
15. Ibid., 194.
16. Ibid., 196.
17. Beasley-Murray, *Jesus and the Kingdom of God,* 344.
18. Ibid., 73.
19. Beasley-Murray quotes W. Trilling, "The unsurpassable future of God has begun" (*Christus Verkundigung in den synoptischen Evangelien. Biblische Handbibliothek,* no. 4, Munich, 1969, p. 48). Cited in *Jesus and the Kingdom of God,* 73. He cites A. M. Ambrozic's view of the two clauses of Mark 1:15: "The first clause enunciates clearly that the divinely decreed time of waiting has come to an end. The decisive manifestation of the saving God, promised in the prophecies quoted in verses 2–3, must therefore be taking place. The second member of the parallel can be seen as interpreting the first; it states the same truth. The only difference is between the members: the first looks backward, while the second looks to present and future. The first announces the end of the old era, the second proclaims the beginning of the new" (*The Hidden Kingdom: A Redaction-Critical Study of the References to the Kingdom of God in Mark's Gospel,* Catholic Biblical Quarterly—Monograph Series, 2. Washington, 1972, pp. 21–22. Cited in *Jesus and the Kingdom of God,* 73). Finally, Beasley-Murray gives the interpretation of E. Lohmeyer,

incorporated nonreductively into Perrin's suggestion that it is the tension between present and future that somehow sets the norm for the present moral life?

Richard Hiers, a New Testament scholar with a developed interest in ethics, also tries to suggest ways in which the eschatological moment can function in ethics, while seeming to agree with Perrin that a suprahistorical kingdom cannot be part of contemporary Christian expectation. While Perrin thinks apocalyptic expectation is an early Christian addition, Hiers understands Jesus to have expected an apocalyptic intervention of God in history; Jesus was simply mistaken, and we no longer share this belief.[26]

Not only do we not expect the imminent arrival of the kingdom, but we hope that somehow our world may continue indefinitely into the future. This makes it all the more impossible and even irresponsible to follow Jesus' sayings about giving away all one's belongings, taking no thought for clothing and shelter, and leaving one's family in order to travel about without possessions or money. Furthermore, most of Jesus' hearers had no prospect of participating in the decisions of their government and affecting the welfare of other persons and nations. Nor did they see themselves as responsible for the welfare of the planetary ecology, which, in any event, they did not view in terms of a progressive movement from plenty to scarcity.[27] How then is future eschatology relevant for us?

Like Perrin, Hiers thinks we can retain the relevance of the eschatological message by looking for analogous but this-worldly functions. He illustrates this in two ways. First, even for us, "time is short." Our lives and those of others are limited. The occasion to do good will quickly pass; delay in acting out of love may mean damage that is past repair. "The victims of war in Vietnam have already paid for our decisions, and more will pay tomorrow for our decisions and indecisions of yesterday and today. All ethics are interim ethics."[28] Eschatology is also relevant to ethics as hope. It means both judgment and deliverance. The eschatological hope is that God's action can overrule our actions, at best partly adequate, and often inadequate or guilty. Because we can trust in God's forgiveness and hope in God's redeeming activity, we can acknowledge our sinfulness and become "liberated for our neighbors."[29]

Certainly recent work has compensated for what might have remained a rather individualistic and spiritualized eschatological sense, the legacy of early twentieth-century scholarship. Not only is present moral action emphasized, but also the social nature of all morality, sinful or converted. Many liberation theologians are represented in Benedict Viviano's claim that the very symbol

26. Hiers, "Pivotal Reactions," 18; and *Jesus and Ethics: Four Interpretations* (Philadelphia: Westminster, 1968), 132, 148–49.

27. Hiers, *Jesus and Ethics,* 151.

28. Ibid., 166.

29. Ibid., 168.

"Kingdom of God" is social and political because "it includes peace and justice without which there is no true holiness."[30]

Wolfgang Schrage, author of a major study on New Testament ethics, recapitulates and confirms many of these themes and also points New Testament eschatology both toward a conversionist rather than rule-based approach and toward a social, liberative ethics. He plays on the teachings of Jesus to compose a full-bodied rendition of the New Testament's moral tones, echoed in other texts, such as the Pauline epistles. First of all, Schrage sees eschatology as the foundation, horizon, and center of Jesus' teaching; moreover, the "simultaneity of present and future is characteristic of Jesus."[31] A consequence of the coming of God's kingdom is a change in human behavior. "The kingdom of God is the foundation of ethics in the sense that it has already irrupted into the present as a joyfully acknowledged discovery, as something that even now brings salvation, joy, and direction."[32] Jesus summons the hearer to turn from self-centeredness "to the neighbor-serving ethics of faith as confidence in and loyalty to God, whose will is love, i.e., whose cause is the well-being of all his children and creatures."[33] Not just obedience but solidarity and compassion are important as responses to the mercy and forgiveness that are characteristic of God. The disciple loves the neighbor not simply as a matter of duty, but because he or she is perceived "as a member of one's own family in the family of being," as "one whose life and joy or sorrow touch our own."[34] And, as Schrage puts it, "Personal renewal must occasion a corresponding structural renewal."[35] Jesus' own teaching has "social and political dimensions,"[36] for the imminence of the kingdom motivates people to act in a way appropriate to it, and Christian action has an integral corporate dimension.

These authors hit the keynote of Jesus' command to love neighbor and enemy. Attentive concern for the other in need is not first of all *self*-sacrifice, a still self-centered focus on one's obligation, loss, or righteousness. It is an identification, an empathy captured in the "as yourself" of the double love command (Mark 12:28ff.). Wolfgang Schrage calls this openness to both neighbor and enemy "the comprehensive solidarity of love," a "fundamental, all-encompassing attitude" and also "the quintessence of all the individual commandments."[37]

## MORAL RULES?

J. L. Houlden has suggested that the interplay between eschatology and ethics takes distinctive alternative shapes, prominent even in the New Testament,

30. Benedict T. Viviano, OP, *The Kingdom of God in History* (Wilmington, Del.: Michael Glazier, 1988), 29.
31. Wolfgang Schrage, *The Ethics of the New Testament,* trans. David E. Green (Philadelphia: Fortress Press, 1988), 19.
32. Ibid., 29.
33. Ibid., 156.
34. Ibid., 157.
35. Ibid., 3.
36. Ibid., 21.
37. Ibid., 78–79.

timeless absolutes does not mean that practical ethics is any less demanding. Even though "the superior status of the law of love" implies that no particular directives have absolute status in their own right—not even a "universally valid law of nonviolence"—it is true nonetheless that "love considers the consequences for others correctly only when it refuses to dispense itself from all material implications."[44]

A further question is whether, even when not providing binding rules, the New Testament provides models for moral reflection and, in particular, some sort of model or pattern for capturing the eschatological tension of discipleship in the moral life. To simply leave the articulation of that tension at the level of a paradox opens the door to inconsistencies and wide variations at both the theoretical and the practical levels of morality. This problem will receive ample demonstration in the following chapters, and it is one to which we shall return at the conclusion of this work.

A focal point for consideration of the ethical meaning of the eschatological tension in Jesus' teaching and in Christian community is the Sermon on the Mount. The Sermon can be used as a point of departure for a further substantive exploration of the eschatological ethics of the New Testament.

## THE SERMON ON THE MOUNT: FOUNDATION OF AN ESCHATOLOGICAL ETHICS

Nowhere in New Testament interpretation are exegesis, theology, and ethics bound more closely together than in approaches to Matthew's Sermon on the Mount (Matthew 5–7). When ethical concerns are foremost, the so-called "hard sayings" (5:38-48) command attention. By demanding nonresistance and love of enemies, Jesus seems both to hold the faithful to impossible standards of concrete action and to break up the foundations of justice on which social cooperation is built. Also problematic are the equally direct and at points more impractical imperatives to avoid anger, lust, divorce, and swearing (5:21-37). The Beatitudes (5:3-11) generally have been of secondary ethical interest, while the Lord's Prayer (5:9b-16) has remained peripheral in most accounts of Christian morality. Before the development in the nineteenth century of a historical-critical method of studying and correlating biblical texts, the ethical attention given to the remainder of Matthew 5–7 was occasional at best, and the Gospel setting of the Sermon was virtually ignored.

Undoubtedly the greatest impact of the historical-critical method on ethical interpretations of the Sermon on the Mount has been made by the discovery that the early church expected the imminent return of Jesus, Risen Lord and Judge, to complete the reign of God begun in his lifetime. Standard typologies of historically and theologically important readings of the eschatology behind the Sermon and its relevance to the Sermon's continuing meaning highlighted

44. Schrage, *Ethics*, 11.

its importance. The model proposed by Joachim Jeremias is simple, representative, and of continuing influence.[45] According to this model, the Sermon usually is seen in one of three ways: (1) as a perfectionist code, fully in line with the legalism of rabbinic Judaism; (2) as an impossible ideal, meant to drive the believer first to desperation, and then to trust in God's mercy; or (3) as an "interim ethic" meant for what was expected to be a brief period of waiting in the end time, and which is now obsolete. Jeremias adds his own fourth thesis: The Sermon is an indicative depiction of incipient life in the kingdom of God, which presupposes as its condition of possibility the experience of conversion. More complex or comprehensive schematizations have been offered, but most major interpreters can be understood in relation to the options posed by Jeremias.[46]

The perfectionist conception becomes a straw theory if taken in the most extreme sense, because it would be impossible to find any representative of the position that every single injunction of the Sermon on the Mount, including the destruction of morally offensive bodily members (Matt. 5:29-30), should be taken literally and strictly. Yet there is a strong tradition of gospel-based nonviolence that takes the commands to love the enemy to the point of nonresistance. Early proponents include Tertullian and Origen; the best Reformation examples are the radicals (such as Menno Simons) who faced extreme persecution for wanting to return to primitive Christianity and the cross of Christ. In more recent times, the Quakers, Mennonites, and other pacifists follow in this current. Even some mainstream theorists of natural rights and just war theory understand the Sermon as in a sense a new law. Augustine, Aquinas, Luther, and Calvin all take Matthew 5:48, for example, as a direct moral precept commanding obedience. To find ways around the prima facie social and political implications of loving the enemy, they do not deny the precept's force as moral law, but limit the law's range. (Augustine applies it to attitude rather than to external action, and is followed by Calvin; Luther distinguishes personal relationships as a Christian from larger social roles; and Aquinas distinguishes precepts meant for all persons from counsels of perfection, and places the "hard sayings" in the latter category.) Even so, none deny that following the law of love in the applicable realm goes beyond sheer extrinsic obedience to require heartfelt faith and charity.

The notion that the Sermon is impossible of fulfillment, but has a pedagogical function, is usually associated with Martin Luther or, as Jeremias puts

45. Joachim Jeremias, *The Sermon on the Mount*, trans. Norman Perrin (Philadelphia: Fortress, 1963).

46. See broader schematizations by Harvey K. McArthur, *Understanding the Sermon on the Mount* (New York: Harper, 1960), who has twelve categories; Krister Stendahl, "Messianic License," in *Biblical Realism Confronts the Nation,* ed. Paul Peachey (Nyack, N.J.: Fellowship of Reconciliation, 1963), 139–52, who adds a thirteenth; and the historical survey in Robert A. Guelich, *The Sermon on the Mount: A Foundation for Understanding* (Waco, Tex.: Word Books, 1982), 13–22. The commentaries of Guelich, W. D. Davies, and Hans Dieter Betz are discussed by Charles E. Carlston, "Recent American Interpretations of the Sermon on the Mount," *Bangalore Theological Forum* 17 (1985), 9–22.

it, with "Lutheran orthodoxy." However, Luther himself maintained that faith is active in works of love, and that it is precisely faith which loving sevice presupposes and of which it is a sign. For this reason, Jeremias's own hermeneutic of the Sermon carries through Luther's most central insights. The Sermon indicates a way of life that presupposes conversion; the Sermon's portrayals of discipleship, while not literal prescriptions, create ideals and set burdens of proof for all concrete embodiments.

Finally, the position that the Sermon on the Mount is an interim ethic represents an extreme or caricatured version of an interest characterizing much contemporary thought. Many recent interpreters of the Sermon on the Mount share the dilemma of Albert Schweitzer: How to build a bridge from the eschatological world view of the primitive church to our own?[47] As we have seen, ethicists as well as exegetes have rephrased the question: What is the continuing relevance of the eschatology that is so definitive a part of the early Christian religious experience?

Contemporary interpreters who reject the interim ethic solution share with the pioneering historical critics the conclusion that the eschatological perspective is key. Also shared is a desire to recover as closely as possible the original setting, process of composition, and meaning of the Sermon on the Mount in the Gospel of Matthew. An important question is whether the Sermon should be read in terms of originally discontinuous sayings and units, or read as finally redacted; and whether even to understand the Sermon on the Mount as final collection requires reference to its place within Matthew's Gospel, the New Testament, and eventually the whole canon. To assert that the literary collection which the Christian community takes as its "Scripture" is authoritative in its final, edited form implies that the normative meanings of texts or units must be balanced out within a larger frame of reference in which other notes are struck. Although not every modern interpreter of the Sermon on the Mount has a full-blown theory of canonical authority, most agree at least on the importance of correlating the most pointedly moral constituents with other elements, and of situating these three chapters within the general program of the Gospel writer, surmised partly with the aid of historical-critical tools.[48]

My method likewise presupposes: (1) at least a de facto functional authority of the canon in Christian theology; (2) the coherence of Matthew 5–7 as a

47. Albert Schweitzer, *The Mystery of the Kingdom of God* (New York: Schocken, 1914). Guelich provides an overview of the development of historical-critical research on the Sermon in the post-Reformation period, *Sermon on the Mount,* 18–22. A constructive, historically based study is Norman Perrin, *The Kingdom of God in the Teaching of Jesus* (Philadelphia: Westminster Press, 1963).

48. A notable exception is Hans Dieter Betz, who theorizes that Matthew took over the Sermon on the Mount from a presynoptic source, with its own (and different) soteriology, in which the death and resurrection of Jesus plays no role. Understood independently from Matthew's Gospel, the Sermon on the Mount pictures the kingdom of God as identical with God's activity of continual creation. The Sermon's central text is taken to be Matt. 6:25-34. *Essays on the Sermon on the Mount* (Philadelphia: Fortress, 1985), 89–123.

unit of meaning if considered from either a literary or a religious perspective; (3) reciprocity of meaning between this unit and the Gospel; (4) the usefulness of historical-critical research in shedding light on the original settings and meanings of both the smaller and larger units; and (5) continuity but not identity of the original meanings of Sermon and Gospel with their meanings for later communities that rely on the canon. I make no pretense in this chapter either of settling or rendering superfluous the answers to two further issues of even greater importance and difficulty: (6) whether the authority of the canon as such is not only a fact but a requirement of Christian theology; and (7) the precise nature and criteria of the continuity between the original and the presently normative meanings of canonical texts. However, these latter questions will be addressed again in the conclusion of the book. I will propose that recent biblical scholarship supports a form of Christian cultural critique developed through the formation of contemporary communities whose challenge to the surrounding culture is analogous to the challenge the New Testament communities posed to their cultures.

## KINGDOM ETHICS AS RELATIONSHIP AND ACTION

Recent hermeneutics of the Sermon reveal a trend to avoid the extremes of Jeremiah's first three types and to appropriate the insights of his fourth by recognizing coherence among several interdependent factors: Matthew's view of Jesus as the Messiah who fulfills Jewish expectations; Jesus' depiction of discipleship in concrete and action-oriented but extreme terms; the Sermon's eschatological kingdom language; and traditional Christian views of ethics, both personal and social. These factors often are tied together in some understanding of converted relationship, which reflects the contemporary hermeneutics of "kingdom of God" in general. The Sermon on the Mount portrays a new relationship to God as Father, a relationship that is epitomized in and somehow made possible for others by Jesus. Individuals actually and presently experience this relationship in their own lives and communities; it transforms their relationships so that, like God, they can look selflessly even on their enemies. It makes them doers of concrete actions concerned foremost with grasping the situation and meeting the needs of others they affect. It is a relationship that would be so radical in its fulfillment that fullness never has been experienced.

The Antitheses and especially the "hard sayings" demonstrate that love is "action that places the other's best interests rather than one's rights foremost."[49] A practical question is whether the Sermon defines these loving acts in any precise way. The divorce texts and the instruction to love one's enemy can be translated into clear moral mandates—however problematic they may be to interpret and apply. However, historical-critical study has cast doubt on

49. Guelich, *Sermon on the Mount,* 254.

whether any apparently self-evident mandate can be taken for granted as original to the texts, and whether even the original specific meaning (to the extent that it can be uncovered) ought to be normative for every cultural and social situation.[50] If the Sermon's specific moral commands are most appropriate to their own historical setting, and if the ethical import of the Sermon derives primarily from its depiction of evangelical discipleship, then it becomes questionable whether the formulation of moral rules ought to play any further part in interpreting the Sermon.

If not, then it remains to account convincingly for the Sermon's endurance and practical forcefulness. Robert C. Tannehill suggests that the Antitheses of Matthew 5:39b-42 function as a literary unit to reverse conventional religious and moral values. These verses can provide effective directives toward action in various historical settings. Although specific extreme commands such as "turn the other cheek" obviously are not literal language, they center on "focal instances" of action that stand "in deliberate tension" with the way in which we "normally live and think."[51] The patterning of instances induces the hearer to enlarge his or her field of reference to other situations calling for overriding attention to others. The hearer is urged to act likewise without being told exactly which acts in which situations will represent substantially similar relationships.

## ETHICS AS IMITATION OF GOD

If it is true that the examples of righteousness in the sermon function as focal instances, what attitude or disposition toward others gives coherence to the pattern represented by the series of exemplary actions? What does the Sermon suggest internally about the substantive relationship out of which the mandated actions are to proceed? That relationship will characterize kingdom life, since the kingdom's presence is the subject of the Sermon on the Mount.

50. On the disputed original senses of the divorce texts, see John R. Donahue, "Divorce: New Testament Perspectives," *The Month* 14 (1981), 113–20. Equally disputed is the original referent of "enemies" in Matt. 5:39. The present consensus appears to be that this referred not to national or political enemies, but religious or perhaps personal ones. See Richard A. Horsley, "Ethics and Exegesis: 'Love Your Enemies' and the Doctrine of Non-Violence," *Journal of the American Academy of Religion* 54 (1986): 3–31; Guelich, *Sermon on the Mount,* on the "evil one," p. 219, and on religious enemies, p. 227; Krister Stendal, "Hate, Non-Retaliation and Love: 1QS X. 17–20 and Romans 12:19–21," *Harvard Theological Review* 55 (1962): 343–55 ; Victor Paul Furnish, *The Love Command in the New Testament* (Nashville: Abingdon, 1972), 47; Stephen Charles Mott, *Biblical Ethics and Social Change* (New York: Oxford Univ. Press, 1982), chap. 9; Luise Schottroff, "Non-Violence and the Love of One's Enemies," in *Essays on the Love Commandment,* ed. Reginald H. Fuller (Philadelphia: Fortress, 1978), 12–13; William Klassen, *Love of Enemies: The Way to Peace* (Philadelphia: Fortress, 1984), 85–88; Perkins, *Love Commands,* 27–40.

51. Robert C. Tannehill, "The 'Focal Instance' as a Form of New Testament Speech: A Study of Matthew 5:39b-42," *Journal of Religion* 50 (1970), 379. Tannehill does not see all the imperatives of Matthew 5–7 as "focal instances," however. Others, like the divorce texts, are of the form "legal rule," because they are practicable as stated, though open to future applications and exceptions (381).

A key theme of the Sermon's depiction of the kingdom is imitation of God;[52] to act as God does, with inclusive forgiveness and mercy, is to live in the kingdom. The Lord's Prayer, an appeal for the fullness of the kingdom, closely associates it with doing on earth the will of the Father (6:10), and especially with forgiving as God does. It is one's forgiveness of neighbor on which one's own forgiveness by God explicitly depends (6:15); the disciple prays to be forgiven as one who also forgives (6:12, 14-15). The command not to judge others' failings (7:1-5) bears out the forgiveness theme of the prayer for the kingdom; it is our attitude toward others that will determine God's attitude of judgment or forgiveness toward us.[53] It is not too much to say, with James Dunn, that Christian love "can be measured by" forgiveness, and that "Jesus clearly saw such readiness to forgive as the mark of discipleship and of the community of disciples."[54]

The purpose of loving even the enemy is to "be children of your Father in heaven" (5:45a); if one is to go beyond merely self-gratifying relationships, then one must aim to be as perfect in the ways of mercy and forbearance "as your heavenly Father is perfect" (5:48). Righteousness in God's eyes is not purity and law-abidingness, but mercifulness effective in compassionate action. Matthew's inclusion of the Golden Rule (7:12) urges the disciple to identify with the other, to perceive the other's concrete need as though it were the disciple's, to act toward the other as though the other were oneself. The morally right act is simply but radically the act that demonstrates the forgiving attentiveness to the needs of others disclosed by Jesus as the will of God. Love is defined in Matthew's Sermon as a way of acting, not as an emotion. However, inferrable from the deeds done is an attitude toward others that might be characterized as empathy, kindness, generosity, or compassion.[55] With this, the dilemmas that are sometimes said to be posed by an ethic of love, such as the conflict between love and justice, or the impasse of a choice between two neighbors, are set aside if not answered. The mandate is not to settle such conflicts in the most prudent or effective way, but to enter into them by identifying the needs of those concerned as one's own.

This theme of love as attentive forgiveness fleshes out the concrete meaning of the "hard sayings," including the baffling instruction not to resist the evildoer (5:39). Although the precise original meanings of nonresistance and

52. The theme is noted by William Spohn, SJ, *What Are They Saying About Scripture and Ethics?* (New York: Paulist Press, 1985), 122. Spohn ties imitation to participation in the life of God by the power of the Spirit, and cites authors such as Augustine, Calvin, Jonathan Edwards, and H. Richard Niebuhr.

53. Elsewhere in Matthew, kingdom "righteousness" also is constituted by forgiveness and mercy, e.g., the parable of the king and the wicked servant (18:23-35), or the giving of a cup of cold water to one of the "little ones" (10:42).

54. Dunn, *Jesus' Call to Discipleship*, 85.

55. On forgiveness and compassion, see Frederick E. Schuele, "Living Up to Matthew's Sermon on the Mount," in *Christian Biblical Ethics: From Biblical Revelation to Contemporary Christian Praxis: Method and Content*, ed. Robert J. Daly (New York: Paulist Press, 1984), 208.

## SOCIAL DIMENSIONS OF THE RIGHTEOUSNESS OF DISCIPLESHIP

Three questions, well-rooted in the tradition and leading into the just war question, surface as soon as one moves out from radical discipleship to contemplate the roles and responsibilities of the disciple as also a member of communities whose identity is not primarily religious: (1) Do the actions mandated for the Christian by the Sermon have necessarily any political, institutional sphere of reference? (2) Is justification of violence definitively excluded from Christian ethics? (3) To what extent is the ethics of the Sermon translatable into public discourse?

The Sermon on the Mount does not suggest a social ethics in any direct or usual sense. It depicts active, personal outflow of a total conversion by virtue of which ordinary religious and moral expectations are shaken to their roots and one is transfixed by Jesus' transparence to the reign of God. Sayings and imperatives with ethical content and even prima facie sociopolitical implications function most obviously and effectively within the parameters of the Sermon as engaging illustrations of the immediate sphere of committed discipleship. Indeed, the energy of the practical moral life must spring up here: in individual commitment within a supportive community. Martin Hengel argues historically that a fundamental difference between Jesus and the Zealot revolutionaries is that Jesus saw the primary source of evil in the world as the evil in the individual's heart, rather than Roman political domination, the priestly aristocracy, or large landowners. Thus the reign of God is not brought about in the first instance by sociopolitical transformation, but by the "transformed heart" that alone "is capable of new human community, of doing good."[65]

Yet, even if the Sermon does not plainly dictate social objectives, it implies them. It is particularly appropriate to draw out such implications if the realization of the kingdom is understood biblically to span races, cultures, nations, and now also generations. Inasmuch as the disciple today has increased capacity to affect whole groups of socially and economically disadvantaged, even oppressed, persons, the broader social duties of discipleship hardly can be ignored. Stephen C. Mott, by emphasizing status as "the key to social ethics" in the New Testament,[66] shows how specific New Testament injunctions can serve as the basis, not of prescriptions, but of a social ethics of consistent discipleship action. The inclusive religion of Jesus challenged the status distinctions on which secular cultures depend, thus destabilizing traditional Roman society and provoking persecution. Compatible with Tannehill's hermeneutic of "focal instances," Mott affirms the continuing social meaning of the inclusive call to discipleship and of merciful action. One

65. Martin Hengel, *Victory over Violence: Jesus and the Revolutionists* (Philadelphia: Fortress, 1973), 47–48.

66. Stephen C. Mott, "Use of the Bible in Social Ethics II," *Transformation* 1 (1984): 24.

hardly can forgive another, show mercy in the face of the other's need, and treat the other as oneself would want to be treated, if the other is perceived as alien and approached in terms of gender, race, national, religious, or class stereotypes. To be perfect in one's compassion is to presuppose that such divisions have ceased to exist, along with the institutions that support and feed on them.

Parallel perceptions of the social implications of the Sermon are represented by the ethics of theologies of liberation. Hermann Hendrickx's commentary lifts up the dawning of the kingdom in Jesus as the key theme, expressed paradigmatically in the Lord's Prayer. God's rule requires identification with the oppressed, mutual solidarity, noncondemnation, liberation from fear, and praxis that enhance human welfare.[67] With good biblical warrants, liberation theologians highlight Jesus' special concern for the outcast (but notably, not only or even particularly the innocent), and suggest that the disciple ought to prefer the most powerless.

## NONVIOLENCE AND NONRESISTANCE

Can love and nonresistance express themselves as sociopolitical resistance to injustice, or even physical violence and killing? The Sermon's answer lies in a further question: Which among available alternatives is truly merciful and forgiving? This question certainly puts the burden of proof on the advocates of violence. Political and economic resistance may be justified, but any attitude of righteous anger likely to result in a less compassionate or more self-assertive act toward the perpetrator of injustice looks dubious.[68]

John Howard Yoder is outstanding among those who have taken seriously the "hard sayings" (and Jesus' nonviolent example) as a part of discipleship witness. Taking due account of canonical complexity and historical-critical research, Yoder arrives at a negative judgment on any Christian use of violence in any situation.[69] Absolute exclusion of violence on the basis of the Sermon (Matt 5:38-48) is challenged by those who, like Richard Horsley,[70] do not identify questions of war, revolution, or even personal self-defense against an attacker as concerns for which it has direct implications; or who, like Stephen Mott,[71] resist the extrapolation from it of moral rules.

It should not be assumed that Christian ethicists who reject violence also reject involvement in the transformation of the social order. Even Yoder, who

67. Hendrickx, *Sermon on the Mount,* 3, 87.

68. I do not find in the Sermon justification for the disciple to seek or use power and anger against injustice; such justification is scant in the New Testament generally. This is no doubt why many Christian defenses of active resistance to injustice rely heavily on the Hebrew Prophets. One of the few New Testament warrants might be Jesus' confrontation with the merchants in the temple, found in each Gospel (Matt. 21:12-13, Mark 11:15-17, Luke 19:45-46, John 2:13-17).

69. John Howard Yoder, *The Politics of Jesus* (Grand Rapids: Eerdmans, 1972).

70. Horsley, "Ethics and Exegesis."

71. Mott, *Biblical Ethics and Social Change.*

"the building of a truly united humanity" by means of "sustained resistance to those forces which divide the world into opposing camps, worship power for its own sake, and capitulate to a concept of reality in which disunity and hostility is considered inevitable."[78] Mauser builds on the letters of Paul to affirm that "the Spirit of God already rules the believer's present, and in this life the peace of God is already established," even though it also has a future aspect.[79]

In relation to the just war debate, these claims imply that the follower of Jesus ought to live first and foremost by the virtues of forgiveness and compassion; that the ideal of forgiving love ought not easily be set aside on grounds of the impossibility of achieving the kingdom in history; that the acts this love sponsors should extend across social and religious boundaries; and that God's judgment will fall on those who hear Jesus but turn aside from the actions his teaching implies.

78. Ibid., 164.
79. Ibid., 133.

# 3 DISCIPLESHIP AND PACIFISM IN THE EARLY CHURCH

ALTHOUGH THE NEW TESTAMENT OFFERS NO concentrated or direct analysis of the ethics of war, it clears the ground for Christian pacifism by establishing compassion and forgiveness as part of discipleship for Jesus' followers. The disciples are to love their neighbors and even their enemies, sacrificing their own needs for the welfare of others (Matt. 5:38-48).

## BIBLICAL AND SOCIAL BACKGROUND

In a survey of the significance of New Testament materials for Christian teaching about war and peace, Victor Paul Furnish reviews several of the historical circumstances of Jesus' ministry and of early Christianity that make it necessary to employ inference and extrapolation in applying the mandates of discipleship to the ethics of defense and violence.[1] For instance, Jesus' life and the early Christian movement had as their setting a Roman Empire relatively secure from international aggression. Further, Christianity itself had never been the religion of a nation-state, and thus had no traditional or historical interest in the problem of religion and political power. Rather, the early Christians saw themselves as inhabiting a new world or way of life that was "in" but not "of" the surrounding culture.[2] Jesus proclaimed the imminence of the kingdom, which God establishes and Jesus' hearers are to receive as a gracious gift; it was not a primary concern of Jesus to direct his audience toward specific programs of social action. Nonetheless, to the extent that conversion and discipleship involve a total reorientation of life, they lead the Christian convert to imitation of God's perfect righteousness and mercy (Matt.

1. Victor Paul Furnish, "War and Peace in the New Testament," *Interpretation* 38 (October 1984), 363–79.
2. Ibid., 364.

Preaching a strict asceticism as a preparation for the imminent return of Christ, they encouraged fasting, celibacy, and martyrdom, and forbade second marriages. Tertullian's Montanist writings reflect an austerity latent even in his earlier works.[8]

Throughout his career as a Christian author, Tertullian draws direct and demanding connections between Christian teaching and the practical moral life. The one treatise he devotes exclusively to the military life, *On the Crown*, is dated in his Montanist phase. However, the skepticism about military service he expresses there echoes earlier works such as *The Apology*. At least three aspects of Tertullian's pacifism have recently been subject to debate: (1) whether he supported the function and endeavors of the state generally, as divinely mandated; (2) whether he forbade military service for Christians entirely, or only participation in anti-Christian practices, such as idolatry and the wearing of the ceremonial laurel crown in honor of imperial supremacy and even deity; and (3) whether he was actually a pacifist at all, or instead objected only to military practices other than killing. Further, it has been argued recently that Tertullian's antimilitary polemics may reflect a counter-strain in Christianity which accepted what he rejected, and that just warfare was warranted by some even before Constantine.[9]

Yet Tertullian is typical of most early Christian writers in that he makes no explicit defense of Christian participation in battle and sees military service as at least a temptation to sin, not only through violence but also (perhaps primarily) through lewdness and idolatry.[10] He recognizes that any Christian soldier will likely be forced to an eventual choice between the requirements of his profession and those of his faith, and that if the latter win out, the likely penalty is death. Tertullian's foundational discussion of war occurs in *On the Crown* (the title refers to the soldier's crown of laurel), and dating from the period when his sectarian inclinations are heightened. The idolatry involved in Roman military pageants primarily motivates his exhortation to Christian

8. For example, Tertullian eventually came to agree with the heretical position that mortal sins such as adultery could not be forgiven after baptism (*De pudicitia* 1, as cited in Arthur Cushman McGiffert, *The West, from Tertullian to Erasmus,* vol. 2 of *A History of Christian Thought* [New York: Scribner's, 1933, 1961], p. 20). However, even in his pre-Montanist period, Tertullian had allowed the possibility of only one more repentance after baptism (*On Repentance* 7, p. 662). For a chronicle of Tertullian's works, see C. John Cadoux, *The Early Christian Attitude Toward War* (London: Headley Bros., 1919; New York: Seabury Press, 1982), xiii–xiv; and Coxe, *Latin Christianity*, 11. Unless otherwise indicated, citations from Tertullian's works are taken from Coxe; page numbers will refer to that volume.

9. Hunter, "A Decade of Research," 93.

10. Cadoux, *Early Christian Attitudes,* cites ancient authors such as Lactantius and Eusebius to support his claim that there was a "strong disapprobation" of war in early Christianity, "both on account of the dissension it represented and of the infliction of bloodshed and suffering which it involved," and that warfare and murder were connected in Christian thought (p. 57). The passages he quotes substantiate an abhorrence of bloodshed and other atrocities, but not necessarily the stronger case that all killing under any circumstances is forbidden on grounds of specifically Christian commitment.

soldiers to repudiate the crown, which they were required to wear on ceremonial occasions.[11] Military life is not singled out in this regard, since the duty of obedience to God and the sin of idolatry are key themes throughout Tertullian's writings. Idolatry is named the "principal crime of the human race"[12] and "the crowning sin."[13] Tertullian makes one well aware that indirect cooperation in pagan cults was a pervasive danger in second-century Roman society. He is disgusted by the circuses, games, and shows that were established in honor of false gods and idols.[14] Festivals honoring the emperor are also idolatrous.[15] He is hardly tolerant of the excuses of servant or tradesman or craftsman, noting, for instance, that the plasterer ought to be as able to mend a roof or lay on a stucco as to draw on walls the gods' likenesses.[16]

Tertullian is skeptical in the extreme that a Christian can hold public office, since the Christian would have to refrain from any participation in or support for temples, sacrifices, and tributes, as well as from judgments on life, condemnations, imprisonments, and torture.[17] Military service is so much more dangerous that Tertullian seems, in *On Idolatry*, to exclude it definitely, stating that there "is no agreement" between service to divine and human masters. He addresses specifically both the question of the believer who volunteers and that of the soldier who converts to Christianity; he includes even the lower ranks who are not required to take part in sacrifices and capital punishment. Even if not direct participants, they wear the garb of a soldier, which represents the "unlawful action" of killing.[18] Tertullian is strict in his exclusion of all near occasions of sin, not so much because external association may contaminate the believer, as because he is rigorous in demanding absolute and uncompromising purity of heart in one's devotion to the Christian life.

Tertullian grounds his prohibitions of killing and of military service on a literal interpretation of Scripture. Scripture leads not only to condemnation of any association with idolatrous practices, but also to the more basic question "whether warfare is proper at all for Christians."[19] In the Ten Commandments, God "puts his interdict on every sort of man-killing by that one summary precept, 'Thou shalt not kill.' "[20] Chronological sequence in the gospels is important to Tertullian in determining Jesus' attitude toward violence; even though soldiers had been received by John the Baptist (Luke 3:12-13); and a centurion had believed in Jesus (Matt. 8:5, Luke 7:2), "*still* the Lord afterward,

11. Cf. Helgelund, Daly, and Burns, *Christians and the Military,* chap. 8, for a general discussion of idolatry in Roman army religion.
12. *On Idolatry* 1, p. 61.
13. *The Shows* 2, p. 80.
14. Ibid., 5, pp. 81–82.
15. *On Idolatry* 15, p. 70.
16. Ibid., 8, p. 65.
17. Ibid., 17, pp. 71–72.
18. Ibid., 19, p. 73; cf. Cadoux, *Early Christian Attitude,* 107–9.
19. *On the Crown* 11, pp. 99–100.
20. *The Shows* 2, p. 80.

also vice versa.[34] When, for instance, God reproves the Israelites, God speaks as well to "all men." Tertullian also is willing to take some biblical references figuratively if to adhere rigidly to the literal meaning of one would make nonsense out of the literal meaning of another. In fact, Scripture itself sometimes transfers names of persons or groups figuratively on the basis of similar characteristics.[35] Thus the various modes of discourse included in the Bible become models for contemporary theological and ethical discourse. In proving the Messiahship of Jesus by prophetic sayings, Tertullian is careful to dissociate him from the literal sword, battles, and weaponry. Even though Tertullian thinks the Psalms prophesy a "warrior," girt with a "sword," they also acclaim his "lenity" and "justice." Since these virtues are inconsistent with war and killing, he concludes that the weapon must be meant of Jesus figuratively. Thus notions of justice and mercy that are not derived strictly from the Bible, or at least not from it exclusively, become the standards of the meaning of biblical references.

> See we, then, whether that which has another action be not another sword—that is, the Divine word of God, doubly sharpened with the two Testaments of the ancient law and the new law; sharpened by the equity of its own wisdom; rendering to each one according to his own action. Lawful, then, it was for the Christ of God to be precinct, in the Psalms, without warlike achievements, with the figurative sword of the Word of God.[36]

Tertullian demonstrates as well the fact that specifically religious sources of ethical reflection rarely can be employed in total disjunction from more philosophical or secular presuppositions and normative ideals. For the rules of Christian living, Tertullian turns first to Scripture, but also relies on "Tradition, and custom, and faith" and believes that reason will support rather than collide with these. The "true interpretation of reason" is, however, given by "authority," or "the apostle's sanction."[37] In *On the Soul*, Tertullian intends primarily to vindicate Christian doctrine against the philosophers and heretics. But since Scripture and even church tradition do not speak extensively on the nature of the soul, he has to substantiate his literalist arguments from Scripture (for example, on the corporeal suffering of persons in hell) with references to such philosophers as the Stoics and Aristotle.[38] As Jaroslav Pelikan remarks, Tertullian's avowed aversion to rationalist thought did not prevent his "quoting the very philosophy against whose pretensions he had spoken so violently."[39] It was perhaps Tertullian's insistence on the literal sense of

34. *Answer to the Jews* 9, p. 162.
35. Ibid., 9, p. 162.
36. Ibid., 9, pp. 162–63.
37. *On the Crown* 4, p. 95.
38. See *A Treatise on the Soul* 5, pp. 184–85. See also J. Pelikan, *Emergence of the Catholic Tradition (100-600),* vol. 1 of *The Christian Tradition: A History of the Development of Doctrine* 1 (Chicago: The Univ. of Chicago Press, 1971), 49–50.
39. Pelikan, *Emergence of the Catholic Tradition,* 50.

all of Scripture, authoritatively defined, combined with his resort to more extrinsic supports when biblical texts or the tradition failed to coincide unambigously with his agenda, that led the nineteenth-century scholar Frederick Farrar, in his Bampton Lectures, to exclaim impatiently, "The eloquent, fiery, uncompromising African practically makes Scripture say exactly what he himself chooses."[40]

Although Tertullian generally is regarded as a pacifist and definitely holds up nonviolence as a Christian ideal, it is less clear that he is a sectarian pacifist who supports Christian withdrawal from the secular enterprise of government. On the one hand, we have seen that he views most secular roles as dangerous to Christian belief and practice. On the other, he appeals for tolerance of Christianity on the grounds that Christians pray for the emperor and for the stability of the Roman Empire. "We respect in the emperors the ordinance of God, who has set them over the nations. We know that there is that in them which God has willed."[41] Even though Christians refuse to worship him, the emperor is "called by our Lord to his office."[42] Tertullian does not expect that the kingdom of God, superseding all temporal authority, will be realized soon.[43]

Moreover, it is clear that at least some Christians were serving in the army in Tertullian's time, and that they were allowed to be buried as Christians with their professions inscribed on their tombstones.[44] Tertullian himself protests against the view that Christian citizens are "useless," contending that "we sail with you, and fight with you, and till the ground with you."[45] He twice tells with pride the legend of the "Thundering Legion" of Marcus Aurelius's army, which its Christian members supposedly saved from a drought with their prayers.[46] On these two occasions, the story is mentioned in a group of other incidents meant to demonstrate that Christian claims have merit and that wise and prudent rulers ought not to persecute Christians. It is dubious that these references represent an acceptance of Christian military participation as such on Tertullian's part. They seem to demonstrate merely that he regarded it as a fact, and that the efficacy of Christian prayer at least was to be commended to the powers that be. In his somewhat later but pre-Montanist treatise *On Idolatry*, he states that a Christian may not enlist, nor may a convert continue to serve, not even in peacetime, and not even if he will not be involved directly in killing, for every soldier must wear the military uniform and weapon which are forbidden by Christ.

40. Frederick W. Farrar, *History of Interpretation: Eight Lectures Preached Before the University of Oxford in the Year MDCCCLXXXV* (New York: E. P. Dutton and Co., 1886), 178–79.

41. *Apology* 32, pp. 42-43.

42. Ibid., 33, pp. 43.

43. *On the Resurrection* 24, p. 18.

44. Cadoux, *Early Christian Attitude,* 105–6, 113; Bainton, *Christian Attitudes, 69.*

45. *Apology* 4, p. 49 (pre-Montanist); cf. *Apology* 37, p. 37; and *Ad Nationes* 1, p. 109.

46. *Apology* 5, p. 22; *To Scapula* 4, p. 107. See Cadoux, *Early Christian Attitude,* 229–30; and Helgelund, Daly, and Burns, *Christians and the Military,* for discussion of other ancient attestation to this story of Christian presence in the military.

Philo of Alexandria and Clement. Hellenistic allegorical techniques were quite intricate and included philology, etymology, and numerology. Allegory, for example, was used to enhance the acceptability of the escapades of the heroes and gods in the Homeric poems.[50] Clement of Alexandria, the first Christian thinker to attempt an explanation of the allegorical method, bases his exegesis on the Jewish thinker Philo. According to Philo, allegory is justified by Scripture itself, which, among other instances, uses the trees in Eden to stand for knowledge and for good and evil.[51] Clement's own interpretation is christocentric, but he agrees with Philo that every word in Scripture is divinely inspired but not every part of Scripture need be taken at its most obvious meaning. Beyond the literal sense, Scripture can have meanings that are theological, moral, or even philosophical. The guide of the interpreter is faith in Christ; impossible meanings are rejected and hidden ones discovered on the basis of this standard.[52]

Origen's approach to Scripture is expounded primarily in *On First Principles*, Book 4, which was composed between 220 and 240.[53] After arguing that the success of the early Christian movement and the fulfillment in Jesus of Old Testament prophecies attest to Scripture's divine inspiration, Origen proceeds to the matter of interpretation. Adopting Philo's method, he assigns to the Scriptures a triple meaning corresponding to the body, soul, and spirit of humanity: the literal, the moral, and the mystical or theological.[54] Although Origen does not dispute the historicity of most biblical events, he maintains that their real significance transcends it. The simple believer grasps only the historical meaning or an obvious religious one, but those who have progressed to greater union with the Holy Spirit will discern deeper or higher levels of significance.[55] Indeed, many "hindrances and impossibilities" have been deliberately inserted into the biblical narratives as "stumbling blocks," with the purpose of leading the reader to reflect more carefully on the highest meanings that Scripture contains.[56] When the sequence of the actual events recorded

50. Trigg, *Origen*, 31–33; Karlfried Froelich, *Biblical Interpretation in the Early Church* (Philadelphia: Fortress, 1984), 18–19.

51. Grant and Tracy, *A Short History*, 52–56.

52. Grant, *The Spirit and the Letter*, 85–89; cf. Grant and Tracy, *A Short History*, 55–56; Danielou, *Origen*, 185; Froelich, *Biblical Interpretation*, 15–16; and Trigg, *Origen*, 54–65, which also includes a discussion of the influence of Platonism on Clement.

53. The edition used is *Origen: On First Principles*, ed. G. W. Butterworth (New York: Harper and Row, 1966). *On First Principles* has been partly preserved in Greek by Basil of Caesarea, but much must be reconstructed from Rufinus's less reliable Latin translation. Butterworth arranges translations from the Greek and Latin in parallel columns. The translation from which quotations are taken here will be indicated in the notes as G or L.

54. This is to state the schema in basic terms. Actually, Origen did not have a particularly systematic or definitive set of principles for assigning interpretations. Daly points out that the three levels sometimes have different meanings: historical, moral, mystical; or historical, mystical, spiritual (von Balthasar, *Spirit and Fire*, xvii). Note also Grant's contention that the distinction of levels "breaks down immediately" (*Spirit and Letter*, 94).

55. *On First Principles*, L: 1. preface. 8, p. 1.

56. Ibid., G: 4.2.9, p. 285. (L: "stumbling blocks," "impossibilities and incongruities.")

does not correspond evenly to the spiritual truths to be communicated, the Holy Spirit occasionally has even inserted less probable, impossible, or possible but fictitious events.[57]

Origen tells us that the " 'key of knowledge' is necessary" to understand Scripture.[58] In fact, he uses multiple and not always consistent criteria to determine which of the narrative's literal meanings the Holy Spirit must have inserted gratuitously. If Origen discerns the immediately apparent sense of a text to be "absurd and impossible,"[59] things which "cannot be accepted as history,"[60] then these elements must have been intended to force inquiry to a higher level. However, Origen's standard of the impossible varies. It can be science (there could have been no "morning and evening" on the first three days of creation if the sun and moon had not yet been created);[61] "irrationality" as uselessness (the Mosaic prohibition to eat vultures, since clearly no one would want to);[62] "irrationality" as immorality (the instruction to pluck out an eye if it is guilty of lust);[63] religious (the anthropomorphism "God walks" does not comport with the Christian view of the Deity);[64] or physical unlikelihood or impossibility (the devil could not have shown Jesus the whole world, for it would be impossible to see it all at once;[65] we cannot be expected to offer the "other" cheek, since an aggressor striking with the right hand will hit the left cheek a second time.)[66] On the other hand, Origen asserts without evident qualm that there is no need of inquiry as to the literal sense of "swear not at all" and the condemnation of hidden lust as adultery.[67] The credibility of the virgin birth, miracles of Jesus, and the appearance of the Holy Spirit as a dove[68] are staunchly defended while the creation of Eve from Adam's rib is given an allegorical interpretation.[69] This combination of assertions makes it quite clear that Origen's calls for "considerable investigation" and an "open mind"[70] are more clearly appropriate than the interpretations themselves. No wonder he compares scriptural interpretation to a hunt for lost treasure in a field,[71] and admits that, even while using

57. Ibid., L: 4.2.9, p. 286.
58. Ibid., G: 4.2.3, p. 274.
59. Ibid., G: 4.3.4, p. 294.
60. Ibid., L: 4.3.1, p. 290.
61. Ibid., L: 4.3.1, p. 288; cf. Gen. 1: 5-13.
62. Ibid., G: 4.3.2, p. 290; cf. Lev. 11:14.
63. Ibid., G & L: 4.3.3, p. 293; Matt. 5:28-29.
64. Ibid., G & L: 4.3.1, p. 288; Gen. 3:8.
65. Ibid., G & L: 4.3.1, p. 289; Matt. 4:8.
66. Ibid., G & L: 4.3.4, p. 289; Matt. 5:39.
67. Ibid., G & L: 4.3.4, p. 295; Matt. 5:34, 28. Butterworth indicates that the inclusion of the text on lust may be the work of Rufinus.
68. Against Celsus 1.37, 36; 1:46, p. 42, in *Origen: Contra Celsum,* trans. Henry Chadwick (Cambridge: Cambridge Univ. Press, 1980).
69. Ibid., 4.38, p. 213.
70. Ibid., 1.42, p. 39.
71. *On First Principles,* G & L: 4.3.11, p. 306; Matt. 13:44

of more souls."[87] In the present, however, Christians must avoid not only violence but also public service, so that they may lead progressively better lives, and through piety be leaders in the salvation of all.[88] Others, non-Christians, might in the meantime be involved in "necessary" wars, which should be kept as "just and ordered" as possible.[89]

In understanding Origen's approach to war it is important to keep in mind that while morality is extremely important for him, he sees sanctification as a gradual process. This applies both to the individual as he or she is united with the Logos through the Spirit; and to the human race, as it is converted. Origen tells us that there is no one in whom Christ reigns so that the power of sin is completely broken. "And the Lord himself at the beginning of his preaching does not say: 'The kingdom of heaven has come,' but: 'The kindom of heaven has drawn near' (Matt. 3:12)."[90] The kingdom "draws near" to a person only as he or she increases in understanding of the Word.[91] The mission of Christians is to make the eschatological reality of the kingdom increasingly present in their lives.

Despite his absolute and insistent rejection of violence, Origen maintains a tension in his view of gospel existence in this life. The Holy Spirit is the agent of sanctification that is progressing; adherence to the Sermon on the Mount will not be expected of Christians so unequivocally by Origen as it is by Tertullian. Here Origen will differ from Menno and the Quakers with their commitment to live in the kingdom now without compromise and at the price of repudiation of and by the world outside the kingdom. Origen agrees that the norm for all Christians is absolute pacifism, but the perfection of the Christian life is not yet realized by all and does not so unequivocally exclude sin. For the Christian, participation in violence represents the continuing mark of sin and a lack of full conversion and unity with the Word.[92]

Although the theologians of early Christianity held up pacifism as an ideal and exhorted their hearers to lay hold of the new life possible in Jesus Christ, we have seen that not all Christians actually realized this ideal, and that a thinker like Origen communicates a subtle resignation to the incomplete accessibility of genuine discipleship. The next chapter will open with Augustine's effort to retain the ideals of self-offering love and redeemed Christian community even while compromising with violence and the practical need to maintain order in the "earthly city."

87. Ibid., 7.68, p. 505.

88. Ibid., 8.74, p. 510.

89. Ibid., 4.82, p. 249.

90. From Origen's *Commentary on Romans,* 5.3, as cited in von Balthasar, *Spirit and Fire,* 351.

91. From Origen's *Commentary on Matthew,* 10.14, as cited in von Balthasar, *Spirit and Fire,* 362.

92. Some authors have noted in Origen the seed of the later "two swords" theory of the relation of church and government. See Gerard E. Caspary, *Origen and the Two Swords* (Berkeley: Univ. of California Press, 1979); Helgelund, Daly, and Burns, *Christians and the Military,* 40–41.

# 4 "In Readiness of Mind"

## *The Emergence of Christian Just War Tradition (Augustine)*

EARLY CHRISTIAN THINKERS WERE LIKELY TO assume that Christian discipleship meant a distinctive way of life which, even if not deliberately separatist in relation to politics and government, would mark the Christian community and its members off against dominant cultural values. The early church was not unequivocally pacifist in practice, but major theologians did see military life as a threat to Christian ideals. Although an author like Origen can refer metaphorically to Christians contributing an "army of piety" to social life, the primitive eschatological horizon is reflected in the difference between Christian and pagan social participation, even as that horizon recedes in the very fact that a parallel between them is drawn. As Louis Swift remarks of later periods, "It is a truism that the reign of Constantine (A.D. 306–337) represents a watershed in the development of Christian attitudes concerning war and military service," inasmuch as "the question is no longer whether participation in war is justified but what conditions should govern the right to declare war (*ius belli*) and what rules should be observed in waging it (*ius in bello*)."[1]

## RELIGIOUS AND SOCIAL CONCERNS

A common theme in justifications of violence is that of Christian responsibility in a broken or fallen world; the Christian's conformity to the kingdom's radical nature is limited by his or her coexistence as a citizen of the world and the necessity of fulfilling moral obligations to and in that world. The ideal of life in the kingdom becomes distanced from the actual political realities. Radical Christian pacifists, on the other hand, emphasize the present and utter ultimacy of the kingdom and the absolute character of Jesus' teaching as defining

1. Louis J. Swift, *The Early Fathers on War and Military Service* (Wilmington, Del.: Michael Glazier, 1983), 80.

membership. If force is recognized as necessary and even useful in the world, then the Christians' participation in the world must in the pacifist view be limited at least to the extent that participation in violent force must be avoided. In either the pacifist or the just war case, of course, the author will have contrary biblical evidence with which to deal.

Whether acknowledged explicitly or not, it has always been necessary for Christianity's ethical interpreters to organize scriptural meaning around a core or essence. Dissonant texts will then be read in a manner that allows them to be reconciled at some level with this core and that permits (or at least does not exclude) activity required by the sort of social participation perceived both as responsible and as consistent with the core. As we have seen in early Christian writings, pacifists occasionally overlook or downplay the occurrence of violence in the Old Testament, especially Yahweh's leadership in battle. They not infrequently come to terms with biblical violence by construing a nonviolent message behind the war imagery. Most just war theorists take the nonviolent thrust of the Sermon on the Mount quite seriously and do not attempt to set aside nonviolence as such, but rather to transmute its practical impact to another level or sphere.

Contrasts among the pacifism of earlier figures and later just war (and even "holy war") positions can be gauged by distinctions, described by James Childress, that are often employed to limit the evangelical imperative of nonviolence: higher/lower, for oneself/for others, inner/outer, private/public.[2] In other words, Christian authors have progressively restricted the practical force of New Testament sayings against violence ("turn the other cheek," "go the second mile," "love your enemies") by making one or more of the following assertions: that the sayings define a "higher" Christian life (for example, of the clergy) but need not be taken literally on the "lower" plane (for example, by the laity); that they must be interpreted strictly regarding actions on one's own behalf but not if one is removing or preventing harm to others; that they apply to the inner realm of loving intention but not to the outer realm of just action; that they apply to the decisions of private citizens but not to those of public authorities acting in an official capacity (who have the right to command their subordinates, for example, soldiers). All of these manuevers are attempts to make the Christian life more feasible in light of the other social obligations of the Christian. They also reflect a growing perception that the life of kingdom discipleship is not only not fully accessible in this life, but must be explicitly deferred in order to accommodate duties entailed by membership in multiple, intersecting communities of identity, both religious and secular.

## AUGUSTINE (354–430)

It is common to begin or to focus studies of just war theory with Augustine, who, appropriating from Roman politics the idea of a "just war" for defense

2. James F. Childress, "Moral Discourse about War in the Early Church," *Journal of Religious Ethics* 12 (Spring 1984): 12.

or punishment, based on it the conditions necessary to legitimate the use of force for Christians. Augustine was born in North Africa, then a Roman province. His father was a well-educated pagan who held a government position and had to overcome financial obstacles in his determination to give his son a classical education. Augustine's pious Christian mother, Monica, figures prominently in his *Confessions*, the story of what he later viewed as a wayward youth, and of his religious conversion at thirty-two.[3]

In his early adulthood, Augustine was attracted to Manicheanism, an aberrant Christian sect that was to have a lasting effect on his attitudes. Contemplating the evil in the world and the struggle in the human soul, the Manicheans resorted to a simple if dualistic explanation: They held two different gods responsible for the creation of darkness and light, as well as the human soul or mind and the body or baser nature, and associated these divine principles respectively with the deities of the Old and New Testaments. Known for its ascetic ideals and strict antisexual morality, the Manichean way of life appealed to Augustine's introspective sense of personal moral (especially sexual) conflict. John Mahoney characterizes Augustine's mentality as "dyadic," an approach to reality that tends to highlight dualities, polarizations, and extremes.[4] Most evident in Augustine's interpretations of sexual desire, a certain dualism also colors his grand social paradigm of the "two cities"—earthly and heavenly.

Augustine gave up Manicheanism after nine years of initiation and went to Italy to study Platonist philosophy, after which he accepted a position as a teacher of rhetoric in Milan. There he eventually was baptized by Ambrose, a compelling preacher and teacher. After his conversion, Augustine gave up teaching in favor of a life of study, prayer, and writing in a small community of friends, at first in Italy and later upon his return to Africa. But only about four years after his baptism, Augustine was reluctantly pressed into service as pastor in the port city of Hippo, from which he eventually was to exercise great influence as a prolific theologian and active bishop.

Augustine saw Christianity as "the one true philosophy," that is, the one way to understand and achieve the "highest good" (*summum bonum*). But no mere human reasons or virtues can lead one to God. Augustine knew from his own struggle that only God's touch and calling can move the sinner to a new way of life. Only God's healing grace can convert the self-enclosed will, centering all one's loves on God above all else. The theme of ordered

3. Augustine's biographer, Peter Brown, describes Monica as "relentless" in her efforts to bring her son's life into line with her own religious ideals and social ambitions; but also remarks that few mothers could survive being seen only through the eyes of their sons (Peter Brown, *Augustine of Hippo* [New York: Dorset Press, 1986; originally published by Univ. of California Press, 1967], 30).

4. John P. Mahoney, SJ, *The Making of Moral Theology* (Oxford: Oxford Univ. Press, 1987), 69.

goods and loves is central to Augustine's social ethics, as based on the "tranquillity of order," and to his view of war, as necessary to restore peace or social harmony.

Because Augustine was an eloquent but unsystematic author, often responding passionately to theological or practical challenges to Christian doctrine, it is difficult to make clear and commanding generalizations about his position on any given issue. Justifications of war put forward with single-minded vehemence can be among Augustine's least persuasive. Augustine recognized many paradoxes in the human condition.[5] His general position on war can be summed up thus: Augustine was willing to commend the use of violence if undertaken at the behest of a legitimate civil authority (understood to have authority from God), if necessary to punish crime or to uphold the peace, and if the combatants intended to establish justice rather than hatefully to inflict suffering on their enemies. Augustine relegated most practical implications of Jesus' "hard sayings" (Matt. 5:38-48) to the Christian's personal affairs, there excluding killing in self-defense. To kill to save one's own life represents an inordinate attachment to a personal temporal good rather than to God's will; but to kill selflessly for the common good may be justified because the good of all is greater than that of one. Moreover, even the killing of the one may be interpreted as an act of love, as we shall see below.

## *Influence of Ambrose (ca. 339–397)*

In the background of Augustine's just war thought stands Ambrose, bishop of Milan. As a young man struggling from Manicheanism toward Christianity, Augustine listened to Ambrose's sermons.[6] The Manicheans rejected the anthropomorphically depicted god of the Old Testament, particularly the deity's apparent endorsement of immorality and violence, seemingly so inconsistent with the spirit of the God of the New Testament, Father of Jesus. Augustine learned from Ambrose that Old Testament events could be allegorized and thus made to yield a higher religious meaning, consistent with the Pauline maxim, "The letter kills but the spirit gives life."[7]

5. William R. Stevenson, Jr., *Christian Love and Just War: Moral Paradox and Political Life in St. Augustine and His Modern Interpreters* (Macon, Ga.: Mercer Univ. Press, 1987), 8. Stevenson adds, "The proper human response to the complexities and perplexities of international politics, for Augustine, would not be prudential deduction from principle, whether a principle of ends *or* means, but rather a prudential induction from circumstance. . . . This response would humbly withhold self-confidence in enduring human achievement and place its hope in a merciful providence" (pp. 8–9). Whether such an approach leaves moral judgment so loose and open that excluding the immoral becomes a rather tenuous possibility remains a question to be answered. For example, see Stevenson's own suggested defense of nuclear deterrence (p. 46).

6. Eugene TeSelle, *Augustine the Theologian* (New York: Herder and Herder, 1970), 30–31.

7. Teselle mentions Augustine's claim to have heard Ambrose cite frequently this text (Conf. 6.4.6), cited ibid., 31. TeSelle also notes (p. 265) that after about 405, Augustine probably had access to all the works of Ambrose, which had been brought to Carthage by a former secretary of Ambrose who participated in the controversy against the Pelagians.

Ambrose, elected bishop while serving as governor of a province in northern Italy,[8] depicts the Christian life as answering a higher calling than that of those virtues ordinarily considered just and honorable. Although he avoids keen opposition between the Christian and pagan life-styles, he makes it clear that the Christian must live by a standard which will be sometimes at odds with worldly wisdom. At the same time, many common moral ideals are shared, especially those that have to do with loyalty and service to one's country. Fundamental virtues are justice and courage. "The splendor of justice is great. Justice exists for the good of all and helps to create unity and society among us."[9] "Those who love justice must first direct it to God; second, to their country; third, to parents; and last, to all people. This is the way in which nature reflects it. . . . Courage reflects justice when it protects one's country in time of war or defends the weak and the oppressed."[10]

And yet, Christian morality does not stop at conventional understandings of justice. "The very duty that the philosophers see to be primary to justice, we reject. They say we should hurt no one except when responding to wrong received. The gospel has taught the opposite," that is, "to give grace and not harm."[11] Ambrose commends compassion as the trait that most helps the Christian to imitate the Father's perfection, and reminds, "It is also written that the Lord has commanded us to love our enemies, to pray for those who plot against us, who persecute us, or who spread false scandal about us."[12]

Ambrose makes a distinction between self-defense and national defense or defense of allies, and considers the latter, as actions on behalf of the common good, to be instances of "courage" and "wholly just."[13] The Old Testament provides examples in figures such as Joshua, Jonathan and Judas Maccabeus.[14] Although "there is nothing that goes against nature as much as doing violence to another person for the sake of one's own advantage," still "any man wins a glorious reputation for himself if he strives for universal peace at personal risk to himself."[15] Ambrose follows the standard Roman view of the right to declare war and the morality of conduct within war, allowing defensive or punitive wars and insisting that the conventions of war be kept.[16] Ambrose also adheres both to civil law and to the example of the Old Testament (Moses' slaying of an Egyptian to defend a Jew) in holding up a duty of courage to come to the aid of innocent third parties.[17]

8. Swift, *The Early Fathers*, 97.

9. Ambrose, *The Duties of the Clergy,* 1.28, in *Morality and Ethics in Early Christianity,* trans. and ed. Jan L. Womer (Philadelphia: Fortress, 1987), 99.

10. Ibid., 1.27, p. 97.

11. Ibid., 1.28, p. 98.

12. Ibid., 1.11, p. 90.

13. *On the Duties of the Clergy* 1.27.129, quoted in Swift, *The Early Fathers,* 98.

14. Ibid., 1.40.195, in Swift, *The Early Fathers,* 98.

15. Ibid., 3.3.23, in Swift, *The Early Fathers,* 98.

16. Swift, *The Early Fathers,* 99–100, who cites *On Duties* 1.176, 3.19.110 and 116; 1.35.176–77; 1.27.129; 2.7.33; 3.8.54. See also *The Duties of the Clergy,* 1.29, in *Morality and Ethics,* 99, on fidelity to agreements in war.

17. *On Duties* 1.36.178; quoted in Swift, *The Early Fathers,* 102.

Ambrose often draws parallels between Christian morality and the morality of "nature" in regard to these basic obligations, including the duty to forego personal self-defense; harming another to save oneself appears ignoble as well as unchristian. But although the virtues of peace and mercy are admired generally, the gospel command to love even the enemy[18] colors the moral life of the Christian differently: "The law calls for reciprocal vengeance; the Gospel commands us to return love for hostility, good will for hatred, prayers for curses. It enjoins us to give help to those who persecute us, to exercise patience toward those who are hungry and to give thanks for a favor rendered."[19] The repudiation of self-defense is stated especially strongly on the basis of the Gospel: "Indeed, even if a man comes up against an armed thief, he cannot return blow for blow lest in the act of protecting himself he weaken the virtue of love. The Gospel supports this position in a clear and obvious way: 'Put up your sword; everyone who kills with the sword will be killed by it' (Matt. 26.52)." Ambrose proposes the example of David, who is said to have hated evildoers rather than their deeds, and who is inferred to have been able to live a violent life without loss of loving attitude.[20]

At the practical level, then, Ambrose only occasionally highlights the disjuncture between the pagan's and the Christian's substantive moral duties. While Christian morality is described in a manner that reaches consistently to the heart of intention, it also presupposes as an ideal the unity of civic responsibility and Christian commitment. The Sermon on the Mount does demand radical spiritual reversal, but the peace of the kingdom as beginning in conversion now makes it possible for the Christian to bring peace to the world. "In the area of peace begin with yourself so that when you have established peace there, you can take it to others."[21]

On the other hand, Ambrose recognizes that the total conversion of the Christian's life, attitudes, and actions remains an incomplete project until the end of history, while in the meantime both the inner and the outer struggle continue.[22] The difficulty of persevering both sincerely and effectively while resorting to violence in the interim is reflected in Ambrose's exclusion of participation in war for the clergy, precisely on the basis of the radical orientation of the religious mentality to the things of God. "According to Ambrose, 'the thought of warlike matters seems to be foreign to the duty of our office [as clergy], for we have our thoughts fixed more on the duty of the soul than on that of the body, nor is it our business to look to arms but rather to the forces of peace.' "[23]

18. Discourse on Psalm 118 12.51, quoted in Swift, *The Early Fathers,* 100.
19. Discourse on Luke's Gospel 5.73, quoted in Swift, *The Early Fathers,* 100.
20. Discourse on Psalm 118 15.22, quoted in Swift, *The Early Fathers,* 103.
21. Discourse on Luke 5.58, quoted in Swift, *The Early Fathers,* 109.
22. Discourse on Psalm 36 22, cited in Swift, *The Early Fathers,* 110.
23. Childress, "Moral Discourse about War," 12, quoting *Duties of the Clergy* (place unspecified).

Augustine, too, explicitly contrasts Christian righteousness with the virtue of the courageous and noble pagan, insofar as the motive and intention are concerned (self-glorification versus glory of God).[24] Augustine is less emphatic than Ambrose in contrasting the specific actions of Christian or pagan. Yet he reflects Ambrose insofar as he allows for the justification of war but disallows self-defense, and insofar as he intends to reconcile an evangelical intention of love with a violent outward action.

## *Kingdom and History: The Two Cities*

Ambrose's tentative distinction between the present realm and its eschatological fulfillment is made more explicit and central through Augustine's imagery of the "two cities." Already in Ambrose, social participation had begun to take precedence over practicing the eschatological imperatives of the Sermon on the Mount, since the peace of the kingdom is not fulfilled in history.

The *City of God*, written when Augustine was an old man, is a deliberate confrontation with Roman culture and its pagan religions, with the great classical traditions of the Roman Empire, which at Augustine's time was in decline. After the sack of Rome in 410 by barbarian invaders, some Roman noblemen reestablished themselves in Africa, presenting a challenge to Christianity there.[25] Moreover, just as Christians were wont to blame their culture's recent ill fortune on the persistence of idolatrous rites, so the pagans tended to blame Christian abandonment of the ancestors' gods. Therefore Augustine was motivated to defend the merits of the Christian religion over competitors by illustrating the positive relation of the Christian church to the common good, even while claiming that Christianity infinitely transcends other interpretations of society, virtue, and happiness.

*The City of God*, a work of central importance for ethics and politics, poses the question, In what does true glory (happiness) consist? Augustine's answer is that the Christian citizens of God's "heavenly city" are only transient sojourners in the "earthly city," and that their gaze must always be fixed on a more distant horizon. At the same time, the happiness of the heavenly community is not wholly inaccessible, even in this life. The opposition and interdependence of the two cities form the context for Augustine's approach to politics and social ethics.

Augustine contrasts two cities which "have been formed by two loves," the earthly city by "the love of self" manifested in love of ruling, strength, and profit; the heavenly city by "the love of God," to whom it offers "true worship."[26] Behind this dualism of spheres lies one standard of human existence, against which partial realizations are measured. The true measure of human virtue

24. *The City of God* 5.13–16, in *On the City of God by St. Augustine,* trans. Marcus Dods (New York: Random House, 1950), 163–66.

25. See Brown, *Augustine of Hippo,* chap. 26.

26. *City of God* 14.28; p. 477.

is love of God and of all other things in relation to God and for God's sake. Augustine establishes this clearly at the outset of Book 19 of *The City of God*, which contains his central discussion of the historical relation of the two cities: "the end of our good is that for the sake of which other things are to be desired, while it is to be desired for its own sake."[27] The one thing to be desired for its own sake is God, as Augustine states over and over.[28]

Perfect peace and happiness come to fruition in the heavenly city where love and worship are given to God alone. "The peace of the celestial city is the perfectly ordered and harmonious enjoyment of God, and of one another in God. The peace of all things is the tranquillity of order."[29] Ordered love of God, "true virtue," can exist only in those who have "true piety,"[30] and true piety (recognition of God as the supreme good) is possible only for those who have been divinely enabled to respond in faith, to pray, and to be helped to live rightly.[31] The "eternal peace which no adversary shall disturb" is "the final blessedness, this the ultimate consummation, the unending end."[32] Christian piety will be fulfilled eschatologically by the perfect interrelationship of the Creator and all that is made.

The heavenly city is Augustine's metaphor for the kingdom of God; "peace" is his term for its inner and definitive nature. The earthly city shares partially in this peace. Theologically, peace is the corollary of love; it is the inner perfection or harmony of all things in their relationships to God, when those relationships are characterized as they should be by an orientation to God above all else. Peace expressed as order in the temporal realm connotes the maintenance or restoration of relationships once threatened or broken, whether by sin in the universal relation of humanity to God or by dissension in the political or ecclesial community. Therefore, for Augustine, social order as a form of peace is also a form of love.

27. Ibid., 19.1, p. 669.

28. A concise, representative example is his definition in *On Christian Doctrine* of the grace-inspired love of God called *caritas* or charity: "I call 'charity' the motion of the soul toward the enjoyment of God for His own sake, and the enjoyment of one's self and of one's neighbor for the sake of God; but 'cupidity' is a motion of the soul toward the enjoyment of one's self, one's neighbor, or any corporal thing for the sake of something other than God" (3.10.16, trans. D. W. Robertson, Jr. [Indianapolis: Bobbs-Merrill, 1958], p. 88). See also *On the Morals of the Catholic Church*, 3–6, in *Basic Writings of St. Augustine*, vol. 1, ed. Whitney J. Oates (New York: Random House, 1948), 320–324; and *The Spirit and the Letter*, .39 and .49, in *Augustine: Later Works*, ed. John Burnaby, Library of Christian Classics 3 (Philadelphia: Westminster, 1955), 223, 233.

29. *City of God* 19.13; p. 690.

30. Ibid., 19.4, p. 680; see also 15.15, p. 165, where Augustine comments that eternal life will not be given to those who practice "virtue" without "true piety . . . which the Greeks call *latreia*." However, pagan virtue may yet deserve "a punishment less severe" in eternity (*The Spirit and the Letter*, .48, p. 232).

31. *City of God* 19.4, p. 676. See also *The Spirit and the Letter*, .60; 245: "Assuredly then it is God who brings about in a man the very will to believe, and in all things does his mercy anticipate us."

32. *City of God* 19.10, p. 686. Or again, "we shall one day be made to participate, according to our slender capacity, in His peace, both in ourselves, and with our neighbour, and with God our chief good" (22.29, p. 859).

Peace is realized provisionally, albeit defectively, whenever order or harmony prevails in earthly relationships, whether they be among members of the body, between body and soul, among members of a family, among citizens and rulers, or between humanity and God.[33] The "greatest ornament" of life on this earth is "temporal peace, such as we can enjoy in this life from health and safety and human fellowship.[34] Although neither the "supreme good" nor true happiness can be attained "in the present life," still, with God's help, the lusts of the flesh—cupidity or concupiscence—can be progressively restrained.[35] Even the life of pagans approximates the perfect harmony of the heavenly city to the extent that self-gratification is overcome and lesser beings and enjoyments are ordered in relation to those that are greater. Yet all of these approximations of peace are judged in light of the highest peace.

By contrast, life in the earthly city is distorted and deficient. Its aims and loves fall far short of, and indeed pervert, the love of God that alone confers real order in human affairs. The noblest forms of self-mastery are "inflated with pride"; "so long as there is no reference to God in the matter," they are "rather vices than virtues."[36] Pagan civic virtue will receive sufficient reward in earthly glory and success.[37]

By developing the antinomy between the earthly and heavenly cities, Augustine relates the kingdom to the incompleteness of Christian life in the world primarily by means of a metaphor of contrast rather than one of congruence. (Examples in the latter category would include the Pauline vocabulary of "body of Christ" in the world, and the more modern ones of "kingdom present" and "kingdom future," or "already" and "not yet.") So often Augustine stresses, not the incomplete but real presence of the kingdom in history, but the absence from the historical struggle of the harmony that will characterize the eschaton. A theological rationale for the kingdom's distance is a view of history as a time of trial and testing. The fullness of kingdom life is delayed, not because of failures of discipleship, but because God's providence designates history as a field on which Christian courage and steadfastness shall be tried, as the furnace in which impurities shall be purged.

> But as it must needs be in this world that the citizens of the kingdom of heaven are troubled by temptations in the midst of the erring and godless, so that they may be tested and tried as gold in the furnace, we should not wish to live before the time with the holy and upright only, that we may deserve to receive this reward in its own time.[38]

33. Ibid., 19.13, p. 690; and 19.13; pp. 694–95.
34. Ibid., 19.13, p. 691.
35. Ibid., 19.4, p. 677.
36. Ibid., 19.25, p. 707.
37. Ibid., 5.15, p. 165.
38. Augustine, "Letter 189, to Boniface," in *Saint Augustine: Letters,* Vol. 4 (165–203), trans. Wilfrid Parsons, SND, vol. 30 of *The Fathers of the Church,* ed. Roy J. Deferrari (New York: Fathers of the Church, Inc., 1955), 269.

In the *Retractationes*,[39] Augustine corrects any impression he might previously have given in *On the Lord's Sermon on the Mount* that the kingdom the Sermon announces can now be present fully, even in the lives of the dedicated few. Even the apostles can realize the eschatological blessings only with "the kind of perfection of which this life is capable, not as those things are to be realized, with that absolute peace for which we hope. . . ."[40] A more negative counterpoint in Augustine's characterization of temporal peace is his remark that "the peace which we enjoy in this life, whether common to all or peculiar to ourselves, is rather the solace of our misery than the positive enjoyment of felicity."[41]

It is not infrequently emphasized by interpreters that Augustine affirms the instrumental use of the peace of this world, even when requiring force or violence, as an aid to members of the heavenly city in their earthly journey. According to Richard B. Miller, the key to Augustine's logic of war is "an overarching theory of the meaning of peace," which is "not the absence of violence, but tranquility, concord, a set of properly ordered relations within or between human beings" that is essential to social fellowship.[42] Emphasizing like Miller the instrumental contribution of earthly peace, John Langan concludes that Augustine "puts more stress on the similarity between earthly peace and heavenly peace" than on their difference. Langan is certainly correct in noting that "a great deal also depends on the gradations of similarity to the ultimate peace one is prepared to recognize among the various forms of earthly peace that may be available as alternatives," especially in regard to the relative justice that accompanies each.[43] An emphasis on similarity would accord with Augustine's Neoplatonic view that lesser beings emanate from higher ones in a cosmic hierarchy, and that the lower differ from the higher in respect of their lesser participation in the good (ultimately God), rather than because of any positive evil (a phrase that for Augustine would be a contradiction in terms).

Yet, because Augustine's affirmations of the relative peace attained in the two cities are always accompanied by a strong caveat, the accent the reader gives to Augustine's view of social and political participation may at least as credibly fall on the pessimistic side of the picture. Every analogy builds both on similarity and on difference, both on derivation and on discontinuity, and

39. "Reconsiderations" in which Augustine both defends and revises earlier positions.

40. Augustine, *Retractations*, trans. Mary Inez Bogan, vol. 60 of *The Fathers of the Church*, ed. Roy J. Deferrari (Washington, D.C.: Catholic Univ. of America Press, 1968), .18, p. 80. Augustine, in *On the Lord's Sermon on the Mount,* 1.4.12, had explained Jesus' saying, "Blessed are the peacemakers for they shall be called children of God," by adding, "And these things can be realized even in this life as we believe they were realized in the apostles."

41. *City of God*, 19.27, pp. 707–708.

42. Richard B. Miller, *Interpretations of Conflict: Ethics, Pacifism, and the Just-War Tradition* (Chicago: Univ. of Chicago Press, 1991), 21.

43. John Langan, SJ, "The Elements of St. Augustine's Just War Theory," *Journal of Religious Ethics* 12 (Spring 1984): 29.

this is true of Augustine's comparison of earthly to heavenly peace. The heavenly city is "a captive and a stranger in the earthly city," though it "makes no scruple to obey the laws of the earthly city" in order to secure the things necessary to the common life of both cities in this world.[44] Miserable is the people that is alienated from God. Yet even this people has a peace of its own that is not to be lightly esteemed—though, indeed, the people shall not in the end enjoy the peace, because they make no good use of it before the end.[45] The "well ordered concord of civic obedience and rule," directed toward the attainment of "the things which are helpful to this life," is not a peace secured by faith. "The heavenly city, or rather the part of it which sojourns on earth and lives by faith, makes use of this peace only because it must, until this mortal condition which necessitates it shall pass away."[46]

Also in Book 19 of *The City of God*, Augustine offers a revealing description of the "wise judge," who serves well as a metaphor for Christian political involvement. The judge, in the course of ensuring the civil peace, cannot avoid perpetrating "numerous and important evils," such as the torture of the innocent. These evils are not sins on his part, not only because he does not intend them maliciously, but also because human society demands the judicial role, however dirty it may turn his hands. The judge's dilemma is enough to make us "condemn human life as miserable," to make the judge himself "recognise the misery of these necessities, and shrink from his own implication in that misery." Well may he cry in "piety" to God, " 'From my necessities deliver Thou me.' "[47] The so-called peace and justice of the earthly order are maintained only with tools and at costs that are abhorrent to the citizen of God's city, and they are employed and paid with revulsion.

In understanding Augustine's theological approach to the political order, it is essential to include in the account the fact that the true peace of the heavenly city could never depend on the coercive balance of power generally suggested by political uses of the term "justice." Thus, insofar as civic authority, government, and so-called peace presuppose coercion and depend on power, they are in radical opposition to the peace that consists in graced conversion of the will to true piety toward God and charity toward God's creatures.[48] Although the Christian has a responsibility to participate in the endeavors of the temporal sphere that make the common life possible, the norm of justice itself is suspect when compared to the gospel ideal of love or charity.

The problematic point for Christian social ethics is what rectifying means are available to Christians when the harmony of peace, interrupted by sin,

44. *City of God* 19.17, p. 696.
45. Ibid., 19.26, p. 707.
46. Ibid., 19.17, pp. 695–96.
47. Ibid., 19.6, pp. 682–83.
48. God willed at the creation that humans should live together in harmonious society. Thus society as such is not evil, but it is now marred by sin so that all its members are lost from proper relationship to God, except for those saved by God's "undeserved grace" (*City of God* 14.1, p. 441).

fails. Augustine's theological principle of the comprehensiveness of love in constituting all positive moral relations makes it difficult for him to account for any approved moral action as systematically outside the realm of love. And for historical as well as theological reasons, he was not willing to uphold the rule of love while excluding the moral acceptability of war and other violent coercion.

On the historical plane, Augustine faced what must have seemed dire concrete threats to a precariously established political and religious culture: barbarian challenges to the empire, and the attacks of heretics on the unity of the African church. The peace established by Constantine was also a peace for Christianity to which it was important to cling tenaciously and whose stability it was crucial to augment. Augustine's schema of the "Two Cities" mediates between the ideal realization of divinely ordained peace and the historical circumstances of Christianity in which the struggle against sin is waged. Order in both the political and the ecclesial sphere is unsurpassably important but fundamentally unstable, so that Augustine is willing to justify extreme means to maintain it.

Loss of the essentially theological horizon of Augustine's political theory will result in a distortion of his perspective on justified political action.[49] *Caritas*, for Augustine the theologian, does not ratify the deepest values of secular politics but calls them to judgment. The choice for which Augustine may have to be held accountable is his willingness to allow considerable leeway in history for Christian compromise with secular and civic values and "necessities," deferring eschatological transformation of major dimensions of Christian practice from history to heaven.[50] (We shall return below to Augustine's specific discussions of the morality of war.)

49. William R. Stevenson agrees: "One cannot adequately present or understand Augustine's thoughts on war unless one enters into intimate contact with his thoughts on God. Indeed, Augustine's thoughts on politics severally cannot be divorced from his thoughts on God" (*Christian Love and Just War*, 9). In many ways provocative, George Weigel's far-reaching analysis of the "catholic" just war tradition lacks the religious and theological dimensions requisite to an interpretation of Augustine (and Aquinas) as self-defined *Christian* just war thinkers (*Tranquillitas Ordinis: The Present Failure and Future Promise of American Catholic Thought on War and Peace* [New York: Oxford Univ. Press, 1987]). Although Weigel recognizes that political peace is a negative conception in relation to heavenly peace, he lifts Augustine's concentrated discussion of "tranquillity of order" out of its larger context of order in relation to God, and treats it as though it referred primarily (not derivatively) to the political arena. The keeping of peace in that realm by coercive power is thus given an autonomy and legitimacy it does not receive in *The City of God*.

50. Contrast in this respect Augustine's position on lying. He disallows the morality of any lie whatsoever, even a lie told in order to avoid grave and unjust harm that will otherwise befall another, and rejects any excusing distinction between what may be falsity in one's speech and what may be purity in the intention of one's heart. In time of temptation, one may be fortified by recalling the contemplation of the "luminous good," real unity, that permits not even the shadow of a lie ("Against Lying," in Treatises on Various Subjects, ed. R. J. Deferrari, vol. 16 of *The Fathers of the Church* [New York: Catholic Univ. of America Press, 1952], chaps. 1, 2, 18.

## *Augustine's Biblical Interpretation*

In justifying and limiting recourse to violence, Augustine is influenced not only by the biblical witness, but also by Roman practice or custom and pagan philosophy (for example, Plato and Cicero). His interpretation of the New Testament's practical moral implications depends on these other sources, which represent contact with and respect for the broader civic or political community within which the Christian community exists concretely. It is difficult to resolve the question whether Augustine begins experientially with the perceived historical necessity of waging war to preserve the civil order, and so tries to square it with the New Testament; or sets out from the Christian ideal of love of neighbor and enemy but meets up with the difficulty of how best to put this ideal into practice in a fallen world.

As a moral and political theorist, Augustine is a self-consciously Christian author. Unlike the modern Christian "just war" thinker, he rarely grounds his views of the social use of violence in commonly held values but sets as his explicit foundation the definitive Christian text, the Holy Scriptures. Most important is the New Testament; Augustine does not avoid the challenge of Jesus' nonviolent example by turning instead to the heroes of the Old Testament, and certainly not by averring (anachronistically) that a revealed text is not an appropriate resource for normative reflection on public behavior. Instead he uses the gospel as a lens through which to envision the meanings both of Israelite examples and of social responsibility in his own age and culture.

Augustine insists repeatedly in his writings that there exists a "harmony" between the Old and New Testaments, a belief whose credibility it was particularly important to defend against the Manichean denial of part of the Old Testament canon. Augustine affirmed a "complete agreement" of the words of the Old Testament with those of the New; he rhapsodizes, "On the wonderful order and divine harmony of the two Testaments, we could discourse at length."[51] Revelation occurring throughout the life of the Chosen People, the mission of Jesus, and the composition of the communities' inspired writings is progressive and pedagogical. Although "fear predominates in the Old Testament and love in the New," the soul is gradually led from fear to love and thus to "the perfection of moral conduct."[52] Some parts of Sacred Scripture apply only to some classes of persons, not all.[53] Superficially inconsistent texts may express the same doctrine in different ways or in different contexts, and the most profound meaning of a passage is not always the one most immediately apparent.

51. Augustine, "The Way of Life of the Catholic Church," in *Saint Augustine: The Catholic and Manichaean Ways of Life,* trans. Donald A. Gallagher and Idella J. Gallagher, vol. 56 of *The Fathers of the Church,* ed. Roy J. Deferrari (Washington, D.C.: Catholic Univ. of America Press, 1966), 45 and 43, respectively.

52. Ibid., 43–44.

53. *On Christian Doctrine* 3.18.25, p. 94. Augustine, unlike Ambrose and Aquinas, does not seem to distinguish explicitly between clergy and laity on the subject of participation in violence.

Under the influence of Ambrose and Neoplatonist philosophy, Augustine adopted an allegorical method of exegesis, according to which biblical texts may have multiple meanings and some elements of the Bible are construed as signs of divine things.[54] Yet Augustine did not allegorize unrestrainedly, and his reliance on the literal readings of texts increased in his later works.[55] Augustine also advocated typological or figurative interpretation—understanding the meaning of one thing by means of another—cautiously using the rules of a Donatist author, Tyconius.[56]

In his treatise *On Christian Doctrine*, which deals essentially with biblical interpretation, Augustine claims that the canon is unified in God's intention, despite diversity of genres and obscurity of some meanings. The key to Scripture is love of God and neighbor.[57] Gordon Hamilton states that a "fundamental point of Augustine's exegesis, which could be added as a principle second only to the primary purpose of interpreting scripture (the enjoyment of God), is interpreting the Bible in the light of Christian doctrine and the life of the Church."[58] It is the church that sets the canon, and it is within its faith and practice that the meaning of Scripture is decided.

However, if employed with a "meek and humble heart,"[59] nonbiblical disciplines can aid interpretation. These include history, descriptions of the natural world, the sciences, and philosophy.[60] That the determination of signs must remain a somewhat circular process, to be undertaken with the commitment of faith and in the context of the needs of the church, is clear from Augustine's instruction to resolve ambiguities by "the rule of faith." This rule is to be found "in the more open places of Scripture and in the authority of the Church." If unclarity still remains, then attention must be given to the context of a problematic passage. Further ambiguities—Augustine seems to suppose they will be minor—may be settled with "whatever blameless interpretation the reader wishes."[61]

Augustine cautions that overly lavish resort to figurative interpretation can result from "erroneous opinion." He warns, "If the minds of men are subject to some erroneous opinion they think that whatever Scripture says contrary to that opinion is figurative."[62] Yet Augustine's own proposed limits on interpretation contain an irreducible circularity. Scripture is the foundation for Christian faith and life, but if a text departs from "virtuous behavior" or seems

54. G. W. H. Lampe, ed., *The West from the Fathers to the Reformation,* vol. 2 of *The Cambridge History of the Bible* (Cambridge: Cambridge Univ. Press, 1969), 546–47.

55. Gordon J. Hamilton, "Augustine's Methods of Biblical Interpretation," in *Grace, Politics, and Desire: Essays on Augustine,* ed. Hugo Maynell (Calgary: Univ. of Calgary Press, 1990), 110.

56. Ibid.,111.

57. *On Christian Doctrine,* 1.35–36, p. 30, and 2.7, p. 39.

58. Hamilton, "Augustine's Methods," 113.

59. *On Christian Doctrine*, 2.41, p. 76.

60. Ibid., 2.28–31, pp. 463–68.

61. Ibid., 3.1–3, pp. 78–81.

62. Ibid., 3.10, p. 88.

to condone vice or crime then it is certain to be figurative. Virtue and vice, in turn, may be defined either in relation to charity or to "the custom of the good men among [one's] neighbors."[63] Even when a religious understanding of love of God and neighbor controls, the meaning of Scripture may not be plain and may require reference to the rule of faith, context, personal judgment, and the concrete social context in which action is proposed, evaluated, and chosen or rejected. The result is to make the moral meaning of Scripture more radically dependent on philosophical and political mediation than ever before. The practical results of Augustine's hermeneutic decisions lead to the question whether the New Testament counsels that have served as his point of departure have really in the end controlled the substance of his positions on war and nonresistance.

## *Christian Justification of Killing*

Christians in the fourth century not only depended on the Roman Empire for protection from barbarian invasion, but received from this same government public recognition and protection that were wholly unanticipated by the earlier pacifist theologians. Augustine's contemporaries were able to contemplate Christian transformation of society in a way unimaginable to their forebears. But large-scale social change may require the use of force against those unconverted to Christianity's truths. Violent coercion construed as punishment protects the common welfare by discouraging future infractions and removing the present causes of discord. As chastisement, punishment may encourage reform, and even if death results, punishment cannot harm its object in any essential (spiritual) way. Augustine carefully observes that only those possessed of ordered and authoritative power have the duty to punish, as "when the soldier kills an enemy or the judge or official puts a criminal to death."[64] Private citizens may not kill, even to protect themselves from a robbery that presents danger of death,[65] or to shorten the suffering of a dying person.[66] Augustine does not connect this prohibition of personal self-defense particularly with Christian commitment. Further, the lawfully commissioned agents should be guided by motives of public interest or reform of the sinner, not hatred:

> In regard to killing men so as not to be killed by them, this view does not please me, unless perhaps it should be a soldier or a public official. In this

63. Ibid., 3.10–16, pp. 88–93.

64. *Free Choice of the Will* 4, p. 9. See also *City of God*, 1.21, p. 27, and "Letter 47, to Publicola," p. 230.

65. *Free Choice of the Will* 5, p. 11. A contradictory or at least anomalous text, which I owe to Richard Miller, permits self-defense to the traveler attacked on the road. See *Saint Augustine, Letters*, vol. 3 (131–164), trans. Wilfrid Parsons, SND, vol. 20 of *The Fathers of the Church*, ed. R. J. Deferrari (New York: Catholic Univ. of America, 1953), 294.

66. Augustine, "Letter 204, to Dulcitius," in *Saint Augustine: Letters*, vol. 5 (204–270), trans. Wilfrid Parson, SND, vol. 32 of *The Fathers of the Church*, ed. Roy J. Deferrari (New York: Fathers of the Church, Inc., 1956), 6.

> case, he does not do it for his own sake, but for others or for the state to which he belongs, having received the power lawfully in accord with his public character. Even to those who are deterred from doing evil by some fear, perhaps some help is offered. Hence it was said: "We are not to resist evil" [Matt. 5:39], lest we take pleasure in vengeance which nourishes the soul on another's wrong, but we are not to fall short in correcting men.[67]

The difficulties of the practical undertaking in a Christian spirit of authorized activities of killing engage Augustine as he interprets the Sermon on the Mount. Commenting on Matthew 5, Augustine handles the face value of the "hard sayings" by employing the interpretive categories of the ideal, the pedagogical, the symbolic, the intentional, and the practical. He uses these categories to mediate between the radical ideal of the kingdom and the lesser arena of political order. Augustine lays out a historical zone in which God's people progresses toward the more perfect understanding and realization of God's will, and defines that zone also as a realm of conflict between the people of God and the people of the earthly city.

In explaining the sayings on nonresistance and self-offering of Matthew 5:38-42, Augustine proposes that "perfect peace" is "to have absolutely no wish for any . . . retribution,"[68] however moderate. However, the Israelite law's dictate, "an eye for an eye and a tooth for a tooth" educates from the lust for immoderate revenge toward even requital for injury. This provision of the law suits "the orderly succession of eras," and holds an educative and transitional "middle position" between unlimited revenge and the ideal of nonretribution, "the principle which the Lord prescribed for the perfecting of his followers." [69] Indeed, even nonretaliation falls short of the Lord's precept, since "the Lord seems to deem it insufficient unless you are ready to receive even further evil."[70]

This readiness is symbolized by the instruction to turn the right cheek after having been struck on the left, to give one's tunic as well as one's cloak, and to go the second mile. The Lord himself did not follow his previous precept literally when struck by the servant of the high priest, although he was prepared to offer his whole body as a sacrifice on the cross.[71] So it may be understood that the precept is not literal but is symbolic of a nonresistant

67. "Letter 47, to Publicola," *Saint Augustine: Letters,* vol. 1 (1–82), trans. Wilfrid Parsons, SND, vol. 12 of *The Fathers of the Church,* ed. Roy J. Deferrari (New York: Fathers of the Church, Inc., 1951), 230.

68. "Commentary on the Lord's Sermon on the Mount," in *Saint Augustine: Commentary on the Lord's Sermon on the Mount with Seventeen Related Sermons,* trans. Denis J. Kavanagh, OSA, vol 11 of *The Fathers of the Church* (New York: Fathers of the Church, Inc., 1951), 1.19.56, p. 80.

69. Ibid., 1.19.57, p. 81.

70. Ibid., p. 82.

71. Augustine makes a similar argument in "Letter 138, to Marcellinus," where he argues that "if we notice the words and imagine that they are to be kept literally, we might suppose the right cheek is not to be offered if the left is struck." In *Saint Augustine: Letters,* vol. 3, p. 44.

and self-offering disposition. It is a "precept with regard to the preparation of the heart, and not with regard to the visible performance of the deed." The Christian "should have his heart prepared for everything."[72] Anyone who perpetrates further injustice against one's person should "be endured with equanimity."[73] Augustine creates a space between preparedness to act on the Lord's commands and the actual embodiment of their literal meaning. In this space it will become necessary to determine exactly which actions—if not the ones literally mentioned as exemplifying the kingdom ideal—are the means by which the disciple moves from preparation to action. The most problematic question will be whether the preparedness for which Jesus calls can come to fruition only in other forms of nonresistance unspecified by him or in nonviolent resistance, or in violence also. How far away from the literal meaning can Christian action move and still be claimed to lie within the symbolic range of Jesus' illustrations?

## *Violence as War*

In writings in which Augustine's point of departure is war or the military profession, these themes are reiterated. Response to evil, legitimate authority, and rightful intention are paramount. It is against a backdrop of ambivalence about the potential for virtue of political life that Augustine moves to *The City of God's* brief justification of war as a means toward the provisional and analogous sort of peace that can be attained in political community. War is waged to gain victory, "conquest of those who resist us," and thus to establish "peace with glory" via the victors' suppression of historical conflict into "a peace that suits them better."[74] Obviously enough from this pejorative and even cynical portrayal, Augustine has in view not a true peace but a barely analogous peace, a peace that derives its name from a reality of which it is the mere shadow. Augustine expands on his view that even robbers, murderers, and domestic tyrants seek a peace of this sort in the midst of violence. At the same time, he does not lose sight of the contribution of a partial peace to social order, especially if established by Christian rulers with motives of service and attitudes of restraint. He exhorts Boniface, governor of Africa, to be a peacemaker (following Matt. 5:9) "even while you make war," for war may be necessary in order to secure peace.[75]

Augustine brings his acceptance of violence in pursuit of peace into contact with the biblical witness against violence in his *Reply to Faustus the Manichaean*. One purpose of this work is to defend the Christian Scriptures against the accusation that the violence and wars recounted in the Old Testament cannot have been commanded by the true God who is good. Augustine

72. *Commentary on the Lord's Sermon,* 1.19.59 and 58, p. 85.
73. Ibid., 1.19.61, p. 88.
74. *City of God,* 19.12, p. 687.
75. Augustine, "Letter 189, to Boniface," 269.

enunciates early in the work his principle that whatsoever the canon shows to have been said even once is true and "all things agree." His agenda, of course, is refutation of his adversaries' claim that the Old and New Testaments cannot be reconciled. In his answer to them, Augustine does not take recourse to symbolical interpretations in explaining Israelite wars (as he sometimes does[76]), but locates Moses' authority, in leading his people's rebellion, in the delegated authority of God and in the fact that the Egyptians were "unrighteous oppressors."[77] The tribune Marcellinus also wrote to Augustine, expressing concern that if the God of the Old Testament is the God of the Christians, then he is a fickle God who changes his requirements.[78] Augustine replies that the Old Testament is "the veil of the New Testament,"[79] that observances in the former may be signs of Christ, and that variation in religious observance may be part of God's eternal plan without implying changeability in God.[80]

Augustine explains that cause and authority are important in evaluating war. "The peace and safety of the community" are the justification for war; where these are the objectives, war is in obedience to God's will. The soldier will be innocent in carrying out even an "unrighteous command" of the king, on whom he ought to rely for the determination of just or unjust cause.[81] The evils in war are not death and destruction but "love of violence, revengeful cruelty, fierce and implacable enmity, wild resistance, and the lust of power, and such like."[82] Thus any supposition that Jesus by his example or teaching forbids war is unwarranted, for nonresistance of evil requires "not a bodily action but an inward disposition."[83] Certainly, it cannot be impossible for a person to fulfill the conditions of the Beatitudes even in the profession of a soldier. Otherwise, John the Baptist would have sent away the soldiers who came to him.[84]

76. As in explaining "wars" of Ps. 46:9 as wars of ungodliness, in Saint Augustine, *Expositions on the Book of Psalms,* vol 2, trans. Members of the English Church, vol. 25 of *A Library of the Fathers of the Holy Catholic Church* (London: F. & J. Rivington, 1848), p. 272.

77. *Against Faustus,* 22.71–74, pp. 460–63. Likewise, Abraham's killing of his son would have been executed at the behest of God, "who alone knows the suitable command in every case."

78. Augustine, "Letter 136, Marcellinus to Augustine," in *Saint Augustine: Letters,* vol. 3, pp. 16–17.

79. Augustine, "Letter 138, to Marcellinus," 51.

80. Ibid., 39–41.

81. *Reply to Faustus the Manichaean,* 22.75, pp. 464–65. In his commentary on Psalm 125, Augustine says that a man "ought not . . . to disdain . . . to serve even a bad master!" This includes the "infidel Emperor" Julian, whom the Christian soldiers served, though "when they came to the cause of Christ, they acknowledged Him only Who was in heaven. If he called upon them at any time to worship idols, to offer incense, they preferred God to him: but whenever he commanded them to deploy into line, to march against this or that nation, they at once obeyed. They distinguished their everlasting from their temporal master; and yet they were, for the sake of their everlasting master submissive to their temporal master." Augustine, *Expositions on the Book of Psalms,* vol. 5, trans. H. M. Wilkins, vol. 37 of *A Library of the Fathers of the Holy Catholic Church* (London: F. & J. Rivington, 1853), p. 543).

82. Ibid., 22.74, p. 463.

83. Ibid., 22.76, p. 465.

84. Ibid., 22.74, p. 464.

Marcellinus, a Roman commissioner in Carthage who sided with Augustine during the Donatist controversy, found it questionable whether genuine observance of Christianity could be compatible with the prevention of evil to the state.[85] Augustine points out that attitudes of forbearance and pardon are praised even in powerful pagan rulers such as Caesar (by Cicero). He continues in a utilitarian mode to state that an ethos of forgiveness would be effective in building up the "bond of common agreement" that is the very foundation of the state.[86] The ideal resolution of instances of social conflict and crime is the overcoming of evil with good, the conversion of wrongdoers by an example of patience and mercy.[87]

The successful nonviolent confrontation of good with evil is, however, more difficult to accomplish on an international level than on an interpersonal one. Thus strict adherence to a norm precluding action against evildoers is neither necessary nor commendable, even for Christians. Although Augustine calls wars of domination mere "robbery,"[88] wars to protect the lawful security of the state ("the protection of the citizens"[89]), or even to punish wrongs committed against it, are a different matter. John Langan notes that Augustine focuses on punishment rather than on self-defense in his discussion of war, because defense to the death of finite goods, which are eventually to be lost anyway, is intrinsically suspect as the motive of a Christian.[90] The state and its agents, in punishing wrongdoers, are analogous to a father who punishes his son.[91] Sinners who escape punishment only grow more bold.[92] The governing authority must occasionally act "with a sort of kindly harshness, when we are trying to make unwilling souls yield, because we have to consider their welfare rather than their inclination"; "even war will not be waged without kindness."[93]

When punishment is the course to be taken, as determined by the practical and political necessity of keeping social order, then the sayings of Jesus about nonresistance are moved to the interior sphere: "those precepts of patience are always to be preserved in the heart, to keep it in readiness, and those kindly feelings which keep us from returning evil for evil are always to be developed in the will."[94] "Finally, those precepts refer rather to the interior

85. Augustine, "Letter 136, Marcellinus to Augustine," 16–17.
86. "Letter 138, to Marcellinus", 42-43.
87. Ibid., 44.
88. *City of God,* 4.6, p.114
89. Saint Augustine, *On Free Choice of the Will,* trans. Anna S. Benjamin and L. H. Hackstaff (Indianapolis: Bobbs-Merrill, 1964), .5, pp. 11–12.
90. Langan, "Elements of St. Augustine's Just War Theory," 27.
91. Letter 138, "to Marcellinus," 46. A parallel text occurs in the "Commentary on the Sermon on the Mount" 20.63, p. 90: "Hence, the only requisite is that the punishment be inflicted by one who really is endued with authority, and that he inflict the punishment as affectionately as a father would punish his little child, because, in view of its youth, the father cannot as yet hate his child."
92. Ibid., 47.
93. Ibid., 46-47.
94. Ibid., 46.

disposition of the heart than to the act which appears exteriorly, and they enjoin on us to preserve patience and kindly feeling in the hidden places of the soul, revealing them openly when it seems likely to be beneficial to those whose welfare we seek."[95]

One wonders how well hidden is the place of kindliness when one reads Augustine's comfort to the Christian who shows patience toward the oppressor. God, says Augustine (echoing Tertullian; and Calvin will echo both), will repay our enemy even if we do not: "A final just vengeance is looked for, that is, the last supreme judgment only when no chance of correction remains."[96] Now the correspondence of violent act to loving intentionality is evidently reversed; when the Christian refrains from personal self-defense, he or she is permitted at least to indulge the fantasy of the foe's perdition.

Augustine's discussion of the prohibition of swearing[97] gives a clear instance of the model he uses in handling practical compromise with the ideals of the kingdom. In Augustine's view an ordered social life demands effective response to "infirmity" or sin, even when such response requires a departure from the literal sense of the Lord's commands. Compromise may be a pragmatic necessity, though it is one from which we pray to be delivered in the prayer of the kingdom (the Lord's Prayer). Augustine's reluctance to discount totally the literal force of Jesus' hard sayings against violence and in favor of love of enemies is captured, however, in his ambiguous remark that the precepts of nonresistance are to be kept in readiness in the heart; though not to be acted upon at present they seem to envision future action that is more consistent with the kingdom ideal. Yet both the exact nature of that action and the criteria for determining the time appropriate to its realization remain unspecified.

In a sense there are two distinct beginning points or emphases in Augustine's view of the necessity of war. One is the practical political perception that social life demands that order be preserved, even if at the cost of violence. The other is the Christian religious conviction that love controls the entire moral life, even when violent coercion is morally demanded to serve the neighbor, punish the enemy, and protect the common good. The present

95. Ibid., 45. See also "Reply to Faustus" 22.76: "what is required here is not a bodily action but an inward disposition."

96. "Letter 138, to Marcellinus," 45.

97. The prohibition is aimed primarily at *false* swearing, against which the absolute statement is a hedge. See "Letter 47, to Publicola," 227; *Commentary on the Sermon on the Mount* 1. 17.51; pp. 74–75: "The Lord's prohibition of swearing is to be understood, therefore, as meaning that no one is to desire an oath as if it were something good, lest—through a habit engendered by the constant repetition of swearing—he gradually descend to false swearing. Accordingly, let a man restrain himself as much as he can, since he understands that swearing is not to be counted among the things that are good, but as one of the things that are necessary. Let him make use of it only through necessity. . . . In other words, if you are forced to take an oath, remember that the necessity for it arises from the infirmity of those whom you are trying to persuade with regard to something. And of course this is the evil from which we make daily supplication to be delivered, when we say, 'Deliver us from evil' (Matt. 6.13)."

emphasis on love as a primary but paradoxical norm in Augustine's just war theory is not intended to deny that peace is important to Augustine; indeed, it grounds that very theory. Ordered love is the essence of peace.

However, the paradox or tension in his approach to war (and to social ethics more generally) results from the fact that he both works with the distant eschatology implied by his contrast of the heavenly kingdom with history, and still wants to retain Christian love as the ground and measure of specific moral actions (such as violent coercion) engendered by the necessity of compromising with political exigency. Because Augustine is unwilling to give up love (*caritas*) as the principle that orders all the Christian's relations, he attempts to explain force as love's work. Even when peacemaking moves into violence, Augustine still tries to align that progression with love, as love's direct consequence. It is an act of love to restore the peace by using violence; in his mind it is even an act of love toward the object of the violence. Augustine links violent actions as well as he can with at least a benevolent intention, and with the hope that a true and integral peace will come to characterize relationships originally ordered by force. But for the present the kingdom in its fullness is distant indeed, and political life and even the life of the church at best approximate it dimly.

## *Violent Defense of Religion*

The particular political body of which Augustine was a member—the post-Constantinian Roman Empire—was not, of course, pagan nor even secular from Augustine's viewpoint. Because of the respect and even hegemony that Christianity had achieved in Roman society, the political projects and moral status of the emperor could not be set on a level with those of the pagan philosophers and rulers with whom Augustine contends in, for instance, *The City of God*. The empire is certainly not to be identified with the City of God, and hence its "peace" is always shadowed by defect. However, political life after Constantine seemed gradually transformed by the influence of Christianity. Says Augustine's biographer, Peter Brown, the church in the fourth century "is a group no longer committed to defend itself against society; but rather, poised, ready to fulfil what it considered its historic mission, to dominate, to absorb, to lead a whole Empire."[98] And inasmuch as the empire and its ruler are Catholic, appeal at least can be made to them on the basis of gospel ideals. Furthermore, their protection and aid can be summoned against heretics who challenge the unity of the faith from within.

Augustine's struggle with the Donatist heresy provides a fascinating nexus of his views of kingdom ideals, ecclesial realities, and practical political power. The Donatist controversy had precisely to do with the nature of the church as a holy community, membership in which is marked by a distinctively

98. Brown, *Augustine of Hippo*, 214.

different life-style, a higher moral and religious standard. It may also have had to do with Augustine's concern that, as schismatics with terrorist tendencies, the Donatists threatened the political as well as the ecclesial order. The Donatists claimed that the validity of the sacraments is affected by the holiness of the minister, and that the Church will be unworthy if it permits unworthy leaders, especially those who cooperated with the civil authorities during Diocletian's persecution (A.D. 303).[99] Augustine, on the other hand, was committed to the expansion of Catholicism's size and influence, not just to preservation of its purity and traditions. Observes Brown,

> A man who feels intensely that the existing bonds of men in society are somehow dislocated, but that the group to which he belongs can consolidate and purify them, will regard the society around him as so much raw material to be absorbed and transformed. He will be very different from the man who feels that he can only create an alternative to this society—a little 'Kingdom of Saints', sheltering beneath a bishop, the only possessor of a divine law in a hostile or indifferent world.[100]

In combating the Donatists, Augustine resorted to political and physical coercion as well as to theological argument. In the process of aligning Church and political community, he imports into the religious community the tools for establishing order in civil society. In his ambition for the success and defensibility of Christianity, he loosens his grip on those qualities that distinguish the life of the disciple from that of other citizens.

Augustine's views on the Donatist threat are summarized in a letter to Boniface, Christian governor of Africa, with whom Augustine corresponded frequently regarding the reconciliation of political duty with Christian faith. Not unaware that his own view of the Church does not emerge easily from the New Testament, Augustine calls attention to the necessity of adapting the teachings of the apostles to different historical circumstances. Those who resist the enactment of civil laws punishing heresy by appealing to the apostolic era "fail to notice that times were different then, and that all things have to be done at their own times." Expanding with an observation on the New Testament context that also would apply to early Christian pacifism, Augustine notes, "At that time there was no emperor who believed in Christ, or who would have served Him by enacting laws in favor of religion and against irreligion."[101] A sovereign serves God by legally commanding goodness and true worship of God.[102] Through such laws "all will be called to salvation," either by fear or conversion.[103]

99. J. N. D. Kelly, *Early Christian Doctrines* (New York: Harper and Row, 1958, 1960), 410.

100. Brown, *Augustine of Hippo,* 225. See also TeSelle, *Augustine the Theologian,* 273: against the Donatists' "earnest perfectionism calling for purity in the Church and in individual lives," Augustine objects that "no man can lead a perfect life, however sincerely he tries."

101. Augustine, "Letter 185, to Boniface," in *St. Augustine: Letters,* vol. 4, chap. 19, p. 159.

102. Ibid., 160.

103. Ibid., 148.

The purpose of coercive laws is to achieve the peace and unity of Christianity, as the church on earth embodying "Jerusalem." [104] This argument is flawed by two points of incongruity, given the manner in which Augustine elsewhere expects the peace of the heavenly city to be completed only eschatologically, and his belief that the reality of that kingdom is present in history only where there is genuine love of God. First, in Augustine's attack on the Donatists the metaphor "Jerusalem" is used to cover the church on earth, understood not as a holy sect or a transhistorical ideal, but as an institutional, ecclesial, and even sociopolitical body encompassing believers at disparate levels of commitment. The practical effect of this near collapse of the ideal into the real is to dislocate Augustine's ecclesiology so that the limitations of the historical church (and its need to live with imperfection) are no longer so well illuminated in their irremediability against an eschatological horizon of judgment and transformation. Second, the methods for enforcing order in civil bodies of equally disparate constituencies are taken to be appropriate for effective control over the church—for enforcing the unity of "Jerusalem" in earthly incarnation. Augustine thus places himself in the position—whose anomolous character he half admits[105]—of espousing violent coercion when persuasion fails to induce religious conversion, an event in which *caritas* supposedly is to order all things through God's grace-filled healing of the will.

Augustine has two ways around this apparent inconsistency between the peace of Christian love and violence. First, he relies heavily on Old Testament examples of divinely sanctioned force and bloodshed to characterize the Donatist debate, and thus to justify violence against the offenders. Second, he returns to the theme of loving punishment, also prominent in his discussion of secular warfare, in order to reconcile violence on behalf of religion with the evangelical commands. The persecution of Hagar by Sarah is said, for instance, to have "prefigured" the affliction of the heretics by "Jerusalem," the "true Church of God";[106] the Donatists are compared to the persecutors of Daniel[107] and to Saul acting wickedly toward David.[108] David himself wept over the death of his son Absalom, but that death was the price of the latter's participation in a war against his own father.[109] Augustine protests, "if the good and holy never persecute anyone but only suffer persecution, whose voice do they think that is in the psalm where we read: 'I will pursue after

104. Ibid., chap. 46, p. 185. See also chap. 9, p. 149, and "185A, to Count Boniface," a fragment, p. 90 of the same volume.

105. "Does anyone doubt that it is better for man to be led to the worship of God by teaching rather than forced to it by fear of suffering? Because the former group is preferable it does not follow that those of the latter, who are not like them, should be neglected." "Letter 185, to Boniface," chap. 21, p. 161.

106. Ibid., chap. 11, p. 151.

107. Ibid., chap. 7, p. 147.

108. Ibid., chap. 9, p. 150.

109. Ibid., chap. 32, p. 172.

my enemies and overtake them, and I will not turn again until they are consumed.' "[110] It is God's voice, but Augustine is willing to identify it not only with the Catholic church, but also with civil authorities acting cooperatively with the ecclesial body.

From the ancient Israelite point of view, it may have been credible to identify the people of God with the nation, and to undertake violence to preserve the purity of the covenant. However, the New Testament sets aside any nationalistic understanding of God's reign, and with it the instruments of power requisite to national survival. Israelite nationalism has more in common with Augustine's post-Constantinian vision of an imperially sanctioned Christianity than it does with Jesus' preaching that to "repent and believe in the gospel" is the proper way to recognize that "the Kingdom of God has come near" (Mark 1:15).

Augustine also tries to retrieve the love command by connecting it with an intention of reform. He cites other Old Testament texts that urge punishment as a means of education of the child.[111] The church punishes the Donatists as a father beats a rebellious son;[112] the motivation is "Christian charity" and "fraternal love," which hopes that the wayward will be converted and saved.[113] In this debate, Augustine has slipped from his dialectic contrast of the two cities in *The City of God* by modeling the relationships constitutive of the heavenly kingdom on temporal relationships. In the City of Babylon, historical imperfection and sin will lead inevitably to strife, so that the harmony of political and social life requires other means of support than grace, faith, and love. Nowhere is the incongruity between the religious identity of the church and its pragmatic compromise with violence more evident or more jarring than in Augustine's supposition that physical force may be used to encourage Christian faith. A defense of Augustine on this point could rest only on the possibility that his actions against the Donatists were primarily a reply to their own violence and attacks on other Christians, in which case coercion of them could be seen to further peace in the practical social order.[114]

## CONCLUSION

Augustine distinguishes the peace of the heavenly city from the peace that can be enjoyed on earth, drawing an analogy between the two. The Christian begins in this world to live by the transcendently ordered love that is *caritas*. Yet the potential for embodying that love socially is severely limited by the radically disordered nature of the "loves" of the political community in which

110. Ibid., chap. 11, p. 151, citing Ps. 17:38 (18:38).
111. Ibid., chap. 21, p. 162, citing Prov. 23:14, 13:24.
112. Ibid., chap. 7, pp. 147–48.
113. Ibid., chap. 14, p. 155, and chap. 11, p. 152.
114. For some evidence in favor of this motive, see Stevenson, *Christian Love and Just War*, 101–4.

the Christian has practical responsibilities. Eugene TeSelle refers to Augustine's "political realism," his "refusal to hold illusions about the nature of political life."[115] Violent action becomes acceptable to the degree that the heavenly kingdom recedes from history and becomes a distant ideal to be fulfilled eschatologically. The distance of the eschatological kingdom is particularly pronounced in Augustine's advocacy of force to preserve the unity of the City of Jerusalem on earth.

Nonetheless, Augustine not only sets limits on violence, but also tries to bring permission of violence into constant contact with the evangelical norm of love. The accommodation to historical necessity occurs at the level of application, where "love" can come to mean, not nonviolence, but a particular attitude motivating violent acts. Augustine unites love to violence by speaking of them together as punishment, which has in view the good of the offender. The duty or prerogative to undertake violent punishment is restricted. A private individual, Christian or not, may not punish a criminal, even in self-defense; this duty belongs to those who have lawful authority, deriving ultimately from God. Wars that the authorities undertake must be guided by concern for the common good, that is, the establishment of the tenuous peace within and among peoples that is possible in this life.

How was it that Augustine as a Christian theologian was able to move from the gospel imperative of love and nonresistance to a pragmatic justification of force? In his historical and critical *The Just War in the Middle Ages*, Frederick H. Russell is unable to discover a fully coherent explanation for the origins of Augustine's defense of the just war and of civilly propelled abolition of heresy, and so Russell describes them as "clusters of ideas grouped around the central theme of sin and punishment."[116] The operational criteria in Augustine's justifications are said to be derived from the Old Testament wars. But it is not altogether on target to say either that punishment or Old Testament examples are the points of departure for Augustine. Augustine's assumption in fact is that war and violence are dubious, and are so in light of the teaching of Jesus. Punishment is a means of responding to the anticipated objection that Jesus did not convert by violent methods: it is a device for incorporating violence into the meaning of love.

Examples from the warfare of the Israelite nation come into the picture in a sort of secondary move. For one thing, they are sometimes brought to Augustine's attention by those who would use them as counterinstances of the biblical unity that Augustine set himself to defend. Augustine may respond

115. TeSelle, *Augustine the Theologian,* 272.

116. Frederick H. Russell, *The Just War in the Middle Ages* (New York: Cambridge Univ. Press, 1975), 25. Similarly, TeSelle warns against an oversimplified rendition of Augustine's thought in relation to modern questions about "Christian realism," about the human potential for social transformation, or about the coincidence of Christian norms with norms of justice. In fact, Augustine's political theory points in several directions at once, and is finally "indecisive." Eugene TeSelle, "Towards an Augustinian Politics," *Journal of Religious Ethics* 16 (1988): 98.

that some of these wars were actually defensive, he may give them an allegorical significance, or, as a last resort, he may offer that God by definition does not command that which it is wrong to do. But they are not the point of departure for his justifications of war. When Old Testament violence comes into the picture as a positive line of argument, it is primarily in relation to heresy, and force is there justified because the nature of the church becomes modeled on that of empire. The core of Augustine's approach to violence is not to be found in any of the excusing rationales he gives for it, precisely because he does realize that it is an activity to be excused in relation to the evangelical requirement of love.

One can undoubtedly find separatist, if not dualist, tendencies in Augustine's thought about the kingdom and political ethics. However, it is possible to give the earthly city a positive though subordinate understanding within the parameters of Augustine's eschatology, or discussion of the ends of human life. Although Augustine develops the contrast model of the two cities primarily to account for the "miserable necessities" of this life, he does provide an orientation for provisional positive activity and change, set against the critical horizon of a transcendent future.

# 5 JUSTICE, WAR, AND THE COMMON GOOD

## *Establishing the Just War Tradition (Thomas Aquinas)*

THOMAS AQUINAS (1225–1274) WAS BORN IN the empire of Frederick II, at the castle of Roccasecca near Aquino, a small town between Naples and Rome.[1] As a very young child, Thomas was sent off to the Benedictine abbey of Monte Cassino for schooling, then went around 1239 to the University of Naples. At about age nineteen, he decided to join the Dominicans, a mendicant order of preachers, whose poverty attracted him. Thomas persevered in this vocation, despite prodigious familial efforts to redirect him toward a more promising ecclesiastical career. Later he entered the University of Paris, where he had the good fortune to study with Albert the Great, became acquainted with Neoplatonist philosophy, and eventually served as one of the University of Paris's greatest professors and scholars. In his later years, Aquinas also traveled extensively on assignments from his order and the pope, in addition to writing extensively. He died at the age of forty-nine, on his way to participate in the Council of Lyons, which was to begin in the spring of 1274.

If Augustine operates out of an intellectual milieu socially influenced by an alliance between Christianity and the political order, Aquinas operates out of a milieu equally influenced by an alliance between Christianity and the academy. As a member of the faculty of theology of the University of Paris, Aquinas was at the heart of the intellectual life of his time and place. Of the thirteenth-century university, M.-D. Chenu writes, "Intellectual corporation of the city, the university was at the same time an official body of the Church, with its own proper 'office,' and with rights and liberties that it enjoyed pursuant to charters granted by authority of the collective Christianity it meant to serve."[2] Moreover, "it was the faculty of theology that formed the soul of

1. For biographical information, see Josef Pieper, *Guide to Thomas Aquinas* (New York: Pantheon Books, 1964), 11–22.
2. M.-D. Chenu, OP, *Toward Understanding St. Thomas* (Chicago: Henry Regnery, 1964), 19.

the university," and that represented as well a novel function in the teaching mission of the church. For the first time the mission of expounding revealed truths was extended from the episcopacy to include the competency "of professors, of a school of men who were professionals in their work, whose energies were devoted to developing a science, and whose juridical status depended on the corporation and was not, properly speaking, a function of the hierarchy."[3]

As today, this close cooperation between church and academy gave birth to problems as well as opportunities. Some of each arose from the fact that, in the Western church, Augustine represented the pinnacle of authoritative exposition of Christian doctrine, while a crucial stimulant to intellectual inquiry was offered simultaneously by the philosophy of Aristotle. On the one hand, Aquinas himself achieved an unparalleled synthesis of Christian teaching and philosophical reflection; on the other, the naturalism of Aristotle seemed to some to pose an intolerable insult to the Augustinian doctrines of providence and grace.

## SYNTHESIS OF AUGUSTINE AND ARISTOTLE

Aristotle had already been known in the West since the eleventh century as a logician, but in the thirteenth, his works in natural science and philosophy of nature gained currency: "man's attention now focused on the world of matter and sense, on the study of life and its laws, on the phenomena of generation. . . . In brief, what now appeared was a world that was *real*, a world *capable of being understood*."[4] The Aristotelian approach to nature—as containing its own principles of intelligibility—prescinded from any reliance on God, religion, or revelation. Not surprisingly, it met with repeated resistance within the church and from the hierarchy, expressed by occasional condemnations within which even Aquinas was included (posthumously). These rejections, of course, did not last. The genius of Aquinas was that he set an appreciation of the intrinsic intelligibility of the universe and its laws within a framework of divine creativity and goodness, naming reason and freedom as the very marks of the divine intention for humanity. Union with God through knowledge and love is the destiny that fulfills natural human capacities even as it elevates them to a qualitatively different level. Human abilities and enterprises are thus given a limited autonomy that permits the development of truly philosophical inquiry, even as the reality of an encompassing realm of divine activity and providence is affirmed.

Because political life is construed, on an Aristotelian model, to have its own coherency and positive raison de être, Aquinas feels less need to struggle constantly with the significance of Jesus' preaching of the kingdom. His analyses of government and the political common good achieve a reasonableness

3. Ibid., 20.
4. Ibid., 33.

and balance that eluded Augustine. At the same time, the obligation of the Christian community to shape its life in accord with that preaching is removed even further by Aquinas from the practical delineation of the life of citizenship. Christian morality is substantively identified with human morality as such; this is the essence of the ethics of the "natural law" that Aquinas shaped for later Catholicism.[5]

Aristotle's naturalism pervades the way Thomas Aquinas approaches "right order" within political community, and hence has influenced at its root the Catholic traditions about justice, civic virtue, the preservation of peace, and the permissibility of killing in defense of self, the community, or the nation. Thomas Gilby notes that, historically, the modern state was at this time being born. "Soon the reflection followed that politics or statecraft constituted a special discipline with rules of its own," rather than being an eclectic combination of patristic theology, Stoic philosophy, Roman law, and various local folk customs. Now politics began to aspire to "the ideals of enlightened self-interest and civic reasonableness."[6] The most significant difference of Aquinas from Augustine is that for the former the commitment to a reasonable moral order, knowable in principle by all human beings and forming the basis of a common morality, moves to center stage. For Augustine, the emphasis is on the divine basis of order (*caritas*) and the disruption of order in history by sin. Certainly, for Aquinas, order and its transcendent grounding are still important. But for the purposes of ethics, ordered relations among persons and things are understood in terms of those entities' finite, particular natures.

In his synthesis of theology and philosophy, Aquinas places considerable trust in human reason and evinces a comparable degree of optimism about the potential of natural humanity, hindered though it may be by sin and ignorance, to establish justice in personal and social relationships, and so to achieve a peaceful political order governed by law. This is not to say that Aquinas disagrees with Augustine that the peace of this world is imperfect, or that he takes the kingdom of God to be present. The preservation of just relations between citizens and nations occasionally will require resort to force. Nonetheless, the kingdom builds on and transforms communities and relationships that are not naturally incongenial to it. In Aquinas's ethical writings, the urgency of life in the kingdom is subordinated to the importance of building human communities in the created order. The Christian is at home within this order, and the gradual sanctification by the Spirit in Christ takes place within it, not over against it.

Gilby cautions that Aquinas's politics were always subordinate to his philosophy and theology, and hence cannot be expected to constitute "a complete

5. See the so-called "Treatise on Law," for Aquinas's fundamental exposition of the basic and rationally intelligible principles ordering human life. Aquinas, *Summa Theologica,* trans. Fathers of the English Dominican Province (New York: Benziger Bros., 1948), 1–2.90–94. (Hereinafter cited as ST.)

6. Thomas Gilby, *The Political Thought of Thomas Aquinas* (Chicago: Univ. of Chicago Press, 1958), xvi.

and self-contained system."[7] Nonetheless, four principles lie at the heart of Aquinas's approach to the political order. First, political authority and the law do not exist merely because of original sin, but correspond to needs and purposes inherent in human nature itself. Second, political authority, although flawed by sin, is distinct from and not in principle subordinate to the authority of the church. This, of course, did not resolve the practical problem of coordinating two distinct sources of power without actually subsuming them either under the ecclesiastical or the secular center. Third, temporal power is directed to temporal affairs, including the cultivation of social virtue. "The foremost task of government was to establish and maintain those objective conditions, principally matters of justice, which allowed citizens to lead the good life."[8] Finally, political judgment is more like an art than a deductive science. Because they answer to practical and contingent matters, government and legislation can never be deduced strictly from premises, nor legitimated absolutely by any philosophical or theological reasons. The decision to go to war is a good example. For, while there may be good moral reasons for going to war, the venture itself is justified only if, practically, it will result in more good than harm.

## JUSTIFICATION OF WAR

The common sources of just war theory in the thirteenth century, in addition to Augustine and other church fathers, were the Scriptures, the *Sentences* of Peter Lombard (published midway through the twelfth century), and Gratian's *Decretals*. The latter, a part of the *Corpus Juris Canonici* or code of canon law, drew together various texts on war from the tradition, especially Augustine. It was thus influential for theologians as well as for canonists.[9] Although Gratian cannot be said to have developed a coherent theory of war, his commentaries on the authorities he cites lend emphasis to justification of defensive war to protect property, person, or community; or to redress wrongs already done.[10] Aquinas shares the same fundamental outlook.

Like Augustine, Thomas Aquinas retains in his comprehensive theological work, the *Summa Theologica*, a negative, provisory context for the discussion of violence. He already puts the enterprise of war on dubious footing with his opening inquiry, "Whether it is always sinful to wage war?"[11] The position

7. Ibid., xxii.
8. Ibid., xxiii.
9. For the historical setting, consult Frederick H. Russell, *The Just War in the Middle Ages* (New York: Cambridge Univ. Press, 1975), 213–14; and James Turner Johnson, *Ideology, Reason, and the Limitation of War: Religious and Secular Concepts, 1200–1740* (Princeton, N.J.: Princeton Univ. Press, 1975), 33–43.
10. Johnson, *Ideology, Reason, and the Limitation of War,* 38.
11. *ST* 2–2.40.1. title, p. 1359.

taken in answer is similar to that of Augustine (whom Aquinas quotes extensively) in that both see as central the authority of the sovereign,[12] peace and the protection of the common good against internal and external offenses, and an intention fixed on the advancement of good. Aquinas goes somewhat beyond Augustine in adding to the reasons for going to war (*jus ad bellum*) at least some consideration of the morality of means in war (*jus in bello*). He provides for the legitimacy of ambushes in war because, although they involve deception of a sort, they do not entail direct falsehood or the breaking of a promise. They are a part of the conventional conduct of war and thus are to be anticipated by both sides.[13]

War is fought to serve the goal of peace. Elaborating on Augustine's premise that "peace is tranquillity of order," Aquinas explains that true peace includes the harmony and fulfillment of all one's desires.[14] Since an agreement may not fully satisfy the desires of parties to it, some may seek to redefine the agreement against the wills of the other parties. "Consequently, men seek by means of war to break this concord, because it is a defective peace, in order that they may obtain peace, where nothing is contrary to their will. Hence all wars are waged that men may find a more perfect peace than that which they had heretofore."[15] Genuine peace among individuals, however, cannot be caused by external constraint, but only—as Augustine had said of the peace of the City of God—by charity. Peace implies a union in which "man loves God with his whole heart, by referring all things to Him, so that his desires tend to one object," and in which "we love our neighbor as ourselves, the result being that we wish to fulfil our neighbor's will as though it were ours."[16] Peace is caused by charity alone; the most that "justice" can do is "remove the obstacles to peace." In the *Summa Contra Gentiles,* Aquinas comments that "an ordered concord is preserved among men when each man is given his due, for this is justice."[17] But he explains that justice can be accomplished

12. See also Aquinas, "Fifth Commandment: Thou Shalt Not Kill," in *The Commandments of God: Conferences on the Two Precepts of Charity and the Ten Commandments,* trans. Laurence Shapcote, OP (London: Burns, Oates & Washbourne, 1937), p. 58. Citing Augustine, Aquinas here argues that the sense of the fifth commandment is "Thou shalt not kill on thine own authority." Thus, "it is lawful for the judge who kills at God's command, since then it is God that kills: because every law is a command of God" In *ST* 2–2.64.2, Aquinas also justifies the killing of a criminal in order to safeguard the common good of the community. (The same point is made in the *Summa Contra Gentiles,* bk. 3, pt. 2, 148.4, cited in n. 17 below.) In *ST* 2–2.64.3, he stipulates that this is the prerogative of a public authority only, not of a private individual. The execution of the wicked can be both for "the chastisement of the offender" and for "the good of the state." (Aquinas, *The Commandments of God,* "The Two Precepts of Charity: On the Love of Our Neighbor," .5, p. 23.)

13. *ST.* 2–2.40.3.

14. *ST.* 2–2.29.1. Aquinas cites Augustine's *City of God,* 19.13.

15. *ST.* 2–2.29.2. r. obj. 2; cf. 2–2.29.4.

16. *ST.* 2–2.29.3.

17. Aquinas, *Summa Contra Gentiles,* bk. 3: *Providence,* pt. 2, trans. Vernon J. Bourke (Notre Dame, Ind.: Univ. of Notre Dame Press, 1975), 128.6. This work (hereinafter referred to as *SCG*), apparently directed to the conversion of non-Christians, in fact contains many arguments from "divine law," and even from the Christian Scriptures. Chenu speculates that Aquinas may have

either "from within" by love or "from without" by force; "the complete fulfillment of the law depends on love."[18]

## NATURAL LAW AND SCRIPTURE

Aquinas does not appeal to Old Testament examples of religious or divinely commanded wars to legitimate violence. His basic moral platform in analyzing social and political obligations is philosophical, and he understands violence to be permissible on the basis of natural obligations and prerogatives, even if those obligations have been established divinely in the creation of what is natural to humanity. In the *Summa Contra Gentiles*, Aquinas asserts, "it is apparent that things prescribed by divine law are right, not only because they are put forth by law, but also because they are in accord with nature."[19]

Although the perfection of the Christian life may transcend the natural virtues, Aquinas does not present the moral choices that respect human nature as such as fundamentally different in content from those to which the Christian person is ordinarily obliged. His vision of ethics is an integrated one, in which the parameters of duty are defined first of all by reason, even if reason is the natural disclosure of God's will and even if reinforced by revelation. Aquinas's basic problem as a theologian as well as a philosopher is how to reconcile a natural duty to wage war with the New Testament, which he understands to have superseded the "Old Law"[20] and which he recognizes to present serious challenges to the legitimacy of self-defense.

Although Aquinas does not abandon the traditional doctrine of the multiple senses of Scripture,[21] he is much less disparaging toward the literal sense.[22] Beryl Smalley[23] notes that in the twelfth and early thirteenth centuries, a considerable but not well-organized terminology for biblical interpretation had developed. There was no universally agreed upon method for defining and relating the literal, historical, allegorical, moral, and anagogical senses. It was generally recognized that Scripture had a literal or historical sense that could not be contradicted by any "spiritual" interpretation. Yet even this standard was difficult to apply. For instance, in a parable or in the Sermon

in mind, to an extent, the Islamic religion, to which Christian missionaries had recently ventured in Spain, and to which the scholarly world had been introduced through the influence of Arabic civilization. More likely, though, this work is presented more generally as "a defense of the entire body of Christian thought, confronted with the scientific Greco-Arabic conception of the universe, henceforth revealed to the West" (Chenu, *Understanding St. Thomas,* 292).

18. *SCG,* bk. 3, pt. 2, 128.8.

19. Ibid., 129.1.

20. *ST* 1–2.107.2.

21. See ibid., 1.1.10.

22. Ibid., r. obj. 1.

23. Beryl Smalley, "The Bible in the Medieval School," in *The West from the Fathers to the Reformation,* vol. 2 of *The Cambridge History of the Bible,* ed. G. W. H. Lampe (Cambridge: Cambridge Univ. Press, 1969), 197.

on the Mount, the allegorical or spiritual meaning is part of the literal or historical meaning.

Eventually the method came to recognize that even historical interpetation includes levels of meaning. Thomas Aquinas's contribution was that he "laid more stress on the human agent of revelation and so made for a broader approach. The literal sense was defined as the sacred writer's full original meaning."[24] The spiritual sense, on the other hand, was defined as the meaning that God had intended to reveal through sacred history, a meaning whose full significance the biblical writers did not yet understand. Hence Aquinas concluded that the spiritual interpretation can be used only for preaching and edification, while the literal must ground theological and moral argument.[25] Aquinas asserts that "in Holy Writ no confusion results, for all the senses are founded on one—the literal—from which alone can any argument be drawn, and not from those intended in allegory." Moreover, "nothing necessary to faith is contained under the spiritual sense which is not elsewhere put forward by the Scripture in its literal sense."[26]

The fact of the matter is, however, that Aquinas is much less likely to begin ethical discussions with citations from Scripture than many of his predecessors. The influence of the biblical witness or model of Christ is simply not as strong in determining the framework as is Aquinas's concern to understand what is natural to humanity, what its inherent inclinations and purposes are, and how justice can best be understood and implemented among individuals and as definitive of the common good. Nonresistance and works of love toward enemies are hard to align with natural justice.

Aquinas takes up Augustine's suggestion that some biblical counsels are meant for some classes of persons only, and he combines this with the idea—extending back to Ambrose's discussion of military service—that the calling of the priest is privileged. Clerics and bishops must not fight because "warlike pursuits . . . hinder the mind very much from the contemplation of Divine things." The clergy have a special vocation to imitate the nonviolence of Christ, one not obligatory for the laity.[27] Thus the ideal of discipleship portrayed in the New Testament is limited even as it is protected, by reserving it as a special responsibility of those Christians most highly called. God may be served, however, not only through the "contemplative life," but also through the "active life," insofar as such a life is concerned with "helping our neighbor and in the service of God." Religious orders may be established for the purpose of active service, and even "for the purpose of soldiering."[28] While the ordained cleric—the eucharistic celebrant— must refrain from violent action, the same is not true of the religiously consecrated layperson. Aquinas cites Augustine's

24. Ibid., 215.
25. Ibid., 216.
26. *ST.* 1.1.10, r. obj. 1.
27. Ibid., 2–2.40.2; cf. 2–2.64.4.
28. Ibid., 2–2.188.3: "Whether a Religious Order Can be Directed to Soldiering?"

readiness by indicating instances where the enemy becomes equally a neighbor in need.[41]

On the whole, however, Aquinas's discussion of Christian obligation to sacrifice self-interests for the sake of others can only be characterized as reserved. It takes on an even less biblical tone in a Lenten lecture on the double love command. Here Aquinas gives as the first reason for love of enemy "the preservation of your own dignity" as a "child of God," and follows it by the motives of victory over the offender and the devil, of gaining a friend, of having one's prayers more easily granted, and of avoiding sin—all more or less self-directed reasons. The discussion of charity in combination with the discussion of war and killing demonstrates that Aquinas was most sympathetic to well-reasoned analysis of the human condition and most receptive to exhortations conducive to fairness in interpersonal and community relations, governed by intellectually intelligible laws.

Thomas Aquinas's Christian identity does bring certain important concerns to the forefront of his discussion—for example, the ideals of mercy and forbearance toward enemies and the location of either private or lawfully organized killing on the extreme boundaries of morally tolerable action. The order of charity no doubt also influences him to emphasize the strong pressure against war in the natural moral order. At one place, he even suggests that public officials are motivated by charity in seeking to further the public good over that of individuals.[42] As Jean Porter states, charity lends to the social body a unity that is unattainable on the basis of finite human values and ends, for the attempt to fulfill them simultaneously will always produce practical conflict.[43] However, Aquinas confronts the more radical implications of Jesus' nonviolent example and teachings, but does not allow them to challenge seriously his essentially philosophical moral perspective.

## RELIGION AND COERCION

This fact shows through with particular clarity in Aquinas's acceptance of the use of force in safeguarding true worship of God. Beside the defense of "public safety" and of "the poor and oppressed," the profession of soldiering "can also be directed to the upkeep of divine worship." Like Augustine, Aquinas bolsters this claim with reference to Old Testament figures (Judas Maccabbeus and Simon).[44] But Aquinas relishes the prospect of violent protection of religion even less than does Augustine. Although Aquinas considers pagan and even Jewish rites to be sinful, he advises moderation in measures taken to eliminate them. The comprehensive common good must be the aim of

41. Ibid.
42. Ibid., 2–2.25.6. r. obj. 2.
43. Jean Porter, *The Recovery of Virtue* (Louisville: Westminster/John Knox, 1990), 67, 169.
44. *ST* 2–2.188.3. For a discussion of other texts in which Aquinas defends the protection of religion by civil authority, see Russell, *The Just War in the Middle Ages,* 261.

human government, as of divine government, and the common good may recommend toleration. The rites of unbelievers "may be tolerated, either on account of some good that ensues therefrom, or because of some evil avoided," for instance, "scandal or disturbance."[45] Moreover, it would be an injustice to baptize the children of unbelievers without parental consent: "it would be contrary to natural justice, if a child, before coming to the use of reason, were to be taken away from its parents' custody, or anything done to it against its parents' wish."[46] Unbelieving persons or groups are to be constrained by force only when necessary to put an end to blasphemy and persecution of Christians: "these are by no means to be compelled to the faith, in order that they may believe, because to believe depends on the will."[47]

Heretics are a separate case, because they have once embraced the faith and have willfully turned from it.[48] They are to be twice admonished before they are excommunicated, in the hope that they will return to the church and be saved. Aquinas connects exhortation rather than violence with the prospect of conversion. Yet if heretics refuse to retract, even death is not an excessive measure to take in order to sever the poison of their influence. Force is accepted not out of consideration for the spiritual welfare of the heretic, to which persuasive means are more appropriate, but for the protection of the community.

To the medieval Christian mind, the public welfare did not immediately indicate a sphere independent of religious considerations; right ordering of social life included its subordination to the divine intention. Aquinas's notion of common good thus presumes that the community's welfare, considered integrally, has both a natural and a spiritual dimension. "For it is a much graver matter to corrupt the faith which quickens the soul, than to forge money, which supports temporal life. Wherefore if forgers of money and other evil-doers are forthwith condemned to death by the secular authority, much more reason is there for heretics."[49] Yet Thomas Aquinas locates religious coercion straightforwardly within the realm of communal justice and peace and makes little attempt to argue that killing can be done out of love for its unwilling victim. In fact, a judge who sentences a sinner to death may be motivated by charity to "*prefer the common good* to that of the individual, although conversion and expiation may also be effects of the sentence in the sinner."[50]

## CONCLUSIONS

Although Aquinas did not write for a culture that was secular in the modern sense of being religiously and morally pluralistic, neither does his approach

45. *ST* 2–2.10.11.
46. Ibid., 2–2.10.12.
47. Ibid., 2–2.10.8.
48. Ibid.
49. Ibid., 2–2.11.3.
50. Ibid., 2–2.25.6. r. obj. 2; my italics.

tend in directions that would set the Christian community at odds with non-Christian culture or with philosophical insights. Aquinas adapted from Aristotle the fundamental postulate that "man by nature was a social and political animal. Politics then became a practical art whose end was right action, defined as a virtuous community life in which the welfare of the community overrode individual claims. In this community law existed to pursue the common welfare whose chief feature was peace."[51] It should also be stressed that for Aquinas, peace in political community is accomplished by justice and the rule of law much more emphatically than for Augustine, for whom the possibility of a genuine earthly peace is constantly overshadowed by the distant peace of the Heavenly City.

In making protection of the faith a proper business of the civil government in cooperation with the church, Aquinas follows Augustine by postponing fulfillment of the most radical demands of charity to another life, and also by superimposing the life of the disciple on that of the citizen. Charity is a friendship for God,[52] which surpasses the capacity of natural virtue and depends on the grace of the Holy Spirit.[53] In this life, no person can love God as much as God deserves. At most, charity will mean that the wayfarer "makes an earnest endeavor to give his time to God and Divine things, while scorning other things except insofar as the needs of the present life demand."[54] The "needs of the present life" include fairness, justice, and a reasonable attempt to discern and live by the demands of the natural law.

The central and tensive Augustinian dialectic between *caritas* and concupiscence has been replaced in Aquinas's attention by an orderly contrast between the natural virtues and their divinely graced transformation. In either perspective, however, the result is to approach the justification of violence from the standpoint of the needs of the political community and its citizens. Augustine more overtly retains the eschatological ideal by banishing self-defense and assiduously struggling to press force into the service of love; Aquinas achieves more prudence and balance by regarding conflict in the light of natural law and the common good and by subjecting violence to the test of justice. For Aquinas, life is a natural good commanding respect and demanding preservation except in the case of an acute conflict of duties. But neither Aquinas nor Augustine ventures clear criteria to determine when and how the disciple will turn into practice his or her ostensible readiness to live up to Jesus' nonviolent word and example, which seem to command the sacrifice of even some goods that could be defended "justly."

51. Russell, *The Just War in the Middle Ages,* 261. Russell in turn cites C. T. Davis, " 'Remigio de' Girolami and Dante. A Comparison of Their Conceptions of Peace," *Studi Danteschi* 36 (1959): 110–14.

52. *ST* 2–2.23.1.

53. Ibid., 2–2.24.3

54. Ibid., 2–2.24.8.

## SUBSEQUENT DEVELOPMENTS

Although both Augustine and Aquinas emphasize the right to go to war over temperance within it, attention to right means was also on the agenda by the end of the Middle Ages, finally yielding the key principle of noncombatant immunity. James Turner Johnson notes that the *jus ad bellum* was affirmed within the church by canon law and by scholastic theology, while two secular sources contributed to the *jus in bello*: the chivalric code of conduct prescribing that warfare and warlike contests of valor were to be conducted with tightly regulated gamesmanship; and the gradual and increasingly detailed specification of the Roman concept of *jus gentium,* which became a sort of common law for Christendom.[55]

The extension of the criteria of the just war beyond this cultural boundary, as well as the recognition that both parties to a conflict may have some right on their side, are the contributions of the sixteenth century Spanish Dominican, Franciscus de Victoria (ca. 1492–1546). Johnson refers to Victoria's formulation of just war doctrine as "the first clear and complete statement of what has come to be conceived as the classic requirements of the doctrine of just war."[56] These requirements, although variously formulated, are generally understood to include, under *jus ad bellum,* legitimate authority (expressed in a declaration of war), just cause, right intention, and the purpose of peace or the common good (with regard to the attainment of which there must be a "reasonable hope of success"); and, under *jus in bello*, discrimination or noncombatant immunity, and proportionality of damage caused to good achieved as a limitation on the weapons or tactics of war.

Born in Burgos, Victoria was educated by the Dominicans there, and later at a Dominican college in Paris and at the University of Paris. He finally achieved a distinguished professorship in theology at the University of Salamanca. Around 1540, Victoria authored two works dealing with war, specifically with the conquest of the native populations by the Spanish in the New World. These are *De Indis* (*On the Indians*) and *De Jure Belli* (*On the Law of War*). Appalled at reports of plunderings and massacres, particularly in Peru, Victoria drew on scholastic theology in endeavoring to establish a common law of nature, entailing reciprocal obligations between the Europeans and the "Indians."[57] Regarding the rights of (European) princes to declare war, he cautions that even the authorities "should first of all not go seeking occasions and causes of war, but should, if possible, live in peace with all men." Moreover, even potential adversaries are "neighbors, whom

55. James Turner Johnson, "Morality and Force in Statecraft: Paul Ramsey and the Just War Tradition," in *Love and Society: Essays in the Ethics of Paul Ramsey,* ed. James Johnson and David Smith (Missoula, Mont.: Scholars Press, 1974), 96–101.

56. Ibid., 95.

57. See also LeRoy Walters, "Historical Applications of the Just War Theory: Four Case Studies in Normative Ethics," in *Love and Society,* 120-24

we are bound to love as ourselves." . . . "For it is the extreme of savagery to seek for and rejoice in grounds for killing and destroying men whom God has created and for whom Christ has died. But only under compulsion and reluctantly should he come to the necessity of war."[58] While medieval just war discussion had for all practical purposes occurred within Christian cultures, Victoria used both humanitarian and religious grounds to extend it to non-Christians, and also excluded religion as a valid cause of war.

In his study of the moral significance of just war criteria, James Childress emphasizes that they deal with the transition from nonviolence to violence at the point of a conflict of prima facie duties, so that the burden of proof is on the decision to override, and the burden is a weighty one, as expressed by the criteria of reasonable hope of success and proportionality.[59] "War is the *ultima ratio*, the last resort."[60] To view just war criteria in terms of a conflict of duties also means that even when the duty to avoid violence is overridden, it continues to function in the course of action via the "moral traces" it leaves in the requirement of restraint.[61] Hence the criteria are able to challenge the status quo and, at least ideally, to undermine cultural assumptions that violence is always warranted in pursuit of political goals.

However, as we have seen, just war theory can be established on different bases, and these beginning points may have different consequences for the coloration given both to hesitation and to restraint. In the Augustinian tradition, the legitimation of violence is grounded in a killing-as-love paradox, and the extension of love to cover killing the "loved" victim is taken up by the Reformers. Reinhold Niebuhr and Paul Ramsey also build violence out of love, though more narrowly as service to the victimized but innocent neighbor. Yet the brake on killing may become weaker once the essential divide is crossed, when violence is accounted as a requirement of Christian love, and when moral ambiguity is accepted as an unavoidable and hence excusing aspect of all human resolutions of conflict. In the Thomistic tradition, killing is legitimated as a requirement of natural justice and right order, and this rationale, adopted by Victoria, is taken up in Roman Catholicism. From one point of view, it could be more dangerous to remove access to armed conflict from the realm governed by love than to subject it to that most stringent criterion. But from another, it is more safe to make the steps of war accountable to clearly defined and "reasonable" standards.

The next chapter will deal with the Reformation development of Augustinian thought. The subsequent one will take up the crusading ideology that

58. This passage occurs near the conclusion of *De Jure Belli.* Franciscus de Victoria, *De Indis et de Iure Belli Relectiones,* ed. Ernest Nys (Washington, D.C.: Carnegie Institution, 1917), 187.

59. Ibid., 76.

60. Ibid., 75.

61. James F. Childress, "Just War Criteria," in *Moral Responsibility in Conflicts: Essays on Nonviolence, War, and Conflicts* (Baton Rouge: Louisiana State Univ. Press, 1982), 72. The term "moral traces" is borrowed from Robert Nozick.

was prevalent during the Middle Ages and lasted into the religious wars of the Reformation period. For crusade and holy war apologists, the sense of paradox about violence is heightened by and finally submerged in a righteous sense that a divinely mandated cause demands the most extreme measures. In the crusade ethic, few traces are left of the tradition's premise of the contradiction inherent in the Christian use of violence, the sense of the humanity of the foe, or the ideal of Christian love as transforming antagonistic relations.

the need of the age was for authority rather than for liberty, for order first and freedom afterward."[2]

The political situation in Germany in Luther's day illustrates that the strong government to which many aspired was far from the actuality. The largest part of the Holy Roman Empire, Germany was divided into practically independent, sometimes aligned and sometimes warring, political units, including duchies, bishoprics, walled cities, and territories of knights. Although the Hapsburgs had managed through prudent marriages to keep the empire in the family, the emperor did not actually inherit his position. During the period of Luther's first revolutionary stirrings, the prospect of a new election was in the offing. When Emperor Maximilian died in 1519, he was succeeded by his grandson, Charles V. Charles was to command a considerable dynasty; but because it comprised relatively autonomous political entities in Europe and the New World, he also was to have difficulty exercising control and in responding to problems in his far-flung holdings.[3]

Meanwhile, the church of the sixteenth century had its own political and economic difficulties. Papal jurisdiction (for example, over trials of ecclesiastical cases) and power of taxation had been increasingly curtailed by the monarchs of the national states, who even began to assume power to appoint bishops. Financial burdens were created by the defense of the papal states, the crusades against the Turks, and the support of the papal court. Costs were passed from the Vatican to the higher clergy, to the parish clergy, and finally to the laity, who were charged heavily for clerical services. The indulgences controversy that set off Luther arises in this context.[4] But even before Luther, there were calls for reform of the power of the pope, of the corruption of ecclesiastical institutions, and of the high level of living of some monastic orders. For instance, the conciliarists had proposed reform through decentralization of church administration and teaching.

Theologically speaking, the fourteenth and fifteenth centuries yielded a legacy of doctrinal pluralism, particularly regarding the Eucharist and the role of Mary.[5] Doctrinal diversity prepared the way for questions about church authority and uniformity in relation to the insights of the individual theologian or believer. Other intellectual and religious movements may also have helped to undermine the relative medieval unity of Christian life—for example, mysticism, nominalism, and humanism.[6] The Christian mystical tradition confirmed the capacity of the individual person to experience God directly. Nominalism emphasized the uniqueness of all individual beings in contrast

2. Ibid., 16.
3. Ibid., 32.
4. Ibid., 39.
5. Jaroslav Pelikan, *Reformation of Church and Dogma* (1300–1700), vol. 4 of *The Christian Tradition* (Chicago: Univ. of Chicago Press, 1984), 10.
6. John Dillenberger and Claude Welch, *Protestant Christianity: Interpreted Through Its Development* (New York: Scribner's, 1954), 4–9.

to their unity in a natural, hierarchical order characterized by universality. By emphasizing revelation over reason, the nominalists may in one respect have enhanced church authority, but they diminished the sense of the unity of reality, truth, and knowledge. Another line of challenge to the monocentric, hierarchical church of the medieval period came from humanism, with its confidence in human rationality and moral potential. Humanism also may have contributed to the erosion of the perceived need for ecclesiastical mediation of Christian truths.

In exploring the question, "What is the essence of Roman Catholicism?" the Jesuit historian Robert E. McNally focuses on its social nature. Catholicism, McNally writes,

> is a religious reality of the social order, of the order of men and their concerns, which envisions and demands that, while human beings ultimately depend on God through faith and charity, they also depend on one another. In the historical and social order the distribution of the fruits of redemption is the cooperative work of man.[7]

Hence the church as a community of believers is of crucial importance. Repudiating individualism, the Catholic "finds it congenial and connatural to live and pray as part of a vast worshipping and believing community which through its adherence to its own traditions imparts a unique vision of life both here below and there above."[8]

Martin Luther, in contrast, stood precisely for the openness of every individual to the gospel as communicated by the word of God in Scripture interpreted through the Spirit. Harbison captures this theme. "This was to be the heart of Protestant belief as it developed later: the Bible and a man's conscience are the channels through which God speaks to human beings, not the Roman Church and its sacraments."[9] One angle on the Reformation problematic concerns the question of authority. The reformers implicitly ask by whose authority the medieval edifice is sustained; their answer is that its authority is not Jesus' own. Their ability to pose this question at all is enabled by the social turmoil and intellectual pluralism that shook irrevocably the assumption of cosmic stability and hierarchy undergirding the ecclesiology, theology, and politics of the Middle Ages.

## SCRIPTURE AS KEY TO THE REFORMATION

In its quest for a new polestar, the sixteenth-century reform of Christianity kept the Bible close to the heart of theology and ethics.[10] Both Luther and

7. Robert E. McNally, SJ, "The Reformation: A Catholic Reappraisal," in *Luther, Erasmus and the Reformation: A Catholic Protestant Reappraisal,* ed. John C. Olin (New York: Fordham Univ. Press, 1969), 42.

8. Ibid., 43.

9. Harbison, *The Age of Reformation,* 50.

10. As a general resource, see Roland Bainton, "The Bible in the Reformation," in vol. 3 of *The Cambridge History of the Bible,* ed. S. L. Greenslade (Cambridge: Cambridge Univ. Press, 1963), 1–37.

room of the monastery at Wittenberg, pondering the meaning of God's "righteousness" in Romans 1:17, Luther was struck by the insight that God's righteousness does not judge but justifies. In his mercy, God imparts the divine righteousness as a gift to those who have faith. This was the seed of the theology that was to carry Martin Luther through the next three turbulent decades. Neither merits nor good works earn faith and grace, which are given freely by God in Christ. The Christian responds to this gift with trust in God and God's promises and by spontaneously living out works of love toward the neighbor.

The events that launched Luther's reform illustrate the temper of the times—the interdependence of ecclesiastical and civil governments, political instability, church power, and the direct passion that fueled religious disputes. Luther formulated his ground-breaking Ninety-Five Theses in 1517 in a letter of protest to the archbishop who had sponsored the Dominican monk Tetzel in his indulgence-selling tour. In 1519–20 Luther was incredibly productive, publishing, among other things, his three famed early works: "Treatise on Good Works," "To the Christian Nobility of the German Nation," and "Freedom of the Christian."

Luther remained the active and often contentious father of the reform movement in Germany, and constantly expected capture and execution as a heretic. However, the German princes never enforced the imperial edict against him issued at Worms (1521) as a result of Pope Leo's condemnation of his views (in the bull *Exsurge Domini*, 1520). In 1525, at age forty-two, he married the twenty-six-year-old former nun, Catherine von Bora. Six children were born to them, of whom four survived to adulthood. Luther conducted debates with theologians such as John Eck (on indulgences), Carlstadt and Zwingli (on the Eucharist) and Erasmus (on free will and grace), and became embroiled in attempts to squelch both radical manifestations of the Reformation spirit (Thomas Müntzer) and the peasant rebellion.[15]

## *Luther's Theology and Ethics*

Luther's education at Erfurt was in nominalist theology, the *via moderna*, derived from the thought of the fourteenth-century British theologian William of Occam. In contrast to the thought of Thomas Aquinas, the nominalist stressed the distinction between reason and faith, making religion dependent on revelation and not reason. Although Luther later fought against all academic theology, his exposure to nominalism may have influenced his insistence on the sole sufficiency of grace and faith. The social consequence of this insistence

15. The biographical source on which I have relied primarily is Gritsch, *Martin Luther—God's Court Jester.* See also John M. Todd, *Martin Luther: A Biographical Study* (Westminster, Md.: Newman Press, 1965); Roland H. Bainton, *Here I Stand: A Life of Martin Luther* (New York: New American Library, 1950); Erik H. Erikson, *Young Man Luther: A Study in Psychoanalysis and History* (New York: W. W. Norton, 1958, 1962); and Edward F. Cranz, "Martin Luther," in Brian A. Gerrish, *Reformers in Profile* (Philadelphia: Fortress, 1967), 86–114.

was a strong contrast between (though not separation of) discipleship and citizenship.

One of the most striking and characteristic features of Luther's theology is its experiential grounding, which contributes to the ad hoc character of most of his writings on social issues. Luther replies to questions as they arise, and his solutions are directed more to immediate duties and outcomes than to long-range interpretations of social life or integrated political programs. Partly due to the historical context of upheaval and uncertainty, a dominant theme in his social writings is fear of anarchy and chaos. At the same time, his religious approach brings radical gospel teaching into the realm of personal moral obligation and away from control of the law. He relates positively to Augustine's tensive construal of the political and religious spheres of life, preserving like Augustine a high sense of Christian demand, even while coming to terms with the necessary conditions of maintaining civil order.

Luther might best be described as an exegete whose theology is preeminently a theology of the Word of God.[16] He understands the Word of God as the concrete action of God, through which God acts redemptively, conferring the forgiveness of sins. Above all, God acts in the crucifixion and resurrection of Jesus, events that the preaching of the Word of God in the church makes contemporary. In relation to the oral Word, the written Word functions both to sustain it and to preserve it from error. That is, study of the Scriptures sustains preaching of the gospel and tests its content.[17]

One of Luther's contributions to the history of exegesis was his strong preference for literal interpretation of the Bible over allegorical. However, the history presented in the biblical narratives is "a special and particular history, the history of the church as the people of God."[18] The historical events and meanings themselves can indicate or stand for God's special purposes, which must be interpreted theologically. Thus Luther's position does not mark a complete break with the medieval approach. On the one hand, even his predecessors had emphasized the priority of the literal and historical meaning of Scripture. On the other, Luther, while avoiding excessive allegorization, still reserved a place for it if "properly . . . understood as metaphorical language in the text itself and not as a spiritual or figurative meaning imposed on the text from outside."[19] Thus Luther agreed with the medieval exegetes that the true sense of Scripture is that intended by the Spirit, though he differed from them by expanding the realm of possible allegorical senses

16. Jaroslav Pelikan so describes it in *Luther the Expositor: Introduction to the Reformer's Exegetical Writings* (Saint Louis: Concordia Publishing House, 1959), 48. According to Paul Althaus, Luther's "theology is nothing more than an attempt to interpret the Scripture. Its form is basically exegesis." *The Theology of Martin Luther* (Philadelphia: Fortress, 1966), 3.

17. Pelikan, *Luther the Expositor,* 68–69.

18. Ibid., 89.

19. Scott H. Hendrix, "Luther Against the Background of the History of Biblical Interpretation," *Interpretation* 37 (July 1983): 231. See also Grant and Tracy, *A Short History,* 94–95.

"the disciples of Christ, whom He is teaching about their personal lives, apart from the secular government."[39] In the Christian's role as a "secular person," "there should be no tolerance shown toward any injustice, but rather a defense against wrong and a punishment of it, and an effort to defend and maintain the right, according to what each one's office or station may require."[40]

The most characteristic aspect of Luther's theory of just war is its well-known backdrop, the "two kingdoms" doctrine. By means of this doctrine, Luther manages to bring his emphases on faith, the individual conscience, and eschatological hope into contact with the life of the person and of the Christian community in history. The essence of this view, developed, nuanced, and expounded in many places and contexts,[41] is that all true believers belong to the kingdom of God under a spiritual government, whose membership is by grace and faith; whereas nonbelievers belong to the kingdom of this world, whose criterion is works and which is disciplined by the law, under a secular government. The Christian participates in the world, however, through stations, vocations, offices, or callings (such as prince, lord, soldier, spouse, parent, or minister) that allow him or her to serve the neighbor under the rule of justice but with the motive of love. The secular order is instituted by God to serve the welfare of humanity and to restrain sin, but Christ and the Church are not directly involved in its government.

Luther writes his treatise of 1522, "On Temporal Authority," as a response to Duke John (brother of Frederick the Wise, Luther's protector), who worries that texts such as Matthew 5:38-48 and Romans 12:19 ("Vengeance is mine, I will repay, says the Lord") will make either his Christianity or his public functions impossible. Luther counters with Romans 13:1 ("Let every person be subject to the governing authorities") to establish the temporal sword, even though there "appear to be powerful arguments to the contrary."[42] He deals with the seeming discrepancy by asserting that there are "two classes" of people and "two kingdoms," and that if everyone were "real Christians" there would be no need for the law or the sword, or even the civil government.[43]

Paul Althaus notes some development from the early to the later Luther toward a less oppositional view of the earthly and heavenly kingdoms. Working at first under the influence of Augustine's doctrine of history, Luther saw the whole sinful world to which unbelievers belong as the realm of the devil. All believers belong to the heavenly kingdom; the earthly kingdom is necessary only because of sin. But eventually Luther came to think of the earthly realm

39. *Sermon on the Mount,* 114.

40. Ibid., 113.

41. *Temporal Authority,* 88, 91–92, 110; *Whether Soldiers, Too,* 99; *Sermon on the Mount,* 105; *On War Against the Turks, Luther's Works* 46, 166, 186; *An Open Letter on the Harsh Book Against the Peasants, Luther's Works* 46, 70–71; and *A Treatise on Christian Liberty,* ed. Harold J. Grimm (Philadelphia: Fortress, 1957); also available in *Luther's Works* 31, 7–8, 32–36.

42. "On Temporal Authority," 87.

43. Ibid., 88–89, 92–95; cf. *Sermon on the Mount,* 108, but see also 111.

not only in terms of the state, coercion, and violence, but also in terms of structures of order such as marriage and property. Insofar as these are necessitated by creation itself, the Christian does participate in them, and not just for the sake of restraining sin. They are the secular or outward government that supports our natural, physical life in community.[44] Hence, although Luther rejects what he perceives to be the medieval Catholic confusion of the secular and salvific orders, he wants to distinguish them without entirely separating them. He distances himself as well from the Reformation "enthusiasts" who wanted Christianity to become again a community set apart from the secular order, defined in terms of its missionary and witnessing roles.[45]

Yet even in the more mature Luther, the coercive and violent functions of the state continue to be seen as contingent upon the sinful nature of the world. The individual Christian is called to live, not by the realities of fallenness, but by those of redemption. Luther is inclined to think that the kingdom of Christ, to the extent that it is established, demands absolute fidelity to a radical New Testament morality. However, not all persons are Christian, and furthermore, not even true believers have won the struggle with sin that would allow them to translate into the reality of their lives their complete acceptance by God through the righteousness of Christ which has been imputed to them. Even the existence of the heavenly kingdom is dependent on the order safeguarded by the earthly one. For this reason, Luther regards the sword as the legitimate instrument of civil authorities in fulfilling their office, which is to keep the civil peace and defend the nation.[46] Luther rejects wars sponsored by the church for religious causes—for example, the proposals that Christians should war against the Ottoman Turks threatening Europe in the fifteenth and sixteenth centuries—and he rejects rebellion against the civil order by those having no authority to wield the sword, such as the 1525 revolution of the Swabian peasants against the German princes.[47]

Luther's interpretation of Matthew 5 is premised on the assumption that it is addressed to those among whom the kingdom has already been established. Jesus tells his followers, "you have the kingdom of heaven"; therefore a Christian will not "seek legal redress in the law courts" nor refuse to "suffer every evil and injustice without avenging himself."[48] In Luther's commentary on the Sermon on the Mount, the kingdom imagery is explicit and predominant, but the understanding that the kingdom of God is not the only kingdom

44. Paul Althaus, *The Ethics of Martin Luther* (Philadelphia: Fortress, 1972), 51–52.

45. See Gerhard Ebeling, *Luther: An Introduction to His Thought* (Philadelphia: Fortress, 1970), 178–82.

46. *Whether Soldiers, Too,* 121–22; *Temporal Authority,* 96, 100; *The Large Catechism,* "The Fifth Commandment," no. 72, in John N. Lenker, ed., Luther's Catechetical Writings, vol. 1 (Minneapolis, 1907), 79.

47. These are the themes of the following treatises, all in *Luther's Works* 46: *On War Against the Turks, Admonition to Peace, Against the Robbing and Murdering Hordes of Peasants,* and *An Open Letter on the Harsh Book Against the Peasants.*

48. *Temporal Authority,* 100–101.

united in both the civil and religious orders under a shared commitment to Christ.

A persistent problem in Calvin's relations with Geneva was the precise nature of cooperation between civil and ecclesiastical authorities. While Calvin was determined that the worship and discipline of the church should be in its own hands, the civil authorities were equally adamant about maintaining control.[59] Calvin left Geneva in 1538 to assume a pastorate in Strasbourg, where he married. There he enjoyed a few happy years as pastor and lecturer. In 1541, Calvin once again succumbed to pressure to return to Geneva, where he was to remain until his death in 1564 at fifty-four.

Calvin ordered the reform in Geneva around the four types of ecclesiastic office that he regarded as scripturally prescribed: pastors (responsible for preaching and sacraments), doctors (who test preaching by Scripture), elders (responsible for church discipline), and deacons (who minister to the needy). Religious and moral discipline were charged to the consistory, composed of the pastors and elders. But the civil authorities still managed to control the election of ecclesiastical officers. Together, the religious and civil authorities, backed by sanctions in both spheres, set upon the improvement of the moral and the spiritual condition of the citizens, vigorously seeking to supervise virtually every area of personal and social conduct.[60] With Calvin's support, the civil authorities at Geneva took on the protection and even enforcement of the "true" religion, conducting, for instance, the heresy trial of Michael Servetus.

## *Calvin as Biblical Theologian*

John Calvin also is a biblical theologian and exegete.[61] In some contrast to Luther's emphasis on the personal experience of the interpreter, the former "vigorously maintains an 'objective' type of interpretation,"[62] even seeing the Bible as "an external and formal authority."[63] States Calvin in the *Institutes*,

> If true religion is to beam upon us, our principle must be, that it is necessary to begin with heavenly teaching, and that it is impossible for any man to obtain even the minutest portion of right and sound doctrine without being a disciple of Scripture. Hence the first step in true knowledge is taken, when we reverently embrace the testimony which God has been pleased therein to give of himself.[64]

59. Gerrish, "John Calvin," 147.
60. Ibid., 148-49.
61. Bainton calls Calvin "a systematic commentator on the whole Bible" ("The Bible in the Reformation," pp. 16-17); while T. H. L. Parker asserts that "Calvin saw himself primarily, not as a systematic but a biblical theologian" ("Calvin the Biblical Expositor," in *John Calvin,* ed. G. E. Duffield [Grand Rapids: Eerdmans, 1966], 177).
62. Grant and Tracy, *A Short History,* 96.
63. Gerrish, *The Old Protestantism and the New,* 62.
64. *Institutes* 1.6.2.

Calvin and Luther were one in rejecting both pope and councils as the indispensable and irrefutable interpreters of the Bible. As Calvin puts it, "the Scriptures are the only records in which God has been pleased to consign his truth to perpetual remembrance."[65] The church finds its "strength . . . only in the word of God." Neither any individual nor the church as a whole has any mandate "to coin some new doctrine."[66] For Calvin the unity of both Testaments, their hermeneutical key, is Christology. What should be sought "in the whole of Scripture" is "truly to know Jesus Christ, and the infinite riches that are comprised in him and are offered to us by him from God the Father."[67]

Like Luther, Calvin sees the presence of the Spirit as an indispensable dimension of the interpretation of Scripture and the preaching of the Word of God.[68] Against Roman Catholicism they both would say the authority of Scripture rests on the Spirit's testimony in the heart of the believer, not the testimony of the church or of tradition: "our conviction of the truth of Scripture must be derived from a higher source than human conjectures, judgments or reasons; namely, the secret testimony of the Spirit."[69] Luther and Calvin were in essential agreement that the sole source of faith and doctrine is Scripture, and that its literal interpretation should control.[70]

Despite this concurrence, Calvin's exegetical approach is given a unique accent by two influences that set him apart from the interpretive principles of the first reformer. The first is Calvin's strong humanist bent, rooted in the classics of Western literature and philosophy.[71] Although only the Spirit could guarantee or prove the validity and truth of Scripture, Calvin employed all the methods and disciplines of contemporary scholarship in order to explicate its meaning. He was familiar with Hebrew and Greek, grammar and rhetoric, medicine and science, geography and history, philosophy and classics, all of which he brought to bear in understanding biblical texts. Calvin rejected allegory. He concerned himself with arriving at clear and distinct meanings derived from a reading of the author's intention based on his peculiar style, his likely historical circumstances and those of his community, and the literal biblical wording.[72] Calvin aimed at a contextual rather than an atomistic

65. Ibid., 1.7.1.

66. Ibid., 4.8.9.

67. Preface to Olivétan's New Testament, in *Calvin's Commentaries,* ed. Joseph Haroutunian (Philadelphia: Westminster Press, 1958), 70.

68. Gerrish, *The Old Protestantism and the New,* 64.

69. *Institutes,* 1.7.4, 1.7.5.

70. Gerrish, *The Old Protestantism and the New,* 64. Gerrish would hardly agree with Grant and Tracy's assessment that Calvin's reliance on Spirit-inspired faith "opened the way for subjectivism" (*A Short History,* 96). Jaroslav Pelikan agrees with Gerrish that, although for Calvin the church is governed by the Spirit, the Spirit has "bound" it to the word (*Reformation of Church and Dogma,* 187; citing Calvin's *Reply to Sadoleto*).

71. See Donald K. McKim, "Calvin's View of Scripture," in *Readings in Calvin's Theology*, ed. Donald E. McKim (Grand Rapids: Baker Book House, 1984), 45–50.

72. See Hans-Joachim Kraus, "Calvin's Exegetical Principles," *Interpretation* 31 (1977), especially 12–13; and McKim, "Calvin's View of Scripture," 66–67.

approach, attempting to understand the biblical culture that is the setting of each biblical passage.[73] For Calvin the divine intention in Scripture is to be captured by a careful and educated study of the literal text in its canonical and historical setting, guided by Jesus Christ as the object of faith and the accommodation to human capacity of the divine command and promise.

A second characteristic stress in Calvin's writing is the ecclesial nature of faith, theology, and biblical interpretation. Although the church is certainly contingent upon and secondary to God's revelation in Scripture, Calvin retains much more than Luther a sense of the inherently communal nature of faith and discipleship. Despite the primacy of the Spirit, "the consent of the Church is not without its weight."[74] The purpose of the Word of God is the edification of the church.[75] Calvin's emphases on the biblical text itself as the basis of doctrine, on the availability of scholarly tools to resolve ambiguities, and on the consent of the community within which the individual interpreter works, all contribute to the objective, systematic character of his biblical exegesis and theology.

The center of faith and theology for Calvin is Christology, that is, the experience of God in Christ. Christ as "Mediator" is a key theme in the *Institutes*. A corollary theme is religion as *pietas* (piety), that is, as thankfulness or gratitude. When our eyes are opened to God's goodness as Creator and Redeemer, we rest secure in our dependence on God's love, which restores the lost image of God in humans. In God's love, we are assured of our salvation. Seen so, the doctrine of predestination, which receives so much attention as characteristic of Calvinism, is understood to be both secondary and derivative from the experience of the believer—not from a detached or universalist inquiry about the justice of the fate of any or all individuals.

For Calvin as for Luther, the believer's justification through acceptance and forgiveness creates a union with Christ, in which he or she becomes a partaker in Christ's righteousness. But for Calvin, the law continues in the life of faith to have an explicit third or pedagogical use "among believers," providing education and moral guidance.[76] Importantly for Calvin's view of ethics, he places significant stress on sanctification, or actual improvement; he discusses sanctification or regeneration in the *Institutes* even before justification. The marks of the Christian life are the bearing of the cross and self-denial. According to Calvin, we will be "required to render account of our stewardship," and that especially includes helping the neighbor. The other's benefit should always be subordinated to one's own advantage, since "the only right stewardship is that which is tested by the rule of love."[77]

73. McKim, "Calvin's View of Scripture," 48.
74. *Institutes,* 1.8.12.
75. Ibid., 1.14.4; 4.7.1. See Kraus, "Calvin's Exegetical Principles," 11; McKim, "Calvin's View of Scripture," 65; and Gerrish, *The Old Protestantism and the New,* 67–68.
76. *Institutes,* 2.7.2.
77. Ibid. 3.7.5.

Although Calvin does not identify the visible church with the elect, nor test the true church by the moral behavior of its members, his ideal is still one of true and fervent commitment, accompanied by moral transformation. He held, for instance, that those who are "openly wicked" should not be admitted to the Eucharist.[78]

Calvin sees the church as an "external help" to the religious and moral maturation of those who have been made members of the body of Christ.[79] The church provides the means to call to faith, through the preaching of the gospel. The marks of the true church are thus the preaching of the Word and the enactment of the sacraments (Baptism and Eucharist).[80] Calvin himself never claims that the Christian is identifiable by his or her external way of life, but he does assume that sanctification follows on conversion.

## *Church, Society, and Coercion*

Brian Gerrish notes that the basis of Calvin's social ethics is his humanistically oriented recognition that despite sin, there is a remnant of God's image in human nature and in reason.[81] The specifically Christian life implies a moral regeneration conducive to ordered social life under God, but even the unregenerate recognize the basic moral law, including the essentials of true worship. In an Augustinian vein, Calvin holds that the image of God in the human person comprehends both the rational nature and its proper orientation toward God (thankfulness). While the latter is obliterated by sin, the former is not entirely destroyed by human revolt, but continues, "by Divine indulgence," to distinguish "the whole human race from other creatures." Although not sufficient for salvation, this surviving natural ability to know the good contributes to social order and enables cooperation between the sphere of Christian discipleship and that of citizenship. Public morality and social concord are made possible by the fact that "in a common nature the grace of God is specially displayed."[82]

The substance of Calvin's vision of social cooperation, in its potential and its limitations, is put forth in Book 4 of the *Institutes of the Christian Religion*. Like Augustine and Luther, Calvin understands there to be essentially two societies at stake in discussion of the social order. "In man government is twofold: the one spiritual, by which the conscience is trained to piety and divine worship; the other civil, by which the individual is instructed in those duties which, as men and citizens, we are bound to perform. . . . We may call the one the spiritual, the other the civil kingdom."[83] Again the crucial question becomes, What is their relationship?

78. Ibid., 4.1.15.
79. Ibid., 4.1.1.
80. Ibid., 4.1.8–9.
81. Gerrish, *The Old Protestantism and the New*, 152.
82. *Institutes*, 2.2.17.
83. Ibid., 3.9.15.

Calvin's descriptions of the earthly kingdom and of civil authority are not marked by the same ambivalence and pessimism that one finds in Augustine. Although the function of the civil government is "widely separated" and "distinct" from that of the "spiritual and internal kingdom of Christ," it is "not adverse" to it, for "while we aspire to true piety we are pilgrims upon the earth."[84] Calvin is careful to state (contra Luther) that not even the inbreaking of the kingdom of God makes the functions of government superfluous,[85] for although "that spiritual reign, even now upon earth, commences within us some preludes of the heavenly kingdom," nonetheless, "perfection ... can never be found in any community of men."[86] In Calvin's mind, however, historical imperfection does not so much amount to misery as to the need for firm social organization in light of religious ideals. To advance the social mission of a godly if limited corporate life, the civil authority "is assigned, so long as we live among men, to foster and maintain the external worship of God, to defend sound doctrine and the condition of the Church, to adapt our conduct to human society, to form our manners to civil justice, to conciliate us to each other, to cherish common peace and tranquility."[87]

Because Calvin considers the duty "to worship with pure faith and piety" to fall under the moral law, he regards it as a proper object of civil authority.[88] Therefore he claims that the magistrate's office "extends to both tables of the law," that is, to both religion and morality proper; its object is "to promote the common peace and security of all"; it may require "the coercion ... of the impious"; and in so doing, as "a minister of God," authority "merely executes the judgments of God."[89] The authority of the king or magistrate is immune from rebellion unless there is "a legitimate command from God," as in Old Testament wars; unless the situation involves an inferior magistrate who, in carrying out the duties of office, resists a superior;[90] or unless the king commands acts against God.[91] On the other hand, a moderating influence on the authority of the king or magistrate is the interdependency in Calvin's political outlook of the magistrate, laws, and people, which implies their reciprocal critical relationship.[92] He even anticipates that God may raise up "avengers" to defend the people from tyranny, and that certain public officials may have as their appointed duty watchfulness against abuse of power.[93]

84. Ibid., 4.20.2.
85. Ibid.
86. Ibid., In the same place, Calvin also states that the spiritual government "begins the heavenly kingdom in us, even now upon earth, and in this mortal and evanescent life commences immortal and incorruptible blessedness."
87. Ibid.
88. Ibid., 4.20.15–16.
89. Ibid., 4.20.9–10.
90. Ibid., 4.20.23–30.
91. Ibid., 4.20.32.
92. Ibid., 4.20.3, 14.
93. Ibid., 4.20.30–31.

Yet Calvin agrees fundamentally with Augustine, Aquinas, and Luther that political authority is from God and is owed a strong presumption of respect and obedience. He relies on Scripture to defend both the official punishment of individuals and authoritatively undertaken "war against any hostile aggression." These two causes of retributive violence have existed both before and after "the coming of Christ"; that coming does not alter the legitimacy of coercion as the appropriate response to them. Like Augustine, Calvin qualifies the legitimation of violence by insisting not only that war should aim at a restoration of peace, but that it should be a last resort and not be conducted with attitudes of hatred.[94] However, in refuting Anabaptist pacifism, he insists that "the Christian man, if according to the order of his country is called to serve his prince, not only does not offend God in taking up arms, but also fulfills a holy vocation, which cannot be reproved without blaspheming God."[95]

In reviewing Calvin's attitudes toward force and Christian responsibility, one sees that, far from contemplating withdrawal from the political sphere, he even enlisted civil authority in support of the Christian religion. Committed though he was to at least a partial realization of the kingdom on earth, he was a realist about the prospects for its advent in history. Perhaps it was because of this tentativeness that Calvin considered the political sphere to be hospitable to a cooperative venture with the religious one. Calvin's convictions about the promise of political life under Christian auspices account for what is frequently referred to as his "theocratic ideal,"[96] and supported his cooperation in the eventually unsuccessful attempt to establish a religious commonwealth at Geneva. Certainly a key premise of that enterprise was the Calvinist doctrine of election, whereby practical and observable sanctification follows upon grace and faith.[97] The tendency naturally followed, as it did also for the Anabaptists, to distinguish the true or false Christian by external signs of faith, conduct, and participation in the sacraments, even though Calvin never taught that such externals were sure signs of salvation.

Calvin is not unaware that the Sermon on the Mount presents difficulties for Christian proposals of violence, even (or especially), in pursuit of religious objectives. In coming to terms with the "hard sayings," he repeats at least twice Augustine's counsel to bear them "in readiness of mind," once in the *Institutes* and once in his *Commentary on the Sermon on the Mount.* In commenting on the Lord's command not to dispute with those who "would

94. Ibid., 4.20.11–12.

95. John Calvin, *Brief Instruction for Arming All the Good Faithful Against the Errors of the Common Sect of the Anabaptists,* in *John Calvin: Treatises Against the Anabaptists and Against the Libertines,* ed. Benjamin Wirt Farley (Grand Rapids: Baker Book House, 1982), 73.

96. Roland Bainton, *Christian Attitudes Toward War and Peace: A Historical Survey and Critical Re-evaluation* (Nashville: Abingdon, 1960), 147.

97. *Institutes* 3.19.2 (on the guidance of the law in the sanctification of the Christian); 4.19–21 (on good works that characterize the Christian life, as a gift of grace); and *Catechism of the Church of Geneva,* in *Calvin: Theological Treatises,* trans. J. K. S. Reid (Philadelphia: Westminster, 1954), 100.

go to law with thee" (Matt. 5:40), Calvin argues that a Christian is "not entirely forbidden recourse to law" and "a fair defence," but that "Christians should be ready" to forfeit patiently their possessions should their case be lost.[98] And again, "resist not evil" means to brace oneself for further injury, but does not exclude "nonviolently deflecting" the injury.[99] The persuasiveness of the argument is hardly enhanced by Calvin's interpretation of "love your enemies" (Matt. 5:44) as meaning that while "the faithful should have no dealings with vengeance," they at the same time do not cease to pray that God "takes vengeance on the reprobate."[100] In the *Institutes*, Calvin cites directly Augustine's "Letter to Marcellinus": the Christian "should be ready to bear with patience the wickedness of those whom he desires to become good," but the Christian might in outward conduct act for the advantage of those toward whom he or she feels benevolently—for example, by restraining their sinful actions. Calvin enlarges on this statement by saying that Christians are "ready to forgive" injuries but may still seek legal redress to preserve property or the public good and to "bring a pestilent offender to justice," even though the penalty be death.[101]

Because of Calvin's consideration of justice and the common good as including the natural good of the individual Christian, his position on justifiable uses of violence resembles that of Aquinas at least as much as that of Augustine. Unlike Aquinas (or Augustine), he allows the civil authority status in the governance of the church. Unlike Augustine but like Aquinas, he specifies Christian conduct in response to injustice in either the public or the private spheres in terms of equity[102] and natural right and duty. He certainly gives Scripture a more explicitly central role in his ethical method than Aquinas, but he permits Scriptural meanings to be nuanced by nonbiblical sources. In interpreting Scripture he refers to both testaments but avoids methods that are either excessively literal or allegorical. He attends to the intention of a text and its original setting and historical meaning, rather than to exact wording. For a final reading he depends heavily on previous consensus and tradition. As it is for Augustine and the church fathers, the context of scriptural interpretation is always the community of the church, with its questions, needs, and commitments. Yet Calvin apparently would not have disagreed with the proposition that, at least in the moral arena, what Scripture demands is not radically discontinuous with the broad insights of reason.

## SUMMARY

The major sources of Reformation thinking about discipleship, the social order, and just war are Augustine and the Bible. However, both Luther and

98. *Calvin's New Testament Commentaries,* ed. David W. Torrance and Thomas F. Torrance (Grand Rapids: Eerdmans, 1975), 194-95.

99. Ibid., 194.

100. Ibid., 198.

101. *Institutes,* 4.20.20.

102. Ibid., 4.20.16.

Calvin are more dedicated than Augustine to the literal sense of Scripture, which is another way of saying that they are more attentive to the biblical narrative itself as a primary source of social ethics. At the same time, they are hardly fundamentalists. Their attention to the preaching of the Word and its Spirit-guided hearing implies a social context for biblical theology and reveals the assumption that some sort of working analogy between the biblical meaning and the contemporary situation can and must be made. Luther is more sensitive than Calvin to the paradox of a Christian just war position in light of the gospel, and hence much more insistent on personal nonviolence, in a protective move toward the distinctiveness of the Christian calling. Calvin's sense of paradox is the lesser, certainly because he is by temperament more systematic than Luther, but also because he is much more explicitly conscious of the multifaceted interpretive process that is necessary insofar as Scripture functions as an authority for the Church. As soon as more philosophical and cultural factors are introduced into the interpretive picture, especially if balance and synthesis are attempted in the final depiction, then Scripture begins to be brought into alignment with a "reasonable" rather than a "confessional" view of the mission of the church or of the individual Christian in the political order. This process will be concentrated and expedited to the extent that church and society are ostensibly united in one harmonious sociopolitical reality—as at Geneva. A social milieu of unusual change and instability contributed to the reformers' tendency to defend by whatever means required any government that could provide security to social life, to defend the virtual unquestionability of God-given power, and to keep at the margins any access to social transformation through challenges to the established sociopolitical hierarchies.

Luther and Calvin not only illustrate the Reformation's restoration of the Scriptures to Christianity, but in fundamental ways underwrite it. On the basis of that renewal, the kingdom of God is reclaimed as a possibility, given new emphasis in contrast to the medieval construal of the social order. However, the distance of the full kingdom and the need for living in a broken world is always maintained, especially in relation to any social and political questions. Perhaps, in being more analytical than Luther and more systematic in his views of social life, Calvin loses the sense of tension and paradox that was Luther's way of keeping the kingdom ideals nearer to hand. Luther ever insists on the Christian's being perfect in his or her own life, however ambiguous and illogical it may be to separate "one's own affairs" from social relations, as Luther himself recognizes. Calvin, by contrast, achieves a more coherent social view, but some sense of the immediate enthusiasm of discipleship is thereby lost, and with it the impact of the love command, its absoluteness and comprehensiveness for every Christian's behavior.

Like Augustine (and to some extent Aquinas), both Luther and Calvin give politically justified violence a Christian coloration by demanding that it is religiously justified only when an outgrowth of a loving intention to serve the neighbor by securing the common good. At the same time, they solidify the hegemony of just war thinking in the response of mainstream Christianity to violence used for morally defensible political ends.

# 7 War in God's Name

## *Crusaders, Joan of Arc, and Puritan Revolutionaries*

THIS CHAPTER FOCUSES ON THE MEDIEVAL Crusades, especially the First Crusade, accompanied by some comparisons with the life of Joan of Arc and with the English Puritan Revolution of the seventeenth century. The problem of the medieval Crusade will occupy the greater part of our attention, inasmuch as these wars covered a longer historical period than did either the fifteenth-century struggle to regain France from the English, or the English Civil War. The Crusades also involved many more people, both as aggressors and victims. Especially since they represent violence that was actually instigated by the church for religious ends, it is arguable that the Crusades are unparalleled as the nadir of Christian advocacy of violence and bloodshed.

Wars flowing from religious inspiration or fought on behalf of religious causes have existed virtually from the outset of Christendom and have been legitimized in the writings of just war theorists from Augustine to Calvin. While violations of the law of nature and natural justice (of "peace" and "the common good") are the primary legitimations of social violence in the mainline Christian tradition, they are not the only ones. Religion also has furnished justifications of coercion, violence, even killing. While he did not concur in the death penalty frequently imposed on heretics by the civil authorities, Augustine advocated the forcible conversion or suppression of the Donatists. Relying on his doctrine of God's predestination of the elect, he held that God could somehow "graft in" even those dragged by force to the body of Christ.[1] During the Reformation, Christians on most sides of any question were willing to use force to quell their opponents. Even wars fought for the sake of public welfare or justice, rather than for properly religious causes, have been given indirect religious justifications. Just war theorists commonly make appeal to

1. Peter Brown, *Augustine of Hippo* (New York: Dorset Press, 1986; originally published by Univ. of California Press, 1986), 235–36.

authority of Christ" as the "most characteristic feature of crusading."[9] His definition of what this might mean in practice is broad enough to include wars against local heretics as well as foreign expeditions. "A crusade was a holy war fought against those perceived to be the external or internal foes of Christendom for the recovery of Christian property or in defence of the Church or Christian people."[10] Moreover, Riley-Smith specifically posits a fundamental similarity between the crusade mentality and the twentieth-century liberation theology "concept of a political Christ."[11] Yet surely the liberationist aim of freedom for the sociopolitically oppressed, as well as its appeal to moral sensibilities that the oppressors are presumed to share with the oppressed, are fundamentally different from the conquest of pagans governing Christianity's sacred places. It hardly needs to be added that the practical consequences of the two concepts have scarcely been comparable. The crusade and the holy war ideas call for better definition, especially in relation to other wars fought primarily for political aims under the civil authority, even if sanctioned also in religious terms.

Contemporaries of the Crusades attach much importance to the offer of a papal indulgence to laypeople as a reward for participation, undertaken through a formal vow. Does this feature reveal a basic quality of the crusade mentality—one that might, for instance, be extended to the Puritan civil war as a Protestant and not papally instigated phenomenon? The present argument will be that the most distinctive feature of the understanding of war as crusade is a reconfiguration of the Christian notions of love and discipleship so that they come not only to exclude enemies, but to intend their annihilation; and to mean by "love" a cultural and political loyalty to other Christians that has as its counterpart a fear of outsiders, a fear that easily turns to hatred. Both the crusaders and the Puritans identify Christian discipleship with hatred, vengeance, and violence to a degree that clearly exceeds justification of violence against heretics by Augustine, Aquinas, or the Reformers.

Referring to the development of the early modern holy war thinking that culminated in the Puritan revolution, James Turner Johnson isolates the just war from the holy war by describing as the latter's "fundamental rationale" "the idea that God is 'a man of war' who directs his people into certain battles in the service of their faith. . . ."[12] Johnson thinks that holy war as a divinely commanded war is a broader and less extreme concept than the crusade, insofar as the former can include wars fought for just political ends, even if divine or church authority instigates them. (Just war, then, would refer to wars for political ends that are also begun by legitimate politicial authorities.)

9. Jonathan Riley-Smith, *The First Crusade and the Idea of Crusading* (Philadelphia; Univ. of Pennsylvania Press, 1986), 17.

10. Ibid., xxviii.

11. Ibid., 256.

12. James Turner Johnson, *Ideology, Reason, and the Limitation of War* (Princeton, N.J.: Princeton Univ. Press, 1975), 82.

But the crusade as a type of holy war, however, focuses exclusion and destruction of outsiders with imagery of Christ, cross, and self-sacrifice.

Both crusade and Puritan thinking share a crucial element: the idea that violence is an integral part of God's own way and of the divine will for Christian disciples. The tone of regret with which Augustine, Luther, or Calvin would approach sanctioned killing is muted or (very often) nonexistent in the crusade, and in Puritan "holy war" advocacy. By arguing that "it is integral to holy war doctrine that one's own side be defined as totally righteous and the other as totally reprobate,"[13] Johnson confirms that holy war tends to eliminate restraint. Supreme confidence in the merit of one's own cause and in the worthlessness of the opposition is congenial to "the idea that holy war has no limits, but is an unrestrained, all-out struggle of good against evil."[14] These two characteristics—identification of violence with the Christian mission and self-righteous abandonment of restraint in war—set off the holy war, and even more the crusading ideology, both from more traditional uses of force in religious conflict (suppression of heretics), and from wars waged for properly political objectives.

The character of both crusade and the Puritan holy war—the eager appropriation of violence as a definitive meaning of Christian love and service—may be appreciated by recalling the way in which other forms of coercion in religion have been handled by the just war theorists thus far examined. Even traditional religious wars against heretics and schismatics are unlikely to share the ethos that lies behind the more radical enterprises that we are about to consider.

It is undoubtedly true that theorists defending both the Crusades and the Puritan Revolution utilized just war terminology, stretching it to meet a new agenda by emphasizing points of contact with standard apologies for the Christian use of violence as a means of sociopolitical control. This project was facilitated by the fact that just war theorists had themselves not only given religious backing for political wars, but had also countenanced violent suppression of heresy. Leroy Walters has argued for a basic similarity between the just war and the crusade, in that they both employ concepts of self-defense (of the fatherland and of the Holy Land; of the innocent and of converts); of aid to the oppressed (the allies and the Eastern churches); of rights of passage (of innocent travelers and of missionaries); and of punishment of wrongs (to society and to church or God).[15]

13. Ibid., 115.

14. Ibid., 104. David Little reinforces the point: "Not only is force undertaken for religious purposes and under direct religious anthorization, but opponents in a holy war or crusade tend to regard each other as cosmic enemies with whom compromise is improbable" ("'Holy War' Appeals and Western Christianity: A Reconsideration of Bainton's Approach," in *Just War and Jihad: Historical and Theological Perspectives on War and Peace in Western and Islamic Traditions,* ed. John Kelsay and James Turner Johnson [New York: Greenwood Press, 1991], 122).

15. LeRoy Walters, "The Just War and the Crusade," *The Monist* 57 (October 1973); 584–94.

Yet differences are substantial. In the first place, religion is a secondary definition or cause of war in standard just war thinking; it is not a primary reason for engagement in armed conflict. Religious obligation is not the fundamental category shaping the moral consideration of socially sanctioned and mass killing to further just political defense. Conversely, war and killing are not high on the agenda of the traditional Christian religious self-understanding, whatever compromises with religious identity the Christian has been willing to make in practice as he or she enters the political arena. Although Aquinas, a contemporary of the Crusades, speaks in the thirteenth century in acceptance of them, his genre, tone, and subject matter are far from the crusade "preaching" by which popes and theologians undertook to convert the laity to their mission against the infidels. Identified much more as a just war theorist, Aquinas takes up only the specific question of whether the promised papal indulgence is to be applied to the crusader who "dies before he can take the journey across the sea" and so does not attain his vowed objective.[16] The problem arises as an ad hoc inquiry put to Aquinas during an open forum of questioning and response. Aquinas comments on the preexisting papal decree but does not make the Crusades a part of his coverage of the general causes of engagement in war,[17] nor address the fundamental moral status of the Crusades.

Secondly, when addressed in the context of just war theory, religious coercion tends to be approached with ambivalence if not reserve, as a far less than optimal way to settle religious differences or instill faith. In response to a letter late in life from an old school friend who had become associated with Donatism, Augustine admits that the decision to inflict punishment in spiritual matters is occasion for "trembling" and "darkness."[18] It should be noted that Augustine was willing for force to be applied only to heretics, who are by definition fallen Christians and hence considered culpable, and who are moreover viewed as still subject to church discipline.

In the case of the Crusades, the issue was not so much conversion—possibly excepting the Jews in Europe whom the crusaders on their way to the Holy Land either murdered or "converted" at swordpoint—but the recapturing of Christian territories and the liberation of the Eastern churches. As Erdmann notes, the Christian tradition of the dubiousness of war, still in latent existence in the period of the Crusades, would make it "an exaggeration to suppose that the church generally desired wars upon pagans in order to

16. Aquinas, *Quodlibetal Questions* 2, Q.8, a.2. Quodlibetal disputations, held periodically in medieval universities, gave the masters the opportunity to demonstrate their learning by responding to a range of questions from a large and mixed audience including both teaching faculty and students. Questions often had to do with issues then being debated in the church or by theologians.

17. Aquinas, *Summa Theologica* 2–2.Q64.

18. Brown, *Augustine of Hippo,* 243, citing Letter 95.

eliminate paganism or to force conversion."[19] Yet upon their arrival in the East, the crusading mobs slaughtered "infidels" en masse, including children, as though the Eastern inhabitants deserved death whether or not they presented a danger to any specific Christian interests. In contrast, Walters affirms that none of the spokesmen for the just war tradition advocated unrestrained violence in either just war or religious war, and all of them seemed to apply to the two a similar standard for conduct in war, including the immunity of noncombatants.[20]

The Crusades represent a change from tradition in that they place violence (and especially killing) at the heart, not the periphery, of faithful discipleship; they involve a turn to decidedly aggressive interpretations of "defensive" violence on behalf of church interests; they involve clergy as real and not merely spiritual knights; and they attach to warring a guarantee of eternal reward. The Crusades were initiated and preached by religious leaders and attracted a transnational following, not dependent on the support of any one civil authority.

The Puritan holy wars represent a similar concept of offensive war for religion, but differ in that they are directed against other Christians and aim at both national political and religious goals through the specific unification of religious and state leadership in the persons of godly magistrates and rulers. Puritan holy war proponents demand that the soldiers be godly or personally holy, while the crusaders place more emphasis on their own sinfulness and the efficacy of war as penance. It has been argued that at least some Puritan revolutionaries even shifted toward secular just war theory in sanctioning their cause.[21] Some but not all of the early modern holy war advocates demand that religious warfare be conducted under limitations similar to those which in just war theory restrain political conflict.[22] But fundamentally, holy war and crusade thinking takes root in a Christian version of exclusivist triumphalism that assumes an obligation to extirpate the opposition in the name of Christ.

How does holy war rhetoric play into the continuing issues of justificatory uses of Scripture and views of the presence of the kingdom of God? Both crusaders and Puritans make use of Old Testament war imagery, and in addition construe the significance of Christ and of Christian love in violent terms (the latter is particularly true of the crusaders). For the crusaders, the kingdom is present and demands immediate responsiveness in a way that distorts New Testament eschatology but coincides credibly with medieval

19. Erdmann, *Origin of the Idea of Crusade,* 97. Jonathan Riley-Smith concurs, but points out one exception, in 1098, when Raymond Pilet led an expedition south of Antioch, where he took a Moslem-occupied fortress and killed all those within it who would not consent to baptism (*The First Crusade,* 1100).

20. Walters, "The Just War and the Crusade," p. 591.

21. Little, "'Holy War' Appeals," 134.

22. See Johnson, *Ideology, Reason,* 132–33.

conceptions of a hierarchy of natural and supernatural worlds. Crusaders conceived of the kingdom primarily as a place of delight, comfort, and repose after death. The kingdom impinges on present action, not by creating a presently actualizable ideal of harmonious and mutually forbearing social existence, but through its function as promise and threat, including its contrast with eternal perdition. The medieval Christian, constantly confronted with the vivid reality of death, feared mightily for his or her soul. The Crusade movement demonstrates that the popular belief in the future kingdom's reality could have direct and extreme effects on present action. The crusaders endured unimaginable hardship in order to ensure their own eventual salvation.

The Puritans were at once more biblical and less susceptible to crass promises of "works righteousness." They sought to make God's reign more present on this earth in the lives of God's elect through the establishment of a religious commonwealth uniting godly living with political control. Though they still rested ultimate hope in a heavenly fulfillment, they, exaggerating Calvin's ideas, sought to actualize in every social sphere a covenanted community of the redeemed.

## THE CRUSADES

The First Crusade and the decades immediately preceding it are of great importance to a critical exploration of the interrelation of social circumstances, biblical argument, and justification of violence. It was during the era of the First Crusade that preexisting just war ideas, especially those of Augustine, were reshaped into a recognizably different form. It was a time when violence moved from the margins of Christian social ethics into the heart of Christian discipleship as pictured and proclaimed by the pope and as embraced by thousands of his followers. The eleventh century, like the sixteenth, was a time of unrest in Europe. In the former case, the unrest was due to the gradual establishment of feudalism, precipitating the decline of the authority of central government. Loss of imperial or royal protection resulted in a general insecurity and the multiplication of private wars, in which churches were sometimes involved. The defense formerly afforded the church by the ruler was now undertaken by circles of knights who became the advocates of bishops and monasteries.[23] Violence was particularly endemic in France, which was to supply the forces for the First Crusade.

French society had long been accustomed to institutionalized violence, first in the expansion of the Carolingian empire, and then in its defense against invasions. When the invasions ceased after 1000, the organization and energy formerly directed at external enemies began to seek internal outlets.[24]

23. Erdmann, *Origin of the Idea of Crusade,* 57–59.
24. Riley-Smith, *The First Crusade,* 3.

The Truce of God and Peace of God movements, which began in France, were attempts to curtail the resultant violence and impose some measure of control on the rampant knighthood. These measures were instigated by the church and ratified with ecclesiastical legislation that required knights and local lords either to forswear war for certain periods or to vow immunity from it for clergy, churches, monasteries, and the poor. Some of these early peace decrees even seemed to promise forgiveness of sins, a precedent to the later crusade indulgence.[25] An ironic outcome of these peace initiatives, however, was the constellation of troops of "enforcers" around the ecclesiastical authorities. The monasteries and bishops themselves had knights committed to take action against breakers of the peace. Hence the church at once condemned the knighthood and its activities and found a positive role for its violence under the church's aegis.[26]

When the First Crusade was preached by Urban II in 1095, the holy war was in part a solution to problems of violence at home.[27] Remarking that the French were hemmed in geographically by mountains and sea, and that their land could scarcely provide for them, Urban concludes, "Because of this you murder and devour one another, you wage wars, and you frequently wound and kill one another." He then appeals, "Let this mutual hatred stop. . . . Begin the journey to the Holy Sepulcher; conquer that land which the wicked have seized."[28]

These developments must also be seen against the background of a reform movement in the church, represented above all by the pontificate of Gregory VII. During this period, the clergy and laity were considered to be two distinct orders, with the former dedicated to the spiritual life and divine worship. There was great concern on the part of the papacy to define the role of the laity, especially since many civil rulers and lords were accustomed to wield considerable influence in the affairs of the local churches. The key theme in the reform was to extend the impact of the church on the laity by associating monastic values with lay roles, preeminently the delineation of God-given vocations of service to the church through action in the political order.

The Investiture Contest represented a struggle for power among the ruling classes of Germany and Italy. It was a prolonged conflict over the relative influence in making ecclesiastical appointments of the pope and the Holy Roman Emperor (who, during Gregory's pontificate, was Henry IV). Gregory asserted the independence of the church from any imperial influence by claiming authority as the successor of St. Peter in both the spiritual and the temporal realms, including resort if necessary to the secular sword wielded

25. Erdmann, *Origin of the Idea of Crusade,* 76.

26. Riley-Smith, *The First Crusade,* 4. See Erdmann, *Origin of the Idea of Crusade,* 60–63.

27. Steven Runciman, *The First Crusade,* vol. 1 of *A History of the Crusades* (Cambridge: Cambridge Univ. Press, 1962), 91.

28. "The Sermon of Pope Urban II at Clermont," an eyewitness account, in James A. Brundage, *The Crusades: A Documentary Survey* (Milwaukee: Marquette Univ. Press, 1962), 19.

by his allies.[29] The ongoing dispute devolved not only into the excommunication of emperor by pope and the installments of anti-pope and anti-king, but also into outright war.

Gregory made the most of the availablity of military men in aid of the church, calling them "soldiers of Christ" and "soldiers of St. Peter" or "vassals of St. Peter," who were called to the "warfare of Christ." This military imagery was already familiar as a description of the monastic life (for example, in the Rule of St. Benedict) and even of the secular clergy (in the writings of Gregory the Great). But Gregory VII meant to transform its function from metaphor for monastic spirituality to exhortation to real military action.[30]

Gregory's creation of a papal army, recruited with offers of forgiveness of sins, did not pass without rebuke from other members of the episcopacy who did not concede the consistency of the Christian ideal of love with the militarization of the church. Gregory's countermove was to gather a number of supporters who sought to justify his concept of Christian warfare with reference to the Bible, tradition, and canon law. At the center of this coterie was Countess Matilda of Tuscany, who lent to the cause invaluable resources, both economic and military, and who harbored the papal theologians in her court.[31] Early on, one of these, John of Mantua, took pains to assure Matilda that Scripture endorsed military force in defense of true religion. He admonished her, "Do not ever be ashamed, O Bride of Heaven," to take up the sword against heretics; for "the God still lives who sanctified such action through the arms of David."[32]

One of the most industrious and influential of these Gregorian theologians was Bishop Anselm II of Lucca, who combed the works of Augustine to compile a systematic theory of war that would unqualifiedly justify violence against heretics, eliminating most of Augustine's ambivalence on the subject.[33] Anselm proposes that killing at the behest of church authorities is grounded ultimately in the command of God and should be embraced as a work of Christian love. Drawing from Augustine's anti-Donatist writings, Anselm allegorizes the casting out of the slave Hagar by Sarah (Gen. 16:6) to work out a concept of holy or blessed persecution of heretics. Not lacking in subtlety, Anslem qualifies his program of violence with a reserve that became all but nonexistent during succeeding centuries when the Crusades were in full bloom. He grants both that the individual Christian may not use the sword in self-defense and that use of the sword even for righteousness' sake does not accord with the full perfection of the Christian life. However, he uses a series of biblical references to draw a distinction between Christian perfection and the exigencies of the

29. I. S. Robinson, "Gregory VII and the Soldiers of Christ," *History* 58 (June 1973): 170–73.
30. Riley-Smith, *The First Crusade,* 6; Robinson, "Gregory VII," 174, 177–80.
31. Robinson, "Gregory VII," 184. See also Erdmann, *Origin of the Idea of Crusade,* 224–25.
32. Cited in Robinson, "Gregory VII," 185, from *Tractatus Iohannis Mantuani in Cantica Canticorum ad semper felicen matildam,* ed. B. Bischoff, 41.
33. Erdmann, *Origin of the Idea of Crusade,* 241–47; Robinson, "Gregory VII," pp. 186–188.

church's actual situation. Anselm justifies violence here and now by asserting a vast distance between God's kingdom and the present life. He notes that, although Paul preferred all to be celibate, he allowed that every man might have his own wife; although the Decalogue prohibits killing, Moses still allowed the Israelites to repay a life with a life.

> Similarly, concluded Anselm, "would that Catholics 'wrestled not against flesh and blood' (Eph. 6:12); would that they might live in peace . . . so that there was no need of "the minister of God, an avenger to execute wrath on evildoers' (Rom. 13:4)." But since some members of the Church prove refractory and threaten schism, the Gregorians have no choice save to punish them.[34]

Although the birth of the Crusades against the pagans was to await the pontificate of Urban II, Gregory and his partisans provided two indispensable conditions that made the Crusades possible. In the first place, they provided what for many medieval people would be an irresistable motivation for undertaking hardship and death: a guaranteed escape from the eternal retribution that one might otherwise expect to deserve. But more importantly for the career of Christian thinking about peace and war, they established an ethos of lay service to the church in which professional violence was soldered firmly to the highest Christian ideals, especially fraternal charity.

The motive of love of the persecuted, whom "punishment" might move to repentance, was not abandoned totally, but neighbor-love came to be used in a nonuniversal or exclusive sense to mean love for the comrades to whom one was bound by ties of nationality, kinship, or religious affiliation and whom one intended to defend against outsiders. Indeed, during his lifetime, Gregory had already appealed for an expedition—which he proposed to lead personally—to succor Constantinople against pagan invaders. Although his plans never came to fruition, they consolidated the reinterpretation of discipleship that the crusades would require.

> The example of our redeemer and the obligation of brotherly love demand that we lay down our lives for the liberation of our brethren, just as he "laid down his life for us and we ought to lay down our lives for our brethren."
>
> We beseech you, therefore, that you be moved to fitting compassion by the wounds and blood of your brethren and by the peril of the aforesaid Empire and that your strength be brought, in Christ's name . . . to the aid of your brethren.[35]

When Urban II preached the First Crusade in a tour of France in 1095–96, he brought to effective expression the sentiment in favor of a war of

34. Robinson, "Gregory VII," 187; citing Anselm of Lucca, *Liber contra Wibertum, cap.6, M.G.H, Libelli de lite* 1.525.

35. Letter addressed "to all those willing to defend the Christian faith," and dated Rome, March 1, 1074. In Brundage, *The Crusades: A Documentary Survey,* 9–10.

liberation on behalf of the Eastern churches that had been gathering momentum in the West for half a century. Urban actually had two aims in announcing the crusade, the interrelation and priority of which have been the subjects of much scholarly debate. These aims were to free the Eastern churches from the Turks, and to make a novel (that is, armed) pilgrimage to the holy sites of Jerusalem with the purpose of recapturing them for Christianity.

Erdmann's thesis, setting the mark for further discussion, was that the liberation of the East was Urban's only central purpose, and that the march on Jerusalem was included within this. "The pope's concern was not for any locality in particular, but for the men who confessed the Christian faith and for ecclesiastical institutions. The motive he featured [was] the idea of the community of all Christendom against the heathen."[36] Riley-Smith eventually challenges Erdmann on this point, seeing Jerusalem as much more central in Urban's original appeal. More important, he argues that the "idea of the crusade" really took shape only during and after the fact. The crusaders' horrific experiences of deprivation and suffering en route to Jerusalem, combined with their almost miraculous triumph there, led to a recasting of the meaning of crusade as divinely inspired and providential warfare, rising to the heights of monastic spirituality and complete with visions, signs, discoveries of relics, and martyrs—as recounted in accounts of eyewitnesses narrating their adventures some years later.[37]

The immediate impetus for Urban's initiative was an appeal from the Byzantine emperor for assistance in fending off the Turks who approached Constantinople. In his opening sermon at the Council of Clermont, recounted by an eyewitness, Urban deplores the fact that "the people of the Persian kingdom, an alien people, a race completely foreign to God . . . has invaded Christian territory" and devastated it "with pillage, fire and the sword." Moreover, he expected his French audience to be "especially aroused by the fact that the Holy Sepulcher of the Lord our Savior is in the hands of these unclean people." He invokes the gospel, recalling Jesus' promise that whoever leaves house, lands, and family "for my name's sake" shall receive "life everlasting." Promising remissions of sins, he enjoins the crusader to take up the cross of Christ: "Whoever shall decide to make this holy pilgrimage and shall take a vow to God, offering himself as 'a living sacrifice, consecrated to God and worthy of his acceptance,' shall wear the sign of the Lord's cross, either on his forehead or on his breast."[38]

The imagery of the cross was the symbolic nexus of the crusading movement and was thoroughly effective in stirring up popular fervor on behalf of the "knights of Christ." As the chronicle of a literate but not high-ranking

36. Erdmann, *Origin of the Idea of Crusade,* 330–31.
37. Riley-Smith, *The Crusades,* 2, 7–8, 118–19.
38. "The Sermon of Pope Urban," 18–20.

participant in the First Crusade reveals, Christ's nonresistant suffering and death were used to justify slaughtering the infidels with relish rather than scruple and to exalt violence into martyrdom and sainthood:

> When that time had already come, of which the Lord Jesus warns his faithful people every day, especially in the Gospel where he says, "If any man will come after me, let him deny himself, and take up his cross, and follow me," there was a great stirring of heart throughout all the Frankish lands, so that if any man, with all his heart and all his mind, really wanted to follow God and faithfully to bear the cross after him, he could make no delay in taking the road to the Holy Sepulchre as quickly as possible.[39]

And again, an arriving band of French crusaders is described to the leader Bohemond in a warlike transposition of New Testament sacrifice imagery: "They are well-armed, they wear the badge of Christ's cross on their right arm or between their shoulders, and as a war-cry they shout all together, 'God's will, God's will, God's will.' "[40]

Riley-Smith estimates that perhaps as many as 136,000 people[41] responded to Urban's appeal, including many whom the pontiff had discouraged, such as women, children, and the infirm. Why such a broad response? Many incurred great financial burdens, including debts and mortgages, and were—surely not unexpectedly—in great danger of disease, injury, hunger, and death on the way, therefore financial gain and adventure cannot have been such forceful motivators in the Crusades as they have sometimes been made out to be. One important motive was fear of punishment after death, a fate to be averted by the tremendous sacrifices to be undertaken voluntarily in the crusade. In addition, the pilgrimage was also a popular form of devotion. Travel to the Holy Land had been going on more or less peacefully since Jerusalem was taken by the Muslims in the seventh century.

The appeal of the reinvigorated military theme and the prospect of shedding the blood of aliens can better be appreciated against the backdrop of the medieval culture of family vengeance. At a time when ties of kinship provided protection and stability, and land holdings were crucial to survival, vendettas or blood feuds were common. Family members joined together in avenging wrongs.[42] After the crusaders conquered Jerusalem, they were "maddened by so great a victory after such suffering."[43] Save the general Iftikhar, who surrendered and with his bodyguard was guaranteed safe passage out, the Christians massacred all the Muslim inhabitants, including women and children in houses and mosques, reputedly filling the temple with blood that

39. Rosalind Hill, ed., *The Deeds of the Franks and the Other Pilgrims to Jerusalem* (Gesta Francorum) (New York: Thomas Nelson and Sons, 1962), 1.

40. Ibid., 7.

41. Riley-Smith, *The Crusades,* 11.

42. Riley-Smith, *The First Crusade,* 9, 114; *The Crusades,* 15–17.

43. Runciman, *The First Crusade,* 286–87.

reached up to men's knees. The rhetoric of the crusade and the violent social settings that spawned it prepared the killers to see their deeds as just retribution for egregious insults to the dominion of God and the proprietary rights of the church. Here Christianity fully absorbed and was transformed by, rather than transforming, the prevailing cultural ethos.

Papal preaching and the popular response were to receive a theological development that allowed the outlook and self-understanding of the first crusaders to be transmitted normatively to their successors. This theological interpretation reveals some of the suppositions about violence and Christian living that fueled the Crusades. For instance, three French Benedictine monks mediated the ideology of the First Crusade by writing shortly after the assault on Jerusalem: Robert the Monk, Guibert of Nogent, and Baldric of Bourgueil. They based their accounts on the *Gesta Francorum*, the anonymous narrative of an Italian Norman knight (the "participant" cited above[44]), aiming to refine his rough style into a more convincing apology. Robert goes so far as to draw a parallel in importance and divine approbation between the success of the crusade and the creation of the world and Jesus' sacrifice on the cross.[45] Again, these writers justify the crusade by announcing the Christians' prior claim to the Muslim-occupied territories, especially the Holy Land, scene of the seminal Christian drama. Moreover, they reinforce a sense of religious chauvinism through a rhetoric of unity in Christ, which allows perpetration of unrestrained injury against those understood to have offended him. Laments Baldric,

> Our brothers, members of Christ's body. . . . Your blood-brothers, your comrades-in-arms, those born from the same womb as you, for you are sons of the same Christ and the same Church. . . . Christian blood, which has been redeemed by Christ's blood, is spilled and Christian flesh, flesh of Christ's flesh, is delivered up to execrable abuses and appalling servitude."[46]

Baldric's connotative uses of kinship metaphors (blood, womb, flesh) allow the Christian hearer to replace the universal and inclusive thrust of the gospel love command with fierce group loyalty.

Such efforts cast the mold for the enthusiasm with which later church theologians were to take up the cause. In the crusading centuries, the voices calling for peace were few, among them Peter Damien and Roger Bacon. More representative was one of the medieval church's greatest theologians and preachers, Bernard of Clairvaux. Bernard devoted the energies of his later years to preaching very convincingly the ill-destined Second Crusade (under Pope Innocent II, beginning 1145). Bernard's surviving letters have been called "the most powerful crusade propaganda of all time."[47] A sample:

> Now is the acceptable time, now is the day of abundant salvation. The earth is shaken because the Lord of Heaven is losing his land, the land in which he

44. See n. 39 above.
45. Riley-Smith, *The First Crusade,* 140.
46. Ibid., 145; citing Baldric of Bourgueil, "Historia Jerosolimitana," RHC oc. 4, 12–13.
47. Riley-Smith, *The Crusades,* 95.

> appeared to men. . . . And now, for our sins, the enemy of the cross has begun to lift his sacrilegious head there. . . . What are you doing, you mighty men of valor? What are you doing, you servants of the cross? . . . Gird yourselves therefore like men and take up arms with joy and with zeal for your Christian name, in order to "take vengeance on the heathen and curb the nations."[48]

Bernard also admonishes his audience to lay aside the sword in their native lands in order to take it up elsewhere.

More than two centuries later, Catherine of Siena shared Bernard's interest in diverting local disruption and trouble to other objects when she urged a crusade that never transpired. She believed that a crusade might repair the deep rifts in the church which had arisen from the fact that for seventy years popes had been absent from Rome, ruling instead from the French city of Avignon. Catherine is best known for her impassioned pleading, ultimately successful, that Pope Gregory XI return to Rome from France.

Catherine's lifetime saw the revolt of several Italian states against Gregory XI and the legates through whom he continued to rule in Italy, who even by Catherine's account were often power-hungry and corrupt.[49] Concerned above all with the reconciliation of the church, she built the need for a crusade into her appeals for unity. She begs Gregory XI to forgive those rebels who have offended him, and "by love" to restore "the wandering sheep to the fold of Holy Church." Using an affectionate name for him, she proposes a further step, to give a common focus and to turn past differences to cooperation. "And then, sweet my 'Babbo,' you will fulfil your holy desire and the will of God, by making the holy Crusade, which I summon you in His Name to do swiftly and without negligence. They will turn to it with great eagerness; they are ready to give their life for Christ."[50] Later she writes to Gregory's successor, Urban VI, in support of the identical program. She begs him "by the love of Christ crucified" to show mercy to "the little sheep who have strayed from the fold." To induce the pope to follow her advice, she adds that "once peace is made, you can raise the standard of the most holy cross. As you can plainly see, the infidels have arrived on our shores to challenge you."[51] Catherine's exhortations continue the now-familiar theme: Christian love, transmuted into group loyalty, is turned as a sword's edge against those to whom love as fellow-feeling does not extend.

Christian love turned V.

A final phenomenon setting crusade theory and practice off from earlier just war thinking is the establishment of clerical orders of knights. In departing from the traditional exclusion of clergy from violent professions, these orders

48. Bernard of Clairvaux, "Letter to the People of the English Kingdom" (ca. 1146), in Brundage, *The Crusades: A Documentary Survey,* 91–92.

49. See Mary Ann Fatula, *Catherine of Siena's Way* (Wilmington, Del.: Michael Glazier, 1987).

50. "To Gregory XI" (ca. 1375), in *Saint Catherine of Siena as Seen in Her Letters,* ed. Vida D. Scudder (New York: E. P. Dutton, 1905), 126.

51. J. Kirshner and K. F. Morrison, *Medieval Europe* (Chicago: Univ. of Chicago Press, 1986), 429.

testify to the inroads made by a transformed consciousness of armed coercion as appropriate to a Christlike life. The most prominent of the military orders are the Order of Knights Templar and the Order of the Hospital of St. John of Jerusalem. The Hospitalers were founded in 1113, originally with the purely charitable motive of caring for sick pilgrims to the Holy Sepulchre. Later they took on the role of defending the frontiers of Christian settlements and began accumulating land, and their ministry to the poor became secondary. In 1118–19, a French knight and eight companions took vows of obedience, poverty, and chastity and swore to protect pilgrims on the road to Jerusalem. The order they formed, the Knights Templar, was supported both by the king, Baldwin II, and by Bernard of Clairvaux, who drafted their rule. Both orders came directly under the authority of the Holy See, which guaranteed them an unusual degree of freedom from the usual civil and ecclesiastical institutions. Eventually they developed into transnational organizations of notable military strength and great wealth, exercising important roles both in defense of the Latin states that had been established in the East and in international finance.[52]

Aquinas was later to offer the defense that, although members of religious communities should not defend by violence any "worldly purpose," the "religious order directed to soldiering" can accomplish work belonging to the active (versus contemplative) part of a consecrated life of service to God. He continues, "a religious order may be fittingly established for soldiering . . . for the defense of divine worship and public safety, or also of the poor and oppressed."[53]

The capture of Jerusalem that ended the First Crusade brought only temporary satisfaction—the city was recaptured in 1187 by the Muslims under Saladin—but the victory was to inspire other initiatives for two centuries, with nearly continual waves of crusaders departing for the East in between the major contingents. In these Eastern initiatives, success tended to be ephemeral, though the crusaders sometimes stayed to settle colonies (the states of the "Latin Kingdom of Jerusalem," the last holdout of which fell again to the Muslims in 1291). The final Ninth Crusade (led by Prince Edward of England in 1271–72) was, like most of its predecessors, a failure.

The term "crusade" was extended to campaigns mounted in Europe, both against non-Christian invaders (for example, the Wends in Germany) and against heretical Christian insurrectionists (the Albigensians and Hussites, for example). Political goals could be intertwined with religious ones: the status and privileges of crusaders were awarded the Teutonic knights who campaigned against the Prussians (1226), and the pope proclaimed a crusade against Holy Roman Emperor Frederick II (1228). Despite their longevity, the

52. See Hans Eberhard Mayer, *The Crusades,* 2d ed. (New York: Oxford Univ. Press, 1988), 77–80; and Riley-Smith, *The Crusades,* 56–60.

53. Aquinas, *ST* 2–2.Q.188.a.4.

high point of the crusades had really been at their beginning. As Riley-Smith tells it, the movement "died a lingering death," its popular energy lost by the late fourteenth century. The crusade of Sebastian of Portugal in 1578 "may have been" the last, although various remaining crusaders still "may well have been found in the late seventeenth or early eighteenth century." The crusading era was definitely brought to a close—in disconcertingly recent history—by the defeat of the last bastion of a military order when Napoleon overtook the Hospitalers on Malta in 1798.[54]

## JOAN OF ARC

A figure who may help to cast into relief the crusading mentality and prepare the transition to the Puritan revolution is Joan of Arc—"la Pucelle" or "the Maid" of Orléans, as she designated herself (1412–31). At first look, Joan in many ways seems to fit into the crusade genre, especially its ethos of Christian knighthood and its sense of divinely appointed mission to recapture occupied lands. But there are crucial differences. Most obviously, those against whom she contended were also Christians, not "infidels," and hence not genuine outsiders to her social vision. Moreover, Joan's martial leadership, while supernaturally inspired, was not yoked to ecclesial aims, nor, in fact, put in the service of religion as such at all. She perceived herself as commissioned for a properly political (justice-based) goal: to conclude the Hundred Years' War by saving France from English dominion, and to ensconce Charles VII on his rightful throne.

More noteworthy from a theological point of view are two facts that distance Joan from the crusade ideology of the medieval period. First, she expressed ambivalence about the enterprise of killing, avowing at the end of her career that she had never personally engaged in it. To have put anyone to death apparently would have offended her sense of the integrity of the mission with which she had been supernaturally charged. (One also notes that she hardly discouraged her troops from measures that were to her personally repugnant.) Second, she expressed repeatedly a hope to make peace with her adversaries, in prospect of forgiveness and reconciliation, not conquest or extermination.

The appeal of the Maid to the imaginations of so many, from her contemporaries to the present,[55] is due not only to her reputed ability to inspire military confidence and hence success, but also to the aura of mystery and

54. Riley-Smith, *The Crusades,* 255.

55. See Ingvald Raknem, *Joan of Arc in History, Legend and Literature* (Oslo: Universitetsforlaget, 1971). Among the many other biographies and works on Joan's influence are Lucien Fabre, *Joan of Arc* (New York: McGraw-Hill, 1954); W. S. Scott, *Jeanne d'Arc* (London: Harrap, 1974); Marina Warner, *Joan of Arc: The Image of Female Heroism* (New York: Alfred A. Knopf, 1981); Anne Llewellyn Barstow, *Joan of Arc: Heretic, Mystic, Shaman* (Lewiston, N.Y.: Edwin Mellen Press, 1986).

miracle, or at least of inexplicability, with which she has constantly been surrounded. Daughter of a French farmer in Domrémy, Joan began as a girl of thirteen to hear the "voices" of St. Michael, St. Catherine, and St. Margaret. When she was about sixteen, they exhorted her to come to the aid of Charles the Dauphin. Shortly after news came in 1428 that the English had taken Orléans, she journeyed to see Charles at Chinon castle. There, in a secret conversation, she convinced him of her mission to raise the siege of Orléans and have him crowned at Reims. (A prevalent theory is that she reassured him, on God's authority, of the legitimacy of his birth, a matter in some doubt in his own mind as well as others. Hence she was able to secure Charles's confidence in his right to the throne and in her ability to lead him to it.)

When the army to march on Orléans was organized at Tours, Joan put on a suit of white armor and carried a standard, the prerogative of a knight, on which were inscribed "Jesu Maria," a depiction of Christ, and the French white fleur-de-lys.[56] She made an unusual request for a special sword, with five crosses engraved on it, which she said would be found behind the altar in the Church of St. Catherine in Fierbois. It was in fact discovered there and brought to her. Joan is said to have prized her banner even more than her sword. "'I truly love my sword,' said the Maid, 'because it was found in the church of St. Catherine whom, too, I love. But I value my standard forty times more highly than my sword.'" When she was asked why she carried it into battle, she replied, "Because while carrying my banner I could avoid the shedding of blood. I have never killed anybody."[57]

Other events and circumstances in Joan's life also contributed to the tremendous power she was able to exercise over the imaginations of her followers and even her enemies. One of these was her seeming ability to predict the future or to know contemporaneous events that had not yet come to light. She predicted accurately that she would be wounded, yet not seriously, at the battle of Orléans; and that a man who at Chinon swore at and insulted her was near his death (which came to pass within an hour). Even before her audience with the Dauphin, she had known of an important defeat of the French near Orléans and told of it to the immediate disbelief and later conversion of her hearers. Joan's mystique was enhanced by her anomolous gender identification, manifest most obviously in her refusal to wear women's clothing and her adoption of knightly garb. She not only was a virgin (evidenced at least three times upon examination by officially commissioned groups of matrons), but also was apparently amenorrheic. According to the testimony of her page and other young men, they considered her to be an utterly inappropriate object of sexual desire, much less advances—despite a

56. Warner reports that in December 1429, Joan "and her family and all their issue in the male and female line were ennobled by Charles in perpetuity" (*Joan of Arc,* 165).

57. Fabre, *Joan of Arc,* 277, from a transcript of Joan's trial; also see 131. See also Warner, *Joan of Arc,* 165. Warner cites *Procès de condamnation de Jeanne d'Arc: Traduction et notes par Pierre Tisset avec le concours de Yvonne Lanhers,* 3 vols. (Paris, 1870), 27 February.

physical appearance that, while sturdy, they seem not to have regarded as unattractive.

After the successful siege on Orléans in 1429, Joan took a place of honor beside Charles VII at his coronation. However, her fortunes were about to turn. The same year, she was unsuccessful in her siege of Paris and was later captured by the Burgundians, who sided with the English, to whom they sold her. Charles, unintelligibly if not reprehensibly, made no attempt to ransom her. She was eventually turned over to the ecclesiastical court at Rouen.

Pierre Cauchon, bishop of Beauvais, indebted both financially and politically to the Burgundians and the English, tried her personally for heresy and witchcraft. Fear caused her finally to sign a statement disavowing the saints whose voices had led her. But after a three-day period in which the voices rebuked her for her faithlessness, she returned to the steadfastness of her original convictions. She did not waver in her beliefs when she was shortly thereafter burned at the stake as a heretic. The events of her death evoked wonder and strengthened rather than undermined her reputation. She begged that a crucifix be brought from a local church so that she might fix her gaze upon it until her death, which she met calling upon the names of her saints and of Jesus Christ. By at least some accounts, her heart did not burn, and was ordered to be cast, along with other potential relics of the execution, into the river Seine.[58] In 1456 Joan was "rehabilitated" in a special trial that repudiated the biased partisan proceedings of the first. In 1920 she was canonized.

That Joan was an avid patriot who sought French independence through allegiance to God as its true sovereign is clear. Certainly she endorsed and personally led troops to the kill in defense of this aim, and she embossed her leadership with the popular ideals and emblems of knightly chivalry. What more is known of her attitudes toward violence and toward the role of divine intervention in the political conflicts that she believed she was sent to resolve? Some evidence comes from letters that she sent to the English prior to the campaign against them at Orléans. Addressing herself to the king, the regent of France, and other high-ranking officers, she implores, "I call upon you to make submission to the King of Heaven, and to yield into the hands of the Maid, who has been sent hither by God, the King of Heaven, the keys of all the fair cities which you have seized and ravished in France." Nevertheless, Joan declares herself "willing to make peace with you if you be willing to hearken to her [the Maid's] demands, which are that you shall leave France in tranquility and pay what you owe."[59] She promises that if her plea be heeded, then the Duke of Bedford, Regent, might join with her "and with the men of France in so high an exploit that the like has never been seen in all Christendom."[60] Later, she was to state at her trial that "I first demanded

58. See Scott, *Jeanne d'Arc,* 125; Fabre, *Joan of Arc,* 323; Raknem, *Joan of Arc,* 18.
59. Quoted in Fabre, *Joan of Arc,* 140.
60. Ibid., 140. Fabre speculates that the "exploit" is a projected crusade.

that peace should be made, and was prepared to fight only if that could not be brought about."[61] Lucien Fabre states that Joan's voices had instructed her to warn the English to surrender before resorting to violence against them. He notes moreover that "it is written in Deuteronomy: 'When thou drawest nigh unto a city to fight against it, then proclaim peace unto it. . . . And if it will make no peace with thee, then thou shalt besiege it.' "[62]

The records of Joan's trials provide her own self-justifications in response to hostile questioning. She firmly refuses to draw either God or her voices into any rhetoric of hatred for the English. In response to the query whether St. Margaret and St. Catherine "hate the English," she replies only that "They love what Our Lord loves, and hate what He hates." When pressed, "Does God hate the English?", her answer is that, although if the English "are beaten it will be because of their sins," still "I know nothing of any love or hatred which God may bear to the English; but I do know that God will give to the Frenchmen the victory against them."[63]

Joan's responses pose a contrast with what Urban is reported to have declaimed at Clermont, urging the "heralds of Christ" to "exterminate this vile race [the Muslims] from the lands of our brethren," the "worshippers of Christ":

> Oh, what a disgrace if a race so despised, degenerate, and slave of the demons, would thus conquer a people fortified with faith in omnipotent God and resplendent with the name of Christ! Oh, how many reproaches will be heaped upon you by the Lord Himself if you do not aid those who like yourselves are counted of the Christian faith![64]

The most overt and easily specifiable difference between Joan and the crusaders is that she was motivated by her interest in restoring what she was convinced was right order in the political realm—not by the expansion or defense of the institutional church, and certainly not by its temporal stakes in civil or political affairs. Such ecclesial interests were, in fact, clearly aligned against her in the trials at Rouen. Although Joan indeed invoked a divine mandate, the military objectives backed by that mandate were judged fundamentally just by political criteria, not religious or revealed ones. The similarity between Joan and the crusaders lies in her confidence in divine guidance in a violent contest over territorial dominion. The guidance is voiced in her case not by the church's institutional representatives, but by divine emissaries who lend her independent and thoroughly compelling counsel.

61. Ibid., 293.

62. Ibid., 140. Fabre gives credit for the link to Deuteronomy to Edmond Richer.

63. Ibid., 278–79.

64. "Pope Urban II: The Call to the First Crusade, 26 November, 1095," from an eyewitness account, in *Readings in Church History,* ed. C. J. Barry (Westminster, Md., Westminster Press, 1960), 328.

This similarity is modulated by a second, even more fundamental, difference: Joan refuses to make grandiose assertions about God's final designs in history, or to identify those designs more than provisionally with the "election" of the historical group with which she identifies. She is Augustinian in her reserve about the worthiness of violence as a Christian measure, but voices that reserve even more directly than did Augustine, who tended to confine it to religious, not political, conflicts.[65] Joan also recalls the tone of Aquinas, who asked, "Is it always a sin to wage a war?" and conceived of the justifications primarily in terms of justice and the common good. Joan does not urge the ultimacy or righteousness of her cause beyond the limited political objective of restoring a French monarch to the French throne. She in no way identifies her adversaries as the accursed of God, nor even suggests that her temporal enmity with them is intrinsic and irremediable. In Joan's mission, Christian love does not become a tool with which to excise from the bounds of neighbor-concern all those who threaten one's religious or civil community. In her attitude the Christian ideal of mercy and forgiveness toward one's enemies moderates rather than capitulates to the then-prevailing ethos of warfare and revenge. However skeptical she may have been of obtaining it, Joan did not rule out in principle the possibility of English and French cooperation in securing justice for the French nation. She rejects what she perceives to be the plain injustice of the English position, but she does not project that perception as a cosmic struggle between good and evil. Strongly convinced as she is of the rightness in God's eyes of the French cause, she does not lose all perspective on the limits of its historical and religious importance.

## THE PURITAN REVOLUTION

The English Civil War of the mid-1600s also was to be anchored in a supposed divine mandate to reform the political order. The grounds would be, not reasonableness and fair play, but the covenanted mission of a religious group, called to establish on earth a society that had its charter in a heavenly contract. The term "Puritan" originated in the 1560s to describe a growing movement to simplify and reform the Church of England. Puritans were critics of the settlement with which Elizabeth I had established order in the English church by making it coterminous with the nation. Repudiating the Roman Catholicism of her predecessor and sister, Queen Mary, Elizabeth established the future contours of Anglicanism by favoring an inclusive Calvinistic Protestantism, which tried to accommodate as norms both Bible and tradition, thus leaning away from the more radical Continental reforms. At the same time, the Church of England retained some of the Roman flavor in its liturgy and episcopal hierarchy.

65. Though he sees even a just war as regrettable (*City of God,* 19.7).

Anglican bishops were successors of Peter in the universal church, and he marshaled both religious and political forces behind a strict following of Anglican ritual. The opposition to the Royalists gradually took control of Parliament, leading to several open conflicts with the king, including his dissolution of Parliament in 1629. After eleven years he was forced to reconvene it, in order to seek its financial aid. But by 1640 the Presbyterians, a Puritan party, had gained a majority in Parliament. Laud was impeached and imprisoned, though there was little agreement within Parliament about the direction that Puritan reforms should take.

Civil war was precipitated when Parliament unsuccessfully demanded from the king control over the army and the appointment of royal ministers. Oliver Cromwell, who had served as a member of Parliament, emerged as a Puritan military leader in 1643. In justification of his military endeavors, he averred that "from brethren, in things of the mind, we look for no compulsion, but that of light and reason." However, in "other things, God hath put the sword into the Parliament's hands, for the terror of evil-doers, and the praise of them that do well. If any plead exemption from it he knows not the Gospel."[72] His regiment, the Ironsides, was to be made up of "godly" men who fulfilled their calling with Christian self-discipline. In 1644–45, the parliamentary army was organized into the New Model Army, shaped to the same ideals. Wrote Cromwell of his troops, who obtained their victories by "faith and prayer": "It's their joy that they are instruments to God's glory, and their country's good; it's their honor that God vouchsafes to use them." And of his conquests: "all this is none other than the work of God. He must be a very great atheist who does not acknowledge it."[73] Yet the godly discipline of Cromwell's army was later to break down on at least one infamous occasion, at Drogheda (1649).

The Puritan army defeated the king at Naseby in 1645. In 1648, under Cromwell's direction, the army purged from Parliament those members still interested in negotiating some agreement with the king, and arranged the trial of Charles I for treason. The king, preserving the remnant of his dignity by refusing to justify himself before the court, was condemned and beheaded in 1649. Upon his death, the government of the British republic was entrusted to the Commonwealth, governed by Parliament. It was in the first year of its rule that Cromwell led a punitive campaign into Ireland—regarded like the crusaders' "infidels" as alien to the common cause—and massacred more than three thousand defenders of the Royalist garrison at Drogheda. Following in a month was the execution of hundreds of civilians in Wexford. Cromwell then implemented a policy of transferring Irish properties to English landlords. He is reported to have looked upon these actions with an opprobrious

72. "Letter from Cromwell" (Bristol, 14 September, 1645), in *The Puritan Revolution: A Documentary History,* ed. Stuart E. Prall (Garden City, N.Y.: Doubleday, 1968), 125.
73. Ibid., 124.

sense of divine approval. " 'The Lord is pleased still to vouchsafe us his presence and to prosper his work in our hands,' he wrote, and he spoke complacently of the 'righteous judgment of God upon these barbarous wretches.' "[74]

During the years of the Commonwealth (to 1653) and of the ensuing Protectorate under Cromwell's reign (to his death in 1658), comprehensive Puritan reforms in theology, church government, and liturgy were enacted in England. After Cromwell's death and a short rule by his son, Richard, the nation was returned to the Commonwealth, and eventually to Charles II in 1660, who reinstated Anglicanism as the official church.

James Johnson notes that the English transformation of just war categories into the idea of holy war spanned the years from 1560 to 1660. Motivated by England's rivalry with Spain as well as its internal conflicts, it was not limited to Puritans.[75] Indeed, wars of religion proliferated all over Europe during this period, and there was heavy rivalry among Christian nations for expansion and colonization. Johnson describes holy war doctrine in the early modern period as derived from the late medieval just war but as taking its bearings from the idea that "God himself inspires and commands some wars." Unlike the version of just war theory that becomes part of modern international law, holy war doctrine does not seek "the presence of certain naturally defined, politically manifested criteria."[76] In this, the Puritan holy war authors resemble the crusaders.

Puritans were enthusiastic depictors of God as commander in war. Their imagery was applied to God as a "man of war" and to Christ as "captain" and the angels as an "army." The earth was described as a "field of war," the Christian as a "soldier" against both spiritual enemies and heretics or persecutors.[77] The Puritans' passionate use of biblical warrants to exhort to violence (against other Christians) evidences a mentality not foreign to the crusades against the Moslems in the Holy Land, but with two important differences. First, the ideal of personal righteousness occasionally offers grounds for some restraint in the means used to pursue the aims of war (as in the writings of Alexander Leighton, but contrasting strongly with Henry Bullinger, William Allen, and Thomas Barnes[78]). Second, Puritan divines like William Gouge have, apparently, enough appreciation of the countercultural thrust of the New Testament love command to realize that defense of holy war is on shaky ground if it takes the lordship of Jesus as its point of departure.

74. C. V. Wedgwood, *Oliver Cromwell* (London: Gerald Duckworth & Co., 1973), 71. See also Antonia Fraser, *Cromwell Our Chief of Men* (London: Weidenfeld and Nicolson, 1973), 338–39; and Bainton, *Christian Attitudes,* 151. The quotations come from a letter to Parliament, via the Speaker, reporting on the Irish expedition.

75. Johnson, *Ideology, Reason,* 84.

76. Ibid., 81–82.

77. Walzer, *Revolution of the Saints,* 277–80, 290.

78. See Johnson, *Ideology, Reason,* 141; and his *Just War Tradition and the Restraint of War: A Moral and Historical Inquiry* (Princeton, N.J.: Princeton Univ. Press, 1981), 234.

are to be associated with it. It defines some but certainly not all defenders of war fought for religious purposes.[85]

Johnson rightly calls for nuance in the classification of holy war authors, and he demonstrates persuasively that it is difficult to develop a "hard" category that clearly sets off either the crusade or the holy war (the two may not be historically or conceptually easy to distinguish from one another) from other types of religious war or violence. What unites Puritans and crusaders, and may in the end stand out as the central feature of a category that could comprehend both, is the elevation and cultivation of violence as a core meaning of faithful following of Christ. It can scarcely be denied that this is a perversion—not just a conflict-driven application—of the gospel as embodied in the life and teaching of Jesus and in his death on the cross. It is this fundamental sanctification which, especially in the case of the Crusades, is promoted through Bible-linked warfare imagery. Undergirded by the assurance that the fallen warrior will be granted an eternal reward, it encourages abandonment of compassion and moderation toward the enemy. Imitation of Christ can hardly function as a curb on violence once killing is assimilated into the very meaning of Christlike behavior.

The present study has suggested that the key to crusading is a transformation of Christian love into group loyalty, fostered historically by the medieval world view. Correlative with it are willingness to use violence against outsiders, especially if they are perceived to threaten the group, and the sanctification of violence as an essential meaning of fidelity to Christ and to God's will. Beyond this core, the conditions and trappings of crusading and holy war can vary. The medieval wars against the inhabitants of the Holy Land are the "purest" form of crusade, with their alienation of the "infidel," their lack of attention to *jus in bello*, their grants of papal indulgence for sin, and their highly developed ethos of warrior sainthood and martyrdom. But the Puritans, at least in some instances, possess an essence in common with the crusade, in that violence against the enemies of church and nation is praised in similar terms of godliness and fidelity to Christ.

Joan of Arc, while resembling the crusaders externally, falls further from their basic outlook on the enterprise of war. Her adversaries are Christian and participate in the same basic culture and political institutions as she does. For her, war is neither an apocalyptic judgment against God's enemies nor a privileged form of discipleship. Though she is commanded to make war on her political opponents, the mission of killing is clearly provisional and limited as an expression of fidelity to Christ. The difference between war and Christian discipleship as such is accentuated by the fact that she fights in an essentially secular cause, not a religious one.

Christians today rarely if ever directly endorse holy war, crusading, or total war. Nevertheless, religious rhetoric is not infrequently introduced into programs of national defense or expansion to give a transcendent legitimacy to

85. Ibid., 137–39.

political aims. Moreover, the insider-outsider mentality is often at the root of political conflict. Thus it remains important to examine the warrants, rhetoric, and outcomes that have been associated historically and normatively with the Crusades' fundamental corruption of Christian social responsibility. The modern mind, imbued with convictions about freedom of conscience, finds it difficult to recapture or even imagine the triumphal ethos for which so much blood was poured in the eleventh century (and even the seventeenth). But consider the fairly recent words of a Roman Catholic author, rendering an account of the Crusades only shortly before the Second Vatican Council was to produce the *Declaration on Religious Liberty*. Henri Daniel-Rops, in his biography of Bernard of Clairvaux, praises the saint's ability "to summon Christianity to a holy war for the empty Tomb."[86] Calling the Second Crusade the "culminating point" in Bernard's "brilliant career,"[87] Daniel-Rops, without evident disapproval, describes the Crusade to be, for Bernard, "the total expression of Christianity" and "a testimony to the Communion of Saints."[88] Here we find not only a romanticization of war for chauvinistic aims of the church, but also tacit identification of violence with Christian saintliness.

The Crusades and their near relatives represent a low point in Christian ethics precisely because they fail utterly in the mission of the Christian community to challenge the sinful ethos of the culture in which it participates. A *Gestalt* of exclusion, competition, conflict, coercion, and killing is permitted to eat into the very heart of the Christian moral life, betraying its witness and offering to the world "false prophets," wolves in "sheep's clothing" (Matt. 7:15) and "whitewashed tombs" (Matt. 23:27). These phrases of Jesus' damn religious groups and representatives who eviscerate God's care for human creatures and God's call to be merciful and to forgive. A particularly pernicious rewriting of the Christian mandate to love occurs when Jesus' inclusive and generous compassion for the outcast and outsider is recast as a defensive in-group loyalty.

The mind of the modern reader cannot help but be drawn to the Holocaust, in which the Christian churches for the most part condoned or actively supported the annihilation of millions of Jews. The Jews were refused recognition as fellow human beings and inclusion under the appellation "neighbor," which in biblical parlance would indicate a strong duty to succor. Going further, many Christians were able to persecute Jews actively out of a dearly held misinterpretation of the death of Jesus; instead of identifying with his own sacrificial suffering, they turned the cross into a false accusation of Judaism and into another weapon of destruction.

Although the New Testament, particularly the Pauline and Johannine writings, encourages members of the body of Christ to love and to bear all things

86. Henri Daniel-Rops, *Bernard of Clairvaux* (New York: Hawthorn Books, 1964), 62.
87. Ibid., 95.
88. Ibid., 100.

grounds to "that of God in every man," and their founder George Fox frequently expresses a near-mystical sense of the unity of all things and persons in Christ.

Nothwithstanding this shared vision, not all Christian pacifist thought is the same, as is evident from the distinction of the Anabaptists and Erasmus above. At least two strands within pacifism may be identified: compassionate pacifism and obediential pacifism. While empathetic identification with "the other" (friend, stranger, or foe) is key to the first, that theme is subsumed in the second under obediential imitation of Christ's sacrifice.[1] In the first category may be placed Erasmus, the Social Gospel movement, Dorothy Day, Thomas Merton, and the Quakers; in the second are Tertullian and Origen, the Anabaptists, John Howard Yoder, and H. Richard Niebuhr. These examples certainly do not exhaust the Christian pacifist tradition. They have been chosen for their individual significance and the representative character of their self-expression. Other examples would also have been appropriate—Leo Tolstoy, James Douglass, and Gordon Zahn, to name a few. Moreover, H. Richard Niebuhr's position as a whole cannot be termed pacifist. He is included here because of the special theological direction of his arguments against resort to violence during the Manchurian crisis.

Among the three pacifist examples in this chapter, the Anabaptists (represented especially by their great theologian Menno Simons) are most radically biblical, while Erasmus is the least so. As a humanist, the latter finds wisdom in classical sources, and also sees the patristic period as a crucial resource for theological interpretation of the biblical models of Christian life. Erasmus does reject violence, but accepts nonetheless the congeniality of Christian life and politics. He wants to change society through rather traditional

1. In a recent essay, James Childress distinguishes four kinds of pacifism: legalist-expressive; consequentialist pragmatic-utilitarian; redemptive witness; and technological, especially nuclear, pacifism. The first holds that pacifism is right religiously, even though it is not effective; the second that pacifism is right morally because it is effective; the third that pacifism is both religiously right and that it will be effective; and the fourth that just war criteria themselves lead to the exclusion of certain measures of war, or even modern war itself so long as it entails such means. My thesis is that the fourth variety is not really pacifism, but an application of just war theory. Moreover, *Christian* pacifism is never based solely on consequentialist grounds, apart from any idea of conformity to God's will in Christ. That leaves Childress's first and third varieties as points of comparison with my two. I am distinguishing types not so much on the basis of whether they view pacifism as effective or not, as on the basis of how they ground pacifism as an aspect of Christian community. The point of similarity between Childress's categories and my own is perhaps this: Obediential imitation of Christ is not focused first of all on the effects of action on fellow humanity, while compassionate pacifism does begin with a transformed relation to other persons. But even in Christian compassionate pacifism, the starting point is not political and social effectiveness, but a change in relationships, which pacifism does not "bring about," but of which it is already *the expression.* In other words, while "nuclear pacifism" is not really pacifism, "effectiveness pacifism" is not really Christian. Christian conversion is fundamental to Christian pacifism and is expressed in the primary mode either of fidelity or of compassion. See James F. Childress, "Contemporary Pacifism: Its Major Types and Possible Contibutions to Discourse about War," in *The American Search for Peace: Moral Reasoning, Religious Hope, and National Security,* ed. George Weigel and John P. Langan, SJ (Washington, D.C.: Georgetown Univ. Press, 1991), 114–20.

means (by appeals to rulers, to patrons, and influential people—by using the power network). Erasmus never absolutely rejected the possibility that even the Christian ruler might be morally bound to resort to arms.

The Anabaptists (or Mennonites) and the Friends (or Quakers), along with the Church of the Brethren, are called the historic peace churches, precisely because, since their institution, they have represented opposition to warfare on the basis of the Sermon on the Mount. The Anabaptists stake everything on Scripture itself and on radical discipleship and have little interest in influencing social life. Menno Simons and his community see government as necessary to keep order, but do not participate in it or other worldly institutions that bring potential for conflict with God's commands. The Quakers (and their founder George Fox), in contrast, make both Scripture and traditions relative to the present working of the Holy Spirit ("the Light within") as a guide to what biblical religion demands now. Quakerism represents a grass-roots and working-class movement where social power lies only in conversion of people to the cause. Yet the Friends maintain a hope that by living in the kingdom they will broaden its base and give it progressive transformative power in the world.[2]

The interest in eschatology—that is, in the presence or distance of the kingdom of God—is an essential and necessary part of the Christian tradition and an essential qualification of its ethics. Traditional authors did not share the critical approach to biblical eschatology that pervades modern biblical scholarship, but grappling with the challenge of the kingdom made present in Jesus is constitutive of the Christian ethical tradition. Minority pacifist groups throughout the history of the Christian church have taken the eschatalogical or kingdom thrust of the gospel seriously by setting an agenda of radical practice and witness for the discipleship community. This seriousness characterizes the Anabaptists and Quakers more decidedly than Erasmus, but it is true of the latter also, to the extent that he refused to divide Christians into higher and lower states of life and expected all to strive to attain the perfection of the kingdom as a real goal in their own lives.

The contribution of the modern hermeneutical approach to the theme of eschatology is to focus our attention on it in a new way, so that we can view and understand the commitments of traditional writers from an important perspective: that of eschatological commitment. At the same time, it is important to remember that the twentieth-century theologian or biblical scholar will articulate the theme of eschatology in categories that differ from those of precritical biblical and theological interpretation.

## ERASMUS

The Dutch humanist Desiderius Erasmus (ca. 1466–1536) embodies the confidence in reason and privileging of classical sources typical of the Renaissance,

2. For one comparison of the varieties of pacifism represented by Erasmus and the Anabaptists, see James T. Johnson, "Two Kinds of Pacifism: Opposition to the Political Use of Force in the Renaissance-Reformation Period," *Journal of Religious Ethics* 12 (1984), 39–60.

and at the same time the return to Scripture and commitment to purifying the church definitive of the Reformation.[3] Erasmus was the illegitimate son of a priest, who contributed to the support of Erasmus and his older brother. After the death of his parents during the plague, Erasmus joined the Augustinians in order to continue his education. His early schooling was in the spirit of the *Devotio Moderna*, the "modern piety" of the Brethren of the Common Life, who were committed both to contemplation and to an active life in serving the sick and the poor and in educating children. Erasmus was to look back with repugnance on their pedagogy of rote learning, as boring, constricting, and anti-intellectual; but there is a similarity between their social commitment and his own empathetic pacifism.

In the Augustinian monastery, Erasmus attracted a sizable peer following and stimulated controversy through his independent inquiries into the Latin classics, as well as into Scripture and Christian authors. After his ordination in 1492, his prior allowed him to become a bishop's secretary, a position that enhanced Erasmus' access to the ecclesiastical, political, and academic worlds of influence that so fascinated him. He subsequently spent some years at the University of Paris, where the influence of nominalism was strong. Erasmus traveled to England and to Italy as tutor to the sons of royalty and their associates, eventually teaching at Cambridge University. He made lasting friendships with great humanists such as John Colet and Thomas More. Having gained a wide European reputation, Erasmus moved in 1514 to Basel, a center of Reformed Protestantism, where he spent most of his remaining years.

Erasmus is noted for his publication of the New Testament based on Greek manuscripts, which he used to correct the Latin Vulgate, and for his controversy with Martin Luther over the freedom of the will. Both involvements reflect his humanist identity. His reconstruction of the New Testament evinces the humanists' interest in the return to classic sources. For centuries, scholars had commented on the Bible without ever reading it in the original Greek. The humanists were confident that if they could pass over the accumulation of arid commentary and return to the original texts, using the study of languages as a tool, they would succeed in turning the minds of Christian leaders and rulers to the true and the good.[4] It also was the humanist in Erasmus who could not allow Luther's strong doctrine of "justification by faith" to imply that God's grace makes the human person an automaton. Yet for his part, Luther detected in Erasmus a strain of the Pelagian "justification by works" against which the former had fought so fiercely—although the two men appear not to have disagreed over what either considered essentials of the faith.

3. A biography of Erasmus, giving an overview of his theology and politics, is Roland H. Bainton, *Erasmus of Christendom* (New York: Scribner's, 1969).

4. See E. Harris Harbison, *The Age of Reformation* (Ithaca, N.Y.: Cornell Univ. Press, 1955), 44.

According to E. Harris Harbison, Erasmus represented Christian humanism's "faith in man's reason and fundamental goodness, its confidence in education, its tolerance and sense of proportion," as well as its exaggerated trust that scholarship and reasonableness could change the world and eradicate human sinfulness.[5] At the same time, humanists had a "grasp of history" inaccessible to the scholastics. In medieval universities history was not taught as a subject, and little accurate information was available about heroes of the past, their exploits, and the cultures out of which they rose.[6] War, for instance, is a problem Erasmus tries to put in historical context, showing that its just causes are exceedingly difficult to determine and that its consequences are almost without exception disastrous. Both as a Christian and as a Renaissance humanist, Erasmus was a reformer, drawing on the critical resources appropriate to both: Scripture, the church Fathers, and classical antiquity. Erasmus's vocation was "to apply the best humanistic scholarship of his day to the key doctrines of the Christian faith with a view to cleansing and purifying the whole religious tradition."[7]

As biblical interpreter, Erasmus adopted the basic medieval scheme of meanings: the literal (grammatical and historical), the tropological (moral), the allegorical (figurative or christological), and the anagogical (eschatological). For Erasmus, the moral was the most important. He also curbed runaway allegorization by insisting that the grammatical sense be derived on the basis of careful linguistic study, and that the spiritual sense be expounded in close reliance on grammatical study. Although Erasmus' writings on the Old Testament are few, he nonetheless resolved some difficulties there via an allegorizing approach to the Hebrew Bible. On war, for instance, he argues that what is meant by calling the Hebrew God a "God of vengeance" is that God destroys vice, and that the slaughter of enemies in the Hebrew Bible refers to "the driving away of wicked affections out of the breast and mind of man."[8]

In advocating a return to New Testament sources, Erasmus acknowledged that they demand intepretation, and that interpretation must rely on extrabiblical tools: the original languages, the classics, the church fathers, and a sense of *pietas* or piety to ground and guide the process.[9] In his debate with Luther, he agreed that the most weight must be given to the Scriptures. But Erasmus insisted that the traditions of the fathers should be taken into account in reading Scripture. Who could leave aside such "a body of most learned men . . . whom not only their skill in divine studies but also godliness of life commend"? If Scripture were "crystal clear," there would not have been

Inter-preting Bible-Method

5. Ibid., 45–46.

6. George Faludy, *Erasmus of Rotterdam* (London: Eyre & Spottiswoode, 1970), 18.

7. E. Harris Harbison, *The Christian Scholar in the Age of Reformation* (New York: Scribner's, 1956), 78.

8. *The Complaint of Peace,* 19; see n. 12 below.

9. See Albert Rabil, Jr., *Erasmus and the New Testment: The Mind of a Christian Humanist* (San Antonio: Trinity Univ. Press, 1972), 109.

confusion among so many respected interpreters, for so many centuries, about matters of such great importance.[10]

On the subject of war, Erasmus seems to transcend centuries of circuitous just war theory, which with disconcerting ease had been able to justify what the New Testament hardly envisions as part of the life of discipleship. He expects all Christians to emulate the example of Christ, and refuses to accept that only a few of the elite are called to live fully the ideals of the gospel. But he does not rest with the fact that nonviolence is a gospel mandate. Erasmus also reproaches humanity's penchant for armed conflict because it is a transgression of what ought to be the species' natural sociability. He especially objects to the involvement of the Vatican and of clergy in power politics and war. He notes that the reasons for which secular rulers engage in armed conflict are usually self-seeking and disingenuously presented, and that the consequences of war for the populations involved are scarcely worth the suffering and bloodshed.

Erasmus wrote for an age in which the breakup of the papal states prepared the way for decentralization of authority and for power politics. His own approach to the avoidance of war was to seek the ear of rulers and their advisers and to advocate to them negotiation and arbitration. Erasmus's most extensive discourses on war are *An Essay on War* (*Bellum*, published originally as a commentary on the adage "War is sweet to those who know it not")[11], and *The Complaint of Peace* (*Querela Pacis*).[12] Other treatments of the subject appear in *Handbook of the Militant Christian* (*Enchiridion militis Christiani*)[13] and *Education of a Christian Prince* (*Institutio principis Christiani*).[14] The latter, his most famous political treatise, commended Christian ideals to princes and was dedicated to the young man who was shortly to become Emperor Charles V.

Although Erasmus's views carried weight with influential personages in nearly every court of Europe, they never were translated into policies to guide

10. Erasmus, "On the Freedom of the Will," in *Luther and Erasmus: Free Will and Salvation*, ed. E. Gordon Rupp and Philip S. Watson (Philadelphia: Westminster, 1969), 43, 44.

11. This essay is included in *Bellum: Two Statements on the Nature of War*, with an introduction by William R. Tyler (Barre, Mass.: Imprint Society, 1972), 11–37. As Tyler states, "The first publication of *Bellum* was as *Adagium 3001*, under the title *Dulce bellum inexpertis*, in the Froben edition of 1515. However, its origins go back to a letter which Erasmus wrote in March 1514 to Antonius van Bergen (abbot of the monastery of St. Bertin at St. Omer), brother of the benefactor of Erasmus, Hendrick van Bergen. It was first published as an independent work by Froben in April 1517."

12. In *The Complaint of Peace by Erasmus*, with an introduction by William James Hirten (New York: Scholars' Facsimiles and Reprints, 1946). First published in 1517 by Froben, this work was translated into French, German, Spanish, and English.

13. In *Erasmus: Handbook of the Militant Christian*, trans. with an introductory essay by John P. Dolan (Notre Dame, Ind.: Fides Publishers, 1962). The *Enchiridion* appeared in Latin in 1514, and had been translated into nine other languages by 1585.

14. Erasmus, *The Education of a Christian Prince*, trans. with an introduction by Lester K. Born (New York: Columbia Univ. Press, 1936). This work was first published in 1516 by Froben, and within a few years went into several editions, which indicates its contemporary popularity.

relationships of states. His champions were ignored, speculates John P. D because "they advocated compromise in an age of growing intolerance. . . . few movements in history have suffered a greater disillusionment than the irenicists of the sixteenth century."[15] The religious and political crises provoked by the Reformation were simply too deep, too polarized, and too vitriolic to permit successful mediation by moderate voices.

The argument of *Bellum* is governed by three favorite themes, which recur in other works of Erasmus. First, war is naturally wrong. Not even the beasts war against members of their own species, much less with weapons whose artifice enhances the creature's natural destructive capacity. How much more, then, should humans respect the lives of their fellows. Humanity was created to exist in cooperation and to develop "the attachments of friendship and love."[16] Second, Christianity forbids war. Sophistry has distorted the gospel message. "Christian disinterestedness" has been rationalized away in favor of self-interest, money, and power.[17] Christ teaches love; all are called actually to live the life Christ presents. "Our Lord did not come to tell the world what enormity was permitted, how far we might deviate from the laws of rectitude, but to show us the point of perfection at which we were to aim with the utmost of our ability."[18] Third, "just cause" in war will be claimed by both sides and will be next to impossible to determine fairly.[19] Hence, the traditional criteria of the just war are nonfunctional.

Bellum—3 Themes

It is instructive to contrast Erasmus's rhetoric to that of the crusaders. One notes immediately that the Dutch humanist depends on a notion that might be characterized as "the brotherhood of man," although he also sees Christians as having among themselves still closer and more morally demanding bonds.

> Man has arrived at such a degree of insanity, that war seems to be the grand business of human life. We are always at war, either in preparation, or in action. Nation rises against nation; and, what the heathens would have reprobated as unnatural, relatives against their nearest kindred, brother against bother, son against father!—more atrocious still!—a Christian against a man! and worst of all, a Christian against a Christian![20]

According to Erasmus, it is impossible to ignore the gospel's many exhortations to peace, or the clear fact that Jesus claimed only one law as his

15. Dolan, "Introduction," in *Erasmus: Handbook,* 11.
16. *Erasmus,* 13.
17. Ibid., 28.
18. Ibid., 32. And the gospel declares "in decisive words" that "we must do good to them who use us ill." Further, not merely the apostles, but "all Christian people," "the whole body," should be "entire and perfect" (33).
19. Ibid., 34.
20. Ibid., 18. See also, If a brother murder his brother, the crime is called fratricide: but a Christian is more closely allied to a Christian as such, than a brother by the ties of consanguinity. . . . How absurd then is it, that they should be constantly at war with each other; who but form one family, the church of Christ" (23).

discipleship. The radical reformers wanted a full restitution of the New Testament way of life and saw persecution and suffering as marks of the true church. Although they preferred the name "Christian Brethren," their opponents called them Anabaptists ("rebaptizers") because they accepted only adult baptism as reflective of early Christian practice. The concrete and practical aspects of discipleship were of utmost importance to them, especially the formation of voluntary and disciplined communities, the integral relation of faith and works, and the rejection of participation in government.

Under Ulrich Zwingli's influence, the city council of Zurich had "decreed the Reformation" in 1523, but the Protestant movements in the city were multivocal. Through a close study of the Bible, which Zwingli encouraged, some groups came to diverge on certain points of practice, especially infant baptism. For Grebel, adult baptism signified a certain view of the church: the church does not belong to "Christians" of lukewarm commitment; it is a fellowship of those who truly believe and live rightly. The first clear profession of nonresistance appears in a letter from Grebel to Thomas Müntzer in 1524:

> The gospel and its adherents are not to be protected by the sword, nor are they thus to protect themselves. . . . True Christian believers are sheep among wolves, sheep for the slaughter. . . . Neither do they use worldly sword or war, since all killing has ceased with them—unless, indeed, we would still be of the old law.[33]

The dissenters met almost immediately with the persecution that was forever to be their lot. Fearing the entire reform movement might be discredited by "extremists," Zwingli tried to persuade them to recant, then tortured them, and finally had some executed by drowning.[34] One among hundreds of eventual casualties was Michael Sattler, author of the Swiss Brethren's Schleitheim Confession, who was executed in 1527. A notorious decree of the imperial Diet of Spiers (1529) pronounced, with the concurrence of both Catholics and Lutherans, the death sentence for all Anabaptists. Luther and Melanchthon personally endorsed severe measures against them.

As far as the sixteenth-century radical reformers were concerned (with few exceptions),[35] the way of Jesus Christ so contradicts the sinfulness which

33. As cited by Peter Brock, from George Hunston Williams's revision of a 1905 translation by Walter Rauschenbusch, in *Pacifism in Europe to 1914* (Princeton, N.J.: Princeton Univ. Press, 1972), 60. The doctrine of nonresistance was further ratified in the Schleitheim Confession of 1527 and had become firmly established as an Anabaptist tenet by the early 1530s (Brock, 87).

34. On the emergence of Anabaptism, see Fritz Blanke, "Anabaptism and the Reformation," in Guy F. Hershberger, *The Recovery of the Anabaptist Vision* (Scottdale, Pa.: Herald Press, 1957). See also William Klassen, "Anabaptist Ethics," in *The Westminster Dictionary of Christian Ethics,* ed. James F. Childress and John Macquarrie (Philadelphia: Westminster Press, 1986), 20–21.

35. Peter Brock believes that even within the Dutch Anabaptist community united by Menno, there was some diversity, especially from 1557 onward. Separate sects developed out of disputes over application of principles; for example, over the strictness of the ban, or whether to sanction the holding of offices (*Pacifism in Europe,* 162–63).

imbues the world that to participate in its institutions at all is to compromise the gospel. They portrayed the love and life of the kingdom, as contrasted to the ethic of the world and of political institutions, in sharply dualistic terms. The magistracy is ordained to punish the wicked and protect the innocent, because it is necessary in the present to maintain good order.[36] However, the Christian cannot participate in this office, although he or she must obey the civil authorities to the extent that their commands do not conflict with the commands of God (as based on Romans 13).[37]

In preaching a return to the primitive church, the Anapabtists see the Christian community as perfectionist, separatist, and pacifist. The essence of Christianity is not faith as such, but a way of life captured as "following Christ" (*nachfolge Christi*).[38] Membership in the church through adult conversion and baptism is followed by rigorous conformity to the example of Christ and his kingdom. The church is to consist only of those who are committed to holy living. The inner experience of faith produces transformed behavior; newness of life is as important a criterion as conversion. Discernment of the proper moral shape of that life takes place within a gathered community that places its trust in biblical guidance. The membership of the church was expanded by preaching and example, for the Anabaptists took with utmost seriousness the Great Commission to "go and baptize all nations" (Matt. 28:16-20).

Most characteristic of the Anabaptist way of life were sharing of goods in common and nonresistance. Some groups, such as the Hutterites, translated brotherly love into complete community of property, but, for all Anabaptists, brotherly love meant at least a willingness to yield one's own possessions to the brother or sister in need. The Anabaptists also took the "hard sayings" of Jesus literally and did not try to accommodate them to survival in the world. As anticipated by the biblical accounts of martyrdom, nonconformity leads to persecution. But Christians must neither use the sword nor engage in war. Neither may they take oaths nor make any other compromises, such as bringing a suit in a court of law.

Even according to their most rabid critics, the morality of the Anabaptists was exemplary. Harold Bender cites the testimony of the Catholic theologian Franz Agricola, offered in his 1582 treatise *Against the Terrible Errors of the Anabaptists*:

> Among the existing heretical sects there is none which in appearance leads a more modest or pious life than the Anabaptists. As concerns their outward

36. See Robert Kreider, "Anabaptists and the State," in Hershberger, *Recovery of the Anabaptist Vision,* 180–93.

37. A primary source for Anabaptist views of government is the Schleitheim Confession prepared by the Swiss Brethren in 1527. This document sees the restraint of evil by force as necessary but "outside the perfection of Christ." An edited version is available in John C. Wenger, "The Schleitheim Confession of Faith," *Mennonite Quarterly Review* 19 (1945) 243–53. Excerpts are included in George W. Forell, *Christian Social Teachings* (Minneapolis: Augsburg Publishing House, 1971), 184–88.

38. See Harold Bender, "The Recovery of the Anabaptist Vision," in Hershberger, *Recovery of the Anabaptist Vision,* 43.

Following further victories over the troops outside the city, Beukels had himself ceremoniously crowned king. But his "religious fanaticism and maniacal wickedness,"[45] along with famine and continued siege, sapped the energy and morale of his constituents. Two deserters finally betrayed one of the gates of the town, and the bishop's forces overtook it in 1535, slaughtering most of the inhabitants.

For centuries, the debacle at Münster was associated with the Anabaptist theologian Thomas Müntzer (ca. 1488–1525), owing to a biography by a contemporary (possibly Luther's associate Melanchthon) that aimed to discredit him. Müntzer was a fellow German priest who took his original bearings from Luther but eventually turned vociferously against him. Recent scholarship has shown that Müntzer had no direct influence on the events constituting the Münster disaster; in fact, he died eight years before the eschatological experiment there began. However, Müntzer's fierce prophecies and warnings illustrate the flavor of those Anabaptist fringe movements that had lost their moorings in pacifist witness and become violently revolutionary. By 1524, Müntzer was advocating insurrection against rulers and against the more conservative leaders of reform. During the peasant uprising in Thuringia, he sided with and preached to the peasants, writing letters to rulers above the name "Thomas Müntzer with the Sword of Gideon."[46] Toward the end of those bloody events, Müntzer was captured, tortured, and beheaded.

Müntzer believed in a Spirit-inspired community of avowed believers, who come to faith through personal suffering and who confirm that faith with practical results. To achieve them, God calls the elect to rise against the godless and will ensure their triumph even in this world. "God will strike to pieces all your adversaries who undertake to persecute you." Although Müntzer often relied upon Israelite examples of war—for instance, the destruction of the Canaanite people when "the Chosen were bent on entering the Promised Land"—he also discovered the occasional supporting text in the life of Jesus. Because Christ's enemies are ruining the government of his church, "Christ our Lord says (Matt. 18:6): Whosoever shall offend one of these little ones, it is better for him that a millstone be hung about his neck and that he be thrown in the depth of the sea." The "true governors" of Christ's church must "drive his enemies from the elect." "The sword is necessary to wipe out the godless (Rom. 13:4)," for "the godless have no right to live except as the elect wish to grant it to them." This extermination should be accomplished by the princes, but if they are remiss, "the sword will be taken from them (Dan. 7:26f.)."

The rabid preaching and extremist social plans of the Münsterites and of Thomas Müntzer bear obvious similarity to the crusading ideals surveyed in

45. Ibid., 380.
46. Hans J. Hillerbrand, "Thomas Muentzer," in *Reformers in Profile,* ed. Brian A. Gerrish (Philadelphia: Fortress, 1967), 219. This essay, along with Williams's chapter on Müntzer, provides the backbone of the biography here.

chapter 7. Despite the similarity of their origins, they just as clearly represent a sharp departure from the form of radical Christianity as preached, for instance, by Menno Simons. What elements of Christianity, retained in what way under what circumstances, seem most likely to lead to such ignominious distortions? One notable fact is that militaristic twists of Christianity are often spawned within groups experiencing oppression and social deprivation, to whom a massive social revolt in God's name appears to offer hope of emancipation and victory, and even a justification to trample their oppressors in a frenzy of vindication. Suffering and persecution past the point of endurance can lead either to martyrdom or fanaticism and delusion. The paradigmatic response of the early Christians, as a persecuted social minority, was to die proclaiming their faith and their trust in a spiritual victory and reward. But once Christians divide the world into the righteous and the godless, locate themselves confidently among the former, and—especially—arrogate a mission to exterminate God's enemies, the guiding ideal "kingdom" becomes a blueprint for religious and social mayhem. The kingdom as a coherent way of life is lost, and in its place is substituted a crazed and myopic literalism that makes biblical events and injunctions subservient to social and political tyranny or vendettas.

## *Menno Simons*

The greatest theologian of the Reformation's characteristically nonresistant left wing, Menno Simons (ca. 1496–1561), was born in Friesland, a Dutch province, and was ordained a Catholic priest. The radical reform movement had been brought to the Netherlands in the early 1530s and was nurtured under the leadership of the brothers Obbe and Dirk Philips. Menno (Simons is a patronymic) did not become familiar with the Bible until after his ordination, when he opened it to verify the doctrine of transubstantiation against the challenges of Protestants. In the end, he was led not only to reject that doctrine, but also the baptism of infants and the authority of the pope.

Personal example contributed to his decision. As a young priest, Menno was disconcerted by reports of the execution of a godly man who had accepted rebaptism. A few years later, Menno felt both judged and inspired by the example of his own brother, killed in 1535 after having been caught up in a revolutionary religious movement. Menno was ashamed that he had not had the courage to stand up for his beliefs. In 1536 he was rebaptized into the brotherhood of Obbe Philips, who stressed one's inner relationship to God (Dirk emphasized communal discipline). Menno became an evangelical pastor, married, and was ordained a bishop or overseer in 1537.[47] His leadership and writings did much to establish the Anabaptist fellowship as a disciplined congregation with a distinctive, separatist, and, above all, scriptural way of

47. On Menno's life, see J. C. Wenger, "Menno Simons," in Gerrish, *Reformers in Profile,* 194–212.

life. Completely rejecting violence either as a way of safeguarding the purity of this way or of fending off persecutors, Menno gave eloquent expression to a strain of pacifist thinking that continues to inspire contemporary Christian countercultural movements.

For the Anabaptists, only the Bible defines the Christian life. They give a most rigorous interpretation to the Reformation principle *sola scriptura* and enjoin every Christian to read the Bible as a source of instruction, admonition, and correction. The Word of God is virtually identified with the written text of Scripture, of whose plain interpretation they are confident. Both Old and New Testaments are authoritative,[48] but both are read through Jesus Christ, and the New takes precedence over the Old.

Menno introduces his most influential treatise, *Foundations of Christian Doctrine*, with a call to discipleship premised on the kingdom's accessibility: "Now is the time to arise with Christ in a new, righteous, and penitent existence, even as Christ says, The time is fulfilled, and the Kingdom of God is at hand: repent and believe in the gospel." Christ leaves and proclaims "an example of pure love, and a perfect life."[49] Unless conversion, repentance, and baptism are followed by regeneration from "this wicked, immoral and shameful life, . . . it will not help a fig to be called Christians."[50] Of the "spiritual strength" the Christian receives, baptism is the "outward sign."[51]

The Lord's Supper is important in the radical fellowship insofar as it signifies the unity and love of the community; "by the Lord's Supper Christian unity, love, and peace are signified and enjoined."[52] By the same token and because of the absolute expectation that conversion brings sanctification, sinners are to be excluded from this fellowship. Any who would "sit at the Lord's table . . . must be sound in the faith and unblameable in conduct and life. None is excepted, neither emperor nor king, prince nor earl, knight nor nobleman."[53] It was because of the near impossibility of reconciling worldly offices such as these with Christianity that the pacifist radicals rejected the magistracy for their members, even while recognizing that civil authority and the sword have a use outside the Christian fellowship.[54] Unlike the Münsterites, Menno does not assimilate worldly ideals, structures, or methods to Christian community, but recognizes that dedication to the latter will demand sacrifice of the former.

48. Menno, *Foundations of Christian Doctrine,* 159–60; *Why I Do Not Cease Teaching and Writing,* 312, both in John C. Wenger, ed., *The Complete Writings of Menno Simons* (Scottdale, Pa.: Herald Press, 1955), from which all subsequent citations of Menno's writings will be taken. See also John C. Wenger, "The Biblicism of the Anabaptist," in Hershberger, *Recovery of the Anabaptist Vision,* 67–93.

49. Menno, *Foundations of Christian Doctrine,* 108.

50. Ibid., 110–11.

51. Ibid., 125.

52. Ibid., 145.

53. Ibid., 150.

54. See Robert Kreider, "The Anabaptists and the State," in Hershberger, *Recovery of the Anabaptist Vision,* 180–93. For another view, see Brock, *Pacifism in Europe.*

Menno devotes extensive attention to the exclusion of sinful and recalcitrant members.[55] His stringent expectations in this regard are a direct outcome of his ecclesiology, and particularly of his view of the church as presently realizing kingdom life. In the *Instruction on Excommunication*, he defines Christ's church as "a congregation of saints."[56] Since the devil can work evil from within the community, the exclusion of any who may serve as Satan's weapons must be absolute.[57] However, Menno's tool for purifying the community is not violent but social. The "ban" even cuts apart marriages and families, though in cases of hardship, Menno makes some exceptions.[58] Unlike excommunication in modern churches, the Anabaptist ban is not a merely juridical matter, a decision of the temporal church; as long as it is in effect, it actually excludes the sinner from the eternal kingdom.[59] Yet it does have as one purpose the conversion and readmittance of the sinner.[60] The ban is usefully placed in relation to the weapons resorted to at that time by other Christian groups trying to induce conformity among their members. The mainline reformers and the Catholic hierarchy, as well as the Anabaptist revolutionaries, used coercive measures against heretics, such as imprisonment, torture, and death; in this coercion they sought the backing of the state. But for typical Anabaptists, the voluntary nature of the church precludes physical force even as it demands total religious and moral conformity.

A dominant theme in Menno's writings is the "persecution of the Lamb" in whose cross, sufferings, and blessings the Christian shares. The kingdom of God, present to believers only through their sufferings, is begun but never completed on earth. "The Lamb is slain"; he enters into glory through the cross and death, and his children and servants must do likewise.[61] As both Testaments demonstrate, persecution will not cease so long as the righteous and the unrighteous abide on the earth together.[62] The Anabaptists do not embrace suffering simply for its own sake, nor even for the sake of imitation alone. Suffering and taking up the cross have a pedagogical function that fits the radicals' emphasis on sanctification. To "pick up and bear daily" the cross is "profitable and advantageous."[63] The Lord Jesus "teaches, admonishes, rebukes, threatens, and chastises, in order that we should deny ungodliness and worldly lusts, die entirely unto the world, the flesh, and the devil, and seek our treasure, our portion, and our inheritance in heaven."[64]

55. Menno, *A Kind Admonition on Church Discipline; A Clear Account of Excommunication;* and *Final Instruction on Marital Avoidance;* as well as letters and other references.

56. Menno, *Instruction on Excommunication,* 962.

57. Ibid., 963.

58. For instance, when there are young children, or when one or both parties cannot live in continence (Menno, *Final Instruction on Marital Avoidance,* 1059).

59. Menno, *Instruction on Excommunication,* 966–67.

60. Ibid., 966–67.

61. Menno, *Foundations of Christian Doctrine,* 109.

62. Menno, *Cross of the Saints,* 582; for Old Testament examples, see 589–90.

63. Ibid., 620.

64. Ibid., 616.

Somewhat paradoxically, Menno cites Israelite paradigms of faith at least as frequently as Christian ones. Although he uses wars against the Israelites as examples of undeserved suffering, he does not address the theological and ethical problems created by the wars the Israelites themselves undertook. Menno does not hesitate to mention killings by Abraham,[65] Moses,[66] and David,[67] while praising their obedience and righteousness. David "did great works in the name of the Lord: he slew the terribly great Goliath; he got him two hundred foreskins of the Philistines."[68] Similarly, Menno lauds the faith and humility of the Roman centurion without taking up the implications of his profession. Menno also makes use of warfare imagery in exhorting the faithful to fervent cross-bearing, calling them "soldiers and conquerors in Christ," and referring to the cross as "an armor and a shield."[69]

Although it is certain that he means the followers of Jesus to rely only upon the "sword of the Spirit" in self-defense and the reproof of wickedness,[70] Menno nonetheless appeals to the civil authorities for relief, arguing as Tertullian and Origen had before him that the separatist Christians are not seditious.[71] His supplication was not to be fulfilled; although Menno himself escaped a martyr's end, his followers continued to suffer the most extreme hatred, torture, and death at the hands of the civil authorities and at the behest of Catholics, Evangelicals, and Calvinists. While never a dominant thread in the Christian tradition, the pacifist churches have nonetheless made an indispensable contribution to its vitality. Significant aspects of the Anabaptists' life and faith continue today among the Mennonites, Amish, and Hutterrian Brethren—for instance, a shared way of life set aside from the world and a commitment to biblical nonviolence.

We will close our survey of the premodern pacifist circle by returning our attention to that profound religious experience of mercy and forgiveness in Christ, which alone seems able to sponsor virtues of love and unity steadfast enough to survive in concrete action when the Christian confronts the world.

## QUAKERS

The seventeenth-century English and eighteenth-century American members of the Religious Society of Friends were in agreement with the Reformation pacifists that the presence of the kingdom makes possible a life in the gospel of which violence has no part. Robert Barclay's *Catechism and Confession of*

65. Menno, *The True Christian Faith,* 346–47.
66. Ibid., 353.
67. Menno, *Cross of the Saints,* 589.
68. Ibid., 589.
69. Ibid., 621.
70. Menno, *Cross of the Saints,* 603–4.
71. Menno, *A Pathetic Supplication to all Magistrates,* 523–31; *Foundations of Christian Doctrine,* 117–20; *Cross of the Saints,* 602–5.

*Faith* (1673) states succinctly the Quaker view of discipleship.[72] Jesus' command to "be perfect" (Matt. 5:48) is interpreted with utmost seriousness. The power of Christ's death allows all Christians who persevere "in this life to be freed from the dominion of sin."[73] When God grants to the believer the Light of Christ within his or her soul, consciousness is transformed and sin abandoned. Like the Anabaptists, the Quakers received their popular name from habits that seemed to outsiders disreputable: "Quaker" fitted the violent trembling that overtook those experiencing a confrontation and struggle with the inner Light or Spirit.[74]

Again like their predecessors, the Friends taught their members to expect persecution and to suffer it patiently. Violence, "defensive war," and even swearing explicitly contradict Christ's sayings. The rule for the Christian is love of enemies and forgiveness of hatred, after Christ's example. A primary difference between Anabaptists and Quakers is that the latter trust nonviolence to evoke a similar response from others. At least in the beginning, they hoped to convert the world. Early Quaker thought was apocalyptic, expecting the Lamb's victory in history and an imminent day of judgment. Though they had no distinct political aspirations, they did expect the eventual rule of Christ on earth. Yet their concentration was not on the implications of the kingdom for civil society as such, but on the real presence of the kingdom in the peace and equality beginning within the community of "the Children of the Light," as they originally called themselves.

For Quakers, to wage the "Lamb's War" means to demonstrate that the kingdom has begun by engaging in nonviolent acts that challenge human pride, violate social expectations (especially those tied to political and class hierarchies), and are aimed at conversion. Among their iconoclastic and egalitarian efforts were the disruption of public worship by challenging the priests, the refusal to pay tithes to support the parish clergy of the Church of England, the refusal to give common forms of respectful greeting to acquaintances or to address social superiors with "you" rather than "thee," and—of dubious practical effect—walking through the streets naked "for a sign."[75] Particularly crucial to later Quakerism were its ethical Testimonies against slavery and war. The Testimonies are often understood more comprehensively by modern Quakers as including concern for four specific qualities of life that embody the kingdom: honesty, equality, simplicity, and peace.

72. Robert Barclay, *Catechism and Confession of Faith,* VII, in *Early Quaker Writings,* ed. Hugh Barbour and Arthur O. Roberts (Grand Rapids: Eerdmans, 1973).

73. Ibid., XII.

74. See Hugh Barbour and J. William Frost, *The Quakers* (Westport, Conn.: Greenwood Press, 1988), 28; and Margaret Hope Bacon, *Mothers of Feminism: The Story of Quaker Women in America* (San Francisco: Harper and Row, 1986), 17. Cf. *The Journal of George Fox,* ed. Rufus M. Jones (New York: Capricorn Books, 1963), 125, where Fox says that in 1650 a judge first gave them the name, "because I bade them tremble at the name of the Lord."

75. James F. Childress, *Moral Responsibility in Conflict: Essays on Nonviolence, War, and Conscience* (Baton Rouge: Louisiana State Univ. Press, 1982), 17.

The Society of Friends grew out of Puritan radicalism in seventeenth-century England. Connections can also be drawn to the theology of the Anabaptists and English Baptists, many of whom joined the early Quaker movement. During the English Civil War (1642–49), many working-class groups began to spring up that totally rejected the ideal of self-governing but uniform parishes linked structurally within the Church of England. These separatists instituted more informal and egalitarian forms of local worship, centering on Scripture, in which laypersons were allowed to comment on the text or sermon. It was common for them to choose relatively untrained ministers who also earned their livelihood by some other craft or trade. Although the separatist Puritans did not withdraw from all involvement with government and the state, and did not at first demand nonviolence (many of them, in fact, were members of Cromwell's army), they did root religion in personal experience and in the shared faith of the immediate community, thus undermining the religious foundations of a united Puritan Commonwealth in England. The Quaker founder, George Fox (1624–91), grew up in a radical Puritan family and community.

The Puritans' Calvinist faith in the sovereignty and power of God in this world led them to expect that those elected to receive God's irresistible grace would transfigure church and state in the Holy Commonwealth. The Quakers shared the Puritans' aim to accomplish a worldwide victory over evil, but at the same time they were radically skeptical of the institutional church and reluctant to participate directly in institutions of government. Hence the Quaker challenge to the Puritan theocracy; Quakers stressed a direct relationship of the individual to God, which was shared in community but was not dependent on ecclesiastical mediation. George Fox saw the Friends "as the fruit of the renewal of the conquest of the world by the Spirit or Light of Christ, the climax of God's plan for world history that had begun with Paul the Apostle, had halted for a thousand years of Catholic apostasy, and had begun again as incomplete renewal in the Protestant Reformation and Puritan Revolution."[76] Quakers rejected the Calvinist and Puritan beliefs in predestination, infant baptism, and national churches; in common with the Anabaptists, they believed in moral perfectability, adult faith commitment, and the church as a gathered body of professed believers willing and able to practice stringent discipleship and simplicity of life. Though less formal and widespread than Anabaptist excommunication, the Quakers used "disownment" as a means of separating the committed from the wayward.

Not willing, as the Puritans did, to unite church and government, the Quakers nevertheless had a more positive view of the magistracy's function than the Anabaptists. Anabaptists accused all historical churches of fatal deviation from the apostolic church; usually refused to compromise with the demands of the state, much less to adopt them; and expected the apocalyptic

76. Barbour and Frost, *The Quakers,* 11.

return and conquest of the Lamb to crown the suffering of his saints. Mistrusting the state, they rejected all coercive measures in matters of faith and preached patience toward enemies. Quakers, on the other hand, did not withdraw from society nor necessarily require refusal of public office; they believed that rulers have authority from God, though secondary to God's. Still, Quakers did not see participation in structures of violence as appropriate for those in whom Christ dwells. Instead, they expected total regeneration of life through God's grace, and took as seriously as the Anabaptists the Christian mission to convert the world and so transform it.

George Fox was born in Leicestershire, England. His father, a weaver, had a local reputation for piety. George's mother, a woman of more than average education, encouraged her son in his reflective and religious pursuits. In his *Journal*, Fox tells of his early formation: "When I came to eleven years of age I knew pureness and righteousness; for while a child I was taught how to walk to be kept pure."[77] Educated in the local primary school, George was apprenticed to a cobbler and a shepherd and began early to seek a better religious understanding than that offered him in his intense conversations with his father, his pastor, and a local squire who supported the Puritan reform. By all accounts, George Fox was a singular person who at an early age came to enjoy what might almost be termed a mystical consciousness of the all-encompassing presence of God in Christ.

The period of searching and spiritual travail Fox endured in his youth caused him to leave home in 1643, hoping to discover some religious teaching or leadership that could answer his doubts and anxieties. About four years later, the Lord "opened" Fox to faith while he was returning from a walk alone. "I was taken up in the love of God, so that I could not but admire the greatness of his love; and while I was in that condition, it was opened unto me by the eternal light and power, and I therein clearly saw that all was done and to be done in and by Christ, and how He conquers."[78] In his redeemed state, George came to appreciate "the greatness and infinitude of the love of God, which cannot be expressed by words."[79]

He also assures us that he and all those enlightened by Christ are restored to Adam's original state. "I knew nothing but pureness and innocency, and righteousness; being renewed into the image of God by Christ Jesus to the state of Adam, which he was in before he fell." Moreover, "the Lord showed" Fox "that such as were faithful to Him, in the power and light of Christ, should come up into that state," in which they too might know and do "the admirable works of the creation, and the virtues thereof."[80] For Fox, two primitive periods were normative: the first days of creation before sin marred the world and human nature, and the years of early Christianity, before the apostasy of the

77. *Journal of George Fox,* 66.
78. Ibid., 84.
79. Ibid., 88.
80. Ibid., 97.

Catholic Church.[81] Through renewal in the Spirit of Christ that dwells within, the believer can return to a pristine spiritual consciousness and moral purity.

By 1648, Fox had begun his own ministry in complete assurance that he was called to serve as an instrument of God. Of imposing appearance, Fox wore his hair long and, according to his contemporaries, had piercing eyes capable of summing up in a glance one's spiritual state.[82] Like Joan of Arc, he seemed to have a telepathic knowledge of events transpiring elsewhere.[83] Fox began to attract large numbers of followers by 1652 and was especially successful in the north of England. He was brought to court sixty times and served a total of six years imprisonment on eight convictions for blasphemy or heresy; persecution of the Quakers continued until the passage of The Toleration Act in 1689. In many instances, crowds in towns where Fox arrived to preach beat him unmercifully, subjecting him to serious physical harm. He attributed his seemingly miraculous recoveries to the healing power of the Lord in him. Fox also wrote and traveled extensively, venturing through the British Isles and to Holland, Germany, and America, where he spent two years.[84] At once assured in his beliefs and generous to his companions, as well as quick to attribute his enemies' misfortunes to God's judgment, Fox had a magnetic and commanding effect on his followers. Many wrote to him or addressed him in terms full of enough adulation to cause their recipient alarm and embarrassment. In his preface to Fox's autobiography, William Penn—first instructed by Fox as a young man, and destined to give Quaker universalism a humanistic retouching in the New World—remembers the Quaker leader this way:

> So meek, contented, modest, easy, steady, tender, it was a pleasure to be in his company. He exercised no authority but over evil, and that everywhere and in all; but with love, compassion, and long-suffering. A most merciful man, as ready to forgive as unapt to take or give offence . . . the most excellent spirits loved him with an unfeigned and unfading love."[85]

Fox argued that in Christ men and women are returned to their prelapsarian state, overcoming the hierarchy and division that entered their relationship in Genesis 3. He also makes appeal to the prophetesses of the Hebrew Bible and to New Testament examples such as Mary Magdalene, sent by Jesus to preach the resurrection, and leaders of the Pauline churches, such as Priscilla

81. See James F. Childress, "'Answering That of God in Every Man': An Interpretation of George Fox's Ethics," *Quaker Religious Thought* 15 (Spring 1974), 2–41.

82. See, for example, *Journal of George Fox,* 344.

83. In his autobiography, Fox tells of feeling in his own body, while in prison in England, the death by hanging of some Friends in New England, after the colonies had enacted laws against Quakers (*Journal of George Fox,* 374).

84. T. Canby Jones, *George Fox's Attitude Toward War* (Annapolis, Md.: Academic Fellowship, 1972), 6–8. These incidents are also related in Fox's *Journal.*

85. "The Testimony of William Penn Concerning That Faithful Servant George Fox," in *The Journal of George Fox,* 58–59.

and Phoebe.[86] Hence, one remarkable feature of the Quaker communities from their inception was the participation of women in leadership roles and in preaching and prophesying in religious services. Such practices had already begun to appear in other sects that sprang from Puritanism. Although it would be anachronistic to call Fox a feminist, he wrote two tracts in which he defended women's activity against literalist readings of the later pastoral epistles that prescribe submissiveness for women, and their silence in church (for example, 1 Timothy 2). Women's preaching was upheld on the basis of the freedom of the Spirit of God to inspire and speak through whom it will.

George Fox and the Quakers relied primarily on religious experience rather than ecclesiastical or doctrinal knowledge of God; Fox says that he "knew experimentally," and "in the pure knowledge of God, and of Christ alone, without the help of any man, book, or writing," that only in Jesus Christ would he find the answers to unbelief and sin. Even though Fox had read the Scriptures, he still knew neither Christ nor God until "the Father of Life drew me to His Son by His Spirit."[87] It is only by the power of the Light that the Scriptures' meaning is clear.[88] In order to know God in Christ through the Scriptures, one must be inspired by the same Spirit that moved the prophets and the apostles who wrote the Scriptures.[89] Fox speaks of himself as having been enlightened by Christ; Christ, he says, "gave me His light" and "His Spirit and grace."[90]

86. See Bacon, *Mothers of Feminism,* 10–13; and Hugh Barbour, *The Quakers in Puritan England* (New Haven: Yale Univ. Press, 1964), 132–33. The titles of the two treatises are *The Woman learning in Silence; or, the Mysterie of the womans Subjection to her Husband, as also, the Daughter prophesying, wherein the Lord hath, and is fulfilling that he spake by the Prophet Joel, I will pour out my Spirit unto all Flesh; and Concerning Sons and Daughters, and Prophetesses speaking and Prophesying in the Law and the Gospel.* At the behest of Quaker women, Fox eventually endorsed separate men's and women's meetings to allow women a sphere in which they would be able to speak freely of women's religious concerns. The first person in England to preach Fox's message was Elizabeth Hooten, already a local Baptist teacher. Even as an elderly woman (her four children were grown when she converted to Quakerism), she suffered brutal beatings and imprisonments but remained undeterred in her missionary work. (Phyllis Mack, "Gender and Spirituality in Early English Quakerism, 1650–1665," in *Witnesses for Change: Quaker Women Over Three Centuries,* ed. Elisabeth Potts Brown and Susan Mosher Stuard [New Brunswich, N.J.: Rutgers Univ. Press, 1989], 31–32).

Even more important to the shape of Fox's life and ministry was Margaret Fell, whom he converted in 1652. The wife of Judge Thomas Fell and mother of eight, she presided over a large country home and was in a position to offer considerable protection and support to the Quakers. Though her husband never became a Quaker, he sympathetically used his influence on their behalf. Eleven years after Judge Fell's death, George Fox and Margaret Fell married. (Margaret, at fifty-five, was a decade George's senior and was to survive him for eleven years.) They continued to travel frequently and to spend long periods apart, whether in missionary outreach (Margaret was called by other Quakers the "nursing mother" of the movement) or in jail. Margaret too was an avid proponent of women's preaching, writing from prison her own treatise on it (Bacon, *Mothers of Feminism,* 13–17). The work of Margaret Fell is entitled *Women's Speaking Justified, Proved and Allowed by the Scriptures, all such as speak by the Spirit and Power of the Lord Jesus.*

87. *Journal of George Fox,* 82–83.
88. Ibid., 102.
89. Ibid., 176–77.
90. Ibid., 83.

Centuries later, H. Richard Niebuhr was to characterize the qualities of the Protestant view of the kingdom of God as vividness, absoluteness, and temporal immediacy.[91] While it is arguable that the reformers themselves, and certainly their heirs, have often struck a bargain between the vivid, absolute, immediate kingdom and its distorted, realistic, and compromising context, the Quakers certainly bear out Niebuhr's claim. Important to them and other pacifists is a sense of closeness to Jesus and his community; radical pacifists envision themselves as living, not in some accommodated interim, but with Jesus in the kingdom he inaugurates on earth. The Scriptures are not just a promise, but bring disciples into the reality out of which the Scriptures communicate God's Word.

Because of the Quaker reliance on experimental knowledge of God and their custom of inspired preaching during meetings, they needed some way to test the genuineness of the "leadings" they received and to convince outsiders that they were not anarchists. Initial indications of validity were moral purity and patient waiting and testing of inspirations to eliminate self-will. More important is the self-consistency of the Spirit, both historically and in comparison with biblical conduct, and among members of the group gathered in faith or for worship. After 1656, the custom developed of testing any one member's leading by submitting it to the group's "sense of the Meeting."[92]

Fox was imprisoned for blasphemy for his claim that Christ's spirit dwells in the believer so fully that sin is eradicated. A more radical claim about kingdom presence can hardly be imagined. Upon an inquiry as to whether he was "sanctified," Fox replied, "Yes; for I am in the paradise of God"; and "Christ my Saviour has taken away my sin; and in Him there is no sin."[93]

Despite its radicality, Fox's conception of the kingdom is neither exclusivist nor separatist; its inclusiveness is the major support of Quaker pacifism. God revealed to Fox that "every man" is enlightened by Christ, although some will "believe in" the Light and others will "hate" it.[94] In certain of his letters concerning Quaker work in the New World, Fox also expresses his belief that the Light is in people of all races, and that the missionary must recognize that Light and evoke a response. "Let your light shine among the Indians, the blacks and the whites, that ye may answer the truth in them and *bring them to . . . Jesus Christ*."[95] James Childress argues that "answering that of God in every man," a phrase central in later Quaker religious thought, may be equally

91. H. Richard Niebuhr, *The Kingdom of God in America* (New York: Harper and Brothers, 1937), 25

92. Barbour, *Quakers in Puritan England,* 119–21; Frost and Barbour, *The Quakers,* 40.

93. Barbour, *Quakers in Puritan England,* 120–21.

94. Ibid., 102, 444.

95. From an epistle of 1690, quoted by Rufus Jones in his Introduction to *Journal of George Fox,* 41. An epistle of 1682 advises colonists to "answer the light of truth, and spirit of God, in the Indians, their Kings and their people" (Epistle 379, in Douglas V. Steere, ed., *Quaker Spirituality: Selected Writings* [New York: Paulist Press, 1984], 135).

key to Fox's own writings.[96] Particularly in the early days of the movement, when hopes of converting the world were still high, there was no sectarian double standard for belief or action. God calls to the moral agent through each and every other person, as well as through Scripture, Christ, and the Spirit; and each person the Quaker meets is to be invited through his or her witness to recognize the Light of Christ within both.[97] All persons "in all Towns, Countries and Nations" have "something of God in them" that enables them to answer and observe the "Royal Law of God."[98]

Yet the Quakers, and particularly George Fox, seem less concerned about ethics or moral purity for their own sake than are Menno and the pacifist Anabaptists. The key for the Friends is the inner experience of joy and light in Christ, of which mercy, forgiveness, and innocence are a result. Notable in Fox's writings is a relative disinterest in expending much attention on morality, except for his disavowal of force. He also commends detachment from family in favor of the gospel. Fox left his own family of birth to pursue his religious quest, though he later was welcomed into a large and supportive stepfamily through his marriage to Margaret Fell. Other distinctively Quaker behaviors—such as the custom of marriage without a priest; the worship form of egalitarian response to the Light via spontaneous preaching; and, to an extent, the refusal to swear—have more a religious basis than a properly moral one.

The main source of the Quaker peace testimony is the actions and sayings of Jesus. Hebrew belligerency is unequivocally rejected, for Jesus introduces a new dispensation and a new law that is in discontinuity with the old. Quaker leaders such as Fox and theologian Robert Barclay are not rigorously literal or legalist in their reading of the Bible, claiming as they do the direct moving of the Spirit, the "Inner Light" or "Light Within," which provides an "experimental" knowledge of God.[99] Apparently inconsistent teachings of Jesus about the "sword" are sometimes explained figuratively on the grounds that they contravene the central and overriding message of the gospel, which is one of repentance, mercy, peace, and nonresistance.[100]

Quaker opposition to war and violence was not absolute and universal from the beginning. It originated in Fox's personal experience of the presence of the kingdom in his own life and extended gradually to others as conversion was followed by a progressive shaping of Christian fellowship in interaction with external events and challenges. For instance, Fox was imprisoned in 1650 for six months for "blasphemy," and, having had some success in converting officers in Cromwell's army, was offered a captaincy upon his release.

96. See Childress, "Answering That of God."

97. Ibid., 7, 30.

98. Ibid., 24; citing *The Royal Law of God Revived* (1671–72).

99. See, for example, Robert Barclay's "Turn Thy Mind to the Light," in *The Quaker Reader*, ed. Jessamyn West (New York: Viking Press, 1962), 226–30.

100. Howard H. Brinton, *Sources of the Quaker Peace Testimony* (Wallingford, Pa.: Pendle Hill Historical Studies, 1941), 10–11.

He refused, telling the soldiers that he "was come into the covenant of peace, which was before wars and strifes were"—thus earning himself an additional and equal jail term.[101] In a subsequent letter to Cromwell, who demanded written assurance that Fox would never bear arms for the king and against Cromwell, Fox identified himself as "the son of God sent to stand a witness against all violence," avowing that his "weapons are not carnal but spiritual."[102] In two 1659 letters advising Friends, Fox insists that all wars and fighting belong to the fall, that fighting for Christ is a deception, and that in Christ's kingdom are only peace, light, unity, and love, which "take away the occasion of wars" (a phrase he repeated often).[103] Although Friends had until that time continued to serve as soldiers, the peace testimony became clear and adamant in 1660, when Charles II was restored to the throne and any hope for a Puritan Commonwealth destroyed. In that year, Fox wrote a letter to the king reiterating the themes of love of enemies and repudiation of any carnal weapons.[104] In the "Declaration of 1660" (sent to Charles II in January 1661), the Quakers publicized their peace testimony in a classic statement. They vowed always to endure wrongs without revenge and to deny all weapons and wars, "because it is contrary to the spirit of Christ, his doctrine, and the practice of his apostles."[105]

At the same time, Fox accepted the concept that the sword can be exercised legitimately as part of the police function of the state, and even that when properly used, it responds to the Light of Christ that the criminal violates within himself or herself. "The Magistrate of Christ . . . is in the light and power of Christ, and he is to subject all under the power of Christ. . . . And his laws here are agreeable and answerable to that of God in every man; when men act contrary to it, they do evil: so he is a terror to the evil doers."[106] In 1654, Fox admonished King Charles to use the "sword of magistracy" to banish the "wickedness" then "at liberty." "Our prayers are for them that are in authority, that under them we may live a godly life in peace."[107]

Fox seems to differentiate between the police function of the state and war with its certainty of massive killing. It is at least clear that Fox knew that genuine Christians experience the presence of Christ and of his kingdom in their own lives, and that war is impossible in the kingdom. The Quaker attitude to war is summed up in Fox's declaration that he "lived in the virtue of that life and power that took away the occasion of all wars."[108] The Rules

101. *Journal of George Fox,* 128–29; cf. T. C. Jones, *Fox's Attitude Toward War,* 24–25.

102. 1654–55, as cited in T. C. Jones, *Fox's Attitude Toward War,* 25–26.

103. Ibid., as cited at 27–29.

104. *Journal of George Fox,* 347–51; cf. T. C. Jones, *Fox's Attitude Toward War,* 30–32.

105. As cited in T. C. Jones, *Fox's Attitude Toward War,* 36; cf. Steere, ed., *Quaker Spirituality,* 105–7.

106. Childress, "Answering That of God in Every Man," 25; quoting Fox's *The Great Mystery of the Great Whore Unfolded.*

107. *Journal of George Fox,* 355.

108. Ibid., 128.

of Discipline, compiled annually at regional Friends' meetings since the seventeenth century, continue to reiterate this witness, its basis in the realized kingdom, and its hope for the conversion of Christian states. One representative expression comes from the London conference of 1883, which recapitulated and revised Quaker teachings since 1672:

> We dare not believe that our Lord and Saviour, in enjoining the love of enemies and the forgiveness of injuries, has prescribed for man a series of precepts which are incapable of being carried into practice or of which the practice is to be postponed till all shall be persuaded to act upon them. We cannot doubt that they are incumbent upon the Christian now . . . and upon nations also. Wherefore, we entreat all who profess themselves members of our Society to be faithful to that ancient testimony . . . that, by a conduct agreeable to our profession, we may demonstrate ourselves to be real followers of the Messiah, the peaceable Saviour, of the increase of whose government and peace there shall be no end.[109]

In later years, however, even pacifism was debated within Quakerism, as the originally iconoclastic movement adapted to civic culture. Thomas Hamm displays the division among Quakers in America that occurred as a result of the American Civil War, during which many Quakers joined the Union army, while others persevered in the Quaker principle that evil cannot be met with evil.[110]

## CONCLUSIONS

In the end, one can surmise that pacifist Christianity does not correlate strictly with a literalist reading of the Bible, nor with the isolation of commands like "Love your enemies" (Matt. 5:44) from their contexts as direct and specific norms for conduct. Erasmus was a pacifist even while insisting on the complexity of biblical interpretation, and the more strongly pacifist Friends make a true reading of Scripture dependent on inspiration by the Spirit; their "experimental knowledge" of God implies in practice the relevance of the many founts of awareness and identity that make up the consciousness of the person the Spirit touches. The pacifist Anabaptists, in their total rejection of violence, are no more fundamentalist than the Münster Anabaptists, though the former privilege New Testament texts over Old Testament ones.

Yet even though pacifism does not equate with biblicism, it does seem to correlate with a return to the sources, whether first to personal religious

109. *Book of Discipline of the Religious Society of Friends in Great Britain* (London: Samuel Harris & Co., 1883), 153–55. Virtually all versions and editions of the *Rules of Discipline,* both English and American, contain such examples. Another is given in George W. Forell, ed., *Christian Social Teachings: A Reader in Christian Social Ethics from the Bible to the Present* (Minneapolis: Augsburg, 1971), 239–40.

110. Thomas Hamm, *The Transformation of American Quakerism* (Bloomington: Indiana Univ. Press, 1988), 66–71.

# 9 Contours of the Recent American Debate

THE TWENTIETH-CENTURY DEBATE ABOUT war and peace, not only in the United States but in Western Christianity generally, has been shaped religiously by the rise and fall of the Social Gospel movement. Politically it has been contoured by the two world wars and the ensuing nuclear anxiety that has shadowed international relations since the century's middle decades. While the former factor furthered the serious engagement of Christianity with social sin and social change, the latter introduced into the agenda of Christian social reformers a strong note of self-criticism and a radical scaling-down of expectations.

Around the turn of the century, the Social Gospel theologians, preeminently Walter Rauschenbusch, held out hope of a society renewed by the kingdom ideal of Christlike love and cooperation; they had every confidence that this ideal could be realized in history without reliance on violent coercion. But the wars that brought devastation in Europe also brought a new kind of realism about political life and the limits of the Christian contribution to it. Reinhold Niebuhr saw war as an inevitable necessity to redress international injustice and held out little prospect that love could temper the harsh requirements of securing an ordered social life. His brother H. Richard Niebuhr debated with him about the proper Christian response to war, maintaining that, after all, ensuring that history take a moral course may not be integral to the Christian's social vocation. Arguing at least in one early instance the purist (noncoercive) pacifist position, H. Richard Niebuhr advanced the proposition that there may be a certain grace in "doing nothing" in time of international conflict, for the calling of the disciple consists above all in trust in the sovereign God who is history's source, sustainer, and end.

Both Niebuhrs wanted a way around what they took to be the rather soft love ethic of liberal Christianity, and both tended to say that to put love at the center of the Christian moral life was misguided. In the 1950s and '60s, however, Paul Ramsey sought to reinstall that Christian virtue, renovating its biblical basis—but to save love both from a relativistic practical interpretation and to unite it with the just war tradition. Taking a more Augustinian route to the problem of violent conflict, Ramsey chose charity rather than justice as a ground of just war thinking. He may be contrasted to the evolving Catholic social tradition, which established the just war on a basis of reason, human rights, and the common good. At this point historically arises the paradox of nuclear deterrence, with its threatened violation of noncombatant immunity and its achievement of an anxious peace. While use of nuclear weapons has been widely (not universally) repudiated by Christian authors, U.S. deterrence policy proved a trickier problem, and one on which Catholic social teaching, along with Ramsey, seemed prepared to compromise.

Recent Christianity has not been lacking its pacifist voices. Two from the Catholic tradition (Dorothy Day and Thomas Merton) and two from the Reformation tradition (John Howard Yoder and Stanley Hauerwas) illustrate that two decisive differences between just war and pacifist thinking lie in interpretations of the presence or futurity of the kingdom, and in a conversion-based or rule-based approach to violence as a moral problem.

## THE SOCIAL GOSPEL

As Robert T. Handy notes, the American social gospel of the late nineteenth and early twentieth centuries was part of a wider movement in Western countries to come to terms with the effects of industrialization and immigration, especially the swelling of urban populations along with vastly unequal distributions of wealth. Growing out of dissatisfaction with current individualistic interpretations of faith and salvation, Christian social movements began to appear that grounded the inseparability of religion and ethics primarily in the teachings of Jesus and the prophets. They also relied upon the historical and social sciences, both to rediscover the gospel message and to mount a critique of exploitative economic relationships.

The movement was largely a middle-class, moderate effort at reform through appeal to social solidarity, to Jesus' kingdom preaching, and to his example of inclusive and sacrificial moral behavior. Making use of emerging historical criticism of the Bible, the social gospel was premised on the recovery of the teaching of the historical Jesus. The love of neighbor at its core could serve as a moral guide of perennial worth, one that is concretely practicable at both the individual and the social levels. The proclaimers of the social gospel saw that sin is perpetrated through social institutions and not only by individual selfishness. Yet they trusted that human response to God's initiative in Jesus could not only challenge those institutions and begin a process of social change, but even lead progressively to greater social equality, cooperation, and harmony and to a real initiation of the kingdom of God in history. Much social gospel thought was pacifist. Their essential optimism about human moral sensitivity and potential allowed these reformers to hope that education, persuasion, and conversion, rather than violent coercion, could accomplish their goals.[1]

Although the social gospelers may have had unrealistically high hopes for moral education and for the historical power of Christian virtue, it is not precisely true, as some critics have charged, that on the whole they either ignored the reality of original sin or reduced the eschatological kingdom and salvation to historical social progress and universal brotherhood. The primary theologian of the social gospel, Walter Rauschenbusch (1861–1918), affirmed the reality of original sin in *A Theology for the Social Gospel*, even as he insisted that sin "is not a private transaction between the sinner and God" and that "we rarely sin against God alone." His contribution was to go beyond the Augustinian projection of the soul's disordered loves onto the social scheme of the "Two Cities," by discerning in social sin, as contrasted to individual, a qualitative and not only incremental difference. Rauschenbusch speaks of the power of "evil collective forces" to assimilate individuals and to impose their own moral standards.[2] Foreshadowing Reinhold Niebuhr, he held that evil can be embodied in permanent social institutions that generate self-justifying theories, idealize evil, and pervert the moral instincts of individual members.[3] Against social evil, Rauschenbusch upholds "the solidarity of the human family," governed by the law of love, and the duty of the strong to "stand with" the weak and defend them.[4]

Deeply informative of Rauschenbusch's theological and social perspective was his experience as pastor of a German Baptist church in the Hell's Kitchen slums of New York City. The suffering there of impoverished working people and the unemployed—a misery that complacent establishment Christianity not only did nothing to remove, but complicitly perpetuated—birthed Rauschenbusch's passionate commitment to economic reform, especially of labor practices. In coalition with his social concerns, Rauschenbusch's use of contemporary biblical studies created hope of social change. The historical study of Jesus' teachings and primitive Christianity makes it possible to recognize "the kingdom idea," whose submergence "was an eclipse of Jesus." "We are getting back to Christ and to his faith in the possibility and certainty of the reign of God on earth."[5]

1. See Robert T. Handy, ed., "Introduction," in *The Social Gospel in America: 1870–1920* (New York: Oxford Univ. Press, 1966), 3–16; and "Social Gospel," in *The Westminster Dictionary of Christian Ethics,* ed. James F. Childress and John Macquarrie (Philadelphia: Westminster Press, 1987), 593–94. See also Douglas F. Ottati, "The Social Gospel," and "Walter Rauschenbusch: The Anatomy of a Theological Ethic" (read in manuscript; available from the author, Union Theological Seminary, Richmond, Va. 23227).

2. *A Theology for the Social Gospel* (Nashville: Abingdon Press, 1945; originally pub. 1917), 71–72.

3. Ibid., 66.

4. Walter Rauschenbusch, *The Social Principles of Jesus* (Boston: Pilgrim Press, 1916), 17, 49.

5. Walter Rauschenbusch, *Christianizing the Social Order* (New York: Macmillan, 1916), 89–90.

The key violation of God's will occurs when "we set our profit and ambition above the welfare of our fellows and above the Kingdom of God which binds them together."[6] Although the kingdom of God does demand human effort so that it can appear as "a community of righteousness in mankind," the kingdom is neither "merely ethical" nor accessible via human good will and social action alone. "The Kingdom of God is divine in its origin, progress and consummation. It was initiated by Jesus Christ . . . it is sustained by the Holy Spirit, and it will be brought to its fulfilment by the power of God in his own time."[7] Yet even while he acknowledged the transcendent character of God's reign, Rauschenbusch was above all devoted to restoring in social terms the keen revolutionary edge of Christianity. Even though "the Kingdom of God is always both present and future," we must "see the Kingdom of God as always coming, always pressing in on the present, always big with possibility, and always inviting immediate action."[8]

Rauschenbusch was greatly affected by the outbreak of the Great War, as was evident in the series of lectures delivered at Yale in 1917 and published shortly before his death as *A Theology for the Social Gospel*. Not only did Rauschenbusch see the war as "the most acute and tremendous social problem of all," a patent violation of everything Christianity stands for, but his own family roots were German, and he had spent years in Germany during his early studies. To Rauschenbusch militarism exemplified perfectly the super-personal forces of evil and of moral self-deception; he goes so far as to term it one of the universal sins of organized society that "cooperated in the death of Christ."[9] In *The Social Principles of Jesus,* published in 1916, he argues that the Great War forced confrontation with the duty to avoid its repetition by "the prevention of armed conflicts," the elimination of causes of war, protection of small nations against big ones, and "the creation of an institutional basis for a great family of nations in days to come."[10] In *A Theology for the Social Gospel* he reiterates that "social righteousness and fraternity," and even "a Christianizing of international relations," are now demanded on a global scale.[11]

Typically enough, Rauschenbusch's deepest objections to war did not stem from a simple obedience ethic of imitation of Christ's self-sacrifice, but from his conviction that war causes immeasurable harm to the welfare of human beings, and that one thing Jesus certainly stood for was the building of a harmonious kingdom among them. Jesus did not experience war firsthand, but "that he had convictions on war is plain from his sayings. 'He that taketh the sword shall perish by the sword,' shows clear comprehension of the fact

6. Walter Rauschenbusch, *A Theology for the Social Gospel,* 48.
7. Ibid., 139–40.
8. Ibid., 141.
9. Ibid., 255.
10. Rauschenbusch, *Social Principles,* 144.
11. Rauschenbusch, *A Theology for the Social Gospel,* 106.

that in war neither side gains, and that the reactions of war are as dangerous as the direct effects."[12]

To Rauschenbusch, it is not at all clear that the radical sayings of Jesus about nonresistance are in the present "unpractical or visionary."[13] In a commentary on "Love your enemies . . . " (Matt. 5:44-45), he commends gentleness as a mark of the kingdom, in contrast to the militant crusade mentality. "Hate breeds hate; force challenges force."[14] He associates with the exemplary "type of primitive Christianity" both the Hebrew prophets and the radical Reformation communities that were against war. He approvingly characterizes the Reformation radicals in the following way, holding them up as models for the social gospel:

> Strong fraternal feeling, simplicity and democracy of organization, more or less communistic ideas about property, an attitude of passive obedience or conscientious objection toward the coercive and militaristic governments of the time, opposition to the selfish and oppressive Church, a genuine faith in the practicability of the ethics of Jesus, and, as the secret power in it all, belief in an inner experience of regeneration and an inner light which interprets the outer word of God.[15]

After World War II, Rauschenbusch's communitarian, pacifist, and ameliorative ideals were severely criticized on two fronts. For the neoorthodox theologies led by Karl Barth, the humanism of the social gospel was insufficiently attentive to the sovereignty and transcendence of God and the ultimate sinfulness of "works righteousness," however benevolently motivated. And for the realist interpretations of Christian ethics, following Reinhold Niebuhr, the social gospel was marked by a naiveté which in the end could only inhibit the accomplishment of genuinely responsible action to curb social evil. Despite a recent resurgence of interest in the contributions of the social gospel,[16] the generally sympathetic but finally distancing judgment of Max L. Stackhouse is not uncharacteristic of the way the next couple of theological generations came to see the movement. "It was and is primarily concerned with *ad hoc* judgments on *ad hoc* problems," and "was and is susceptible at many points to the charges of idealism, immanentism, perfectionism, and culture Christianity, not to mention a longer list of more formal heresies."[17] But one thing

12. Ibid., 255.
13. Ibid., 158.
14. Rauschenbusch, *Social Principles,* 156–57.
15. Ibid., 195.
16. See, for example, Roger Haight, SJ, "The Mission of the Church in the Theology of the Social Gospel," *Theological Studies* 49 (1988): 477–97; and a focus issue on "The Ethics of the Social Gospel," *Journal of Religious Ethics* 18 (1990), 103–28, edited by Diane Yeager and including essays by Christopher Lasch, Reinhard L. Hutter, Grace C. Long, Susan H. Lindley, Roger Haight, SJ and John Langan, SJ.
17. Max L. Stackhouse, "The Continuing Importance of Walter Rauschenbusch," in Walter Rauschenbusch, *The Righteousness of the Kingdom,* ed. and introduced by Max L. Stackhouse (Nashville: Abingdon, 1968), 25.

It is not difficult to see why Reinhold Niebuhr, who had himself been a pacifist in World War I, eventually rejected pacifism[43]: both because of its political idealism and its moral absolutism. His own early pacifism was pragmatic; his hope that it could be an effective social tool ended with the war. Niebuhr finally concluded that the only nonheretical type of pacifism was one that gave up all involvement in politics to function separately as a reminder of the relativity of justice.[44] He also came to question the distinction between violent and nonviolent coercion, referring to the latter as "covert violence."[45] Impatient with those who rejected violence but participated in or benefited from other forms of coercion—like, he said, the Quakers—Niebuhr thought "pure religious idealism" had to result both in total nonresistance and in renunciation of any aspiration to be socially efficacious or politically responsible.[46] Such idealism or perfectionism might have a general social function as a stimulant to greater justice, but must always accept as its end "the Cross" and not social change.[47] In the end, Reinhold Niebuhr's position on the use of violence, like many of his other positions, may exhibit some internal inconsistency, which would not be out of step with his own view of the historical and ambiguous nature of the human moral situation. James Childress sees a contradiction in Niebuhr's attempt to contend, on the one hand, that violence is a legitimate option to pursue order and justice in history; and, on the other, that even when justified it is always a "necessary evil," in violation of humanity's most essential nature.[48] As we have seen, however, a paradoxical position on this point is congenial to the Augustinian just war tradition.

Reinhold Niebuhr's occasional writings, contributed throughout the war years to publications such as *The Christian Century*, *Christianity and Crisis*, and *Christianity and Society*, offer particularly bold examples of his timely and results-oriented approach to ethics.[49] Frequently, he is forthrightly utilitarian, though not without a Christian sense of guilt about violations of moral principle. The bombing of Germany, for instance, which he supported because he saw it as the only alternative to capitulation to a less scrupulous foe, he nonetheless described as "a vivid revelation of the whole moral ambiguity of warfare. . . . It is not possible to engage in any act of collective opposition

43. See Reinhold Niebuhr, "Why I Leave the F.O.R.," *Christian Century* (January 3, 1934), in *Love and Justice: Selections from the Shorter Writings of Reinhold Niebuhr,* ed. D. B. Robertson (Gloucester, Mass.: Peter Smith, 1976), 254–59.

44. Reinhold Niebuhr, *Christianity and Power Politics,* 5.

45. Reinhold Niebuhr, "Why I Leave the F.O.R.," 257.

46. Reinhold Niebuhr, *Moral Man,* 264.

47. Reinhold Niebuhr, "Perfectionism and Historical Reality," *Christian Century* (December 14, 1940), in *Love and Justice,* 277.

48. James F. Childress, *Moral Responsibility in Conflicts: Essays on Nonviolence, War and Conscience* (Baton Rouge: Louisiana State Univ. Press, 1982), 49; cf. 57.

49. For Niebuhr's general view of the necessity of war, see his "A Critique of Pacifism," *Atlantic Monthly* (May 1927), in *Love and Justice,* 241–47; and "Pacifism and the Use of Force," *The World Tomorrow* (May, 1928), in *Love and Justice,* 247–53.

to collective guilt without involving the innocent with the guilty"; this is the price one has to pay.[50]

Reinhold Niebuhr was effective in influencing the political scenario of his day, certainly a rare accomplishment for a theologian, because he was remarkably persuasive in his readings of just what current events really meant.[51] As Robin Lovin notes, Niebuhr's activism may not have resulted in a consistent social theory, but it does teach a critical consciousness toward our own most strongly held beliefs, and it preserves Christianity not as a set of ideas or a social program, but as "a locus of possibilities" that reflects "the incoherences of real experience" even as it prompts transcendence of immediate contexts, thoughts, and actions.[52] Niebuhr stood firm against metaphysics, whatever stability and coherence it claims to offer. For him, both the human person and the Christian truth are irreducibly historical, established in "dramatic and historical media," while remaining to an extent ontologically ambiguous. "The encounter between God and man, as the encounters between men in history, must be by faith and love and not by the discovery of some common essence of reason and nature underlying individuals and particulars."[53] (It is not out of the question that the elder Niebuhr's appreciation of the historical nature of Christianity was strengthened in conversation with his brother, as, for instance, in the debate discussed below.)

Reinhold's and H. Richard's theological approaches contrasted superficially, though they bore deep resemblances in some aspects, for example, the social and communal natures of personhood and of faith. The brothers clashed in a published exchange only once, and that was on the issue of a pacifist Christianity—specifically, on the nature, wisdom, and viability of a pacifist response to the Japanese invasion of Manchuria in 1931. Since Japan had violated clear nonaggression agreements and went on to bomb civilians in 1932, many pacifists were willing to advocate coercive economic measures against Japan by the League of Nations and the United States. Reinhold supported these. An economic embargo or a consumer boycott of Japanese products, however, would harm the civilian population at least as much as its military leaders. The resultant moral impasse in Western opinion was seen by Reinhold as proof of the inadequacy of absolute pacifism as Christian social policy. The issue for him was not whether to resort to coercion, but how to find the least destructive form of doing so. Any purely just and noncoercive alternative would surely be ineffective in deterring what was generally seen as Japan's bold-faced imperialism.[54] And for Reinhold, such deterrence was a nonnegotiable moral objective.

50. Reinhold Niebuhr, "The Bombing of Germany," *Christianity and Society* (Summer 1943), in *Love and Justice,* 222.

51. Gustafson, "Theology in the Service of Ethics," 36.

52. Robin W. Lovin, "Reinhold Niebuhr, Past and Future," *Religious Studies Review* 14 (1988), 101–2.

53. Reinhold Niebuhr, "Intellectual Autobiography," 21.

54. Fox, *Reinhold Niebuhr,* 132.

H. Richard, however, took a different stand, in an essay revealingly titled, "The Grace of Doing Nothing."[55] Although he was not a lifelong or absolute pacifist,[56] the younger Niebuhr saw human inaction as an occasionally appropriate testimony to the providential effect of divine action. Part of his objection to American intervention resided in his sensitivity to the fact that America hardly acted out of disinterested motives—a cynicism about the morality of nations that would certainly have been shared by Rauschenbusch as well as Reinhold Niebuhr. But more essentially, H. Richard Niebuhr discerned in early Christianity, in radical Christianity, and even in communism the insight that profound change in the world order cannot be brought about without occasions of destruction. Nevertheless, this apparently bleak conviction is accompanied by "the belief in the inevitably good outcome of the mundane process"—not because that outcome is contrived by human control, but because the whole process resides within and depends on the ultimate "meaningfulness of reality."[57] The task of the community in the interim, then, is neither self-reliant action nor patient resignation, but a sort of quiet preparation—a creation of the conditions of real reconstruction through hopeful and faithful repentance.[58]

The elder Niebuhr's response, while empathetic at points, amounted to a rebuttal of what he took to be the premises of his brother's position, a position that it is not entirely clear Reinhold understood. At one point he does acknowledge that H. Richard does not counsel "humility and disinterestedness" in order to "change the course of history," but because these attitudes constitute "a prayer to God for the coming of his kingdom."[59] Yet at the same time, he persists in referring to his brother's position as "ethical perfectionism" and "a pure love ethic."[60] Reinhold seems to want to collapse H. Richard into the Social Gospel movement and to reject him on the same grounds, grounds with which H. Richard himself would not have agreed. Somewhat querulously, Reinhold expresses his root skepticism that "a pure love ethic can ever be

55. H. Richard Niebuhr, "The Grace of Doing Nothing," *Christian Century* (March 23, 1932), in *The Christian Century Reader*, ed. Harold E. Fey and Margaret Frakes (New York: Association Press, 1962), 216–221.

56. Gustafson, who was a student of Niebuhr at Yale, testifies that Niebuhr made a case for " 'conscientious participation in war,' the call to be the restrainer, as well as to be restrained." The context for this position was the Christian's ethic of self-denial as an acceptance of limitation. "It is acceptance of our responsibility to limit others, even in the knowledge of the fact that our action is never fully right, that our action causes suffering to others (as in war). It is the acknowledgement that our restraining activity (for example, in family or in nation) is under the restraint of others, and thus is not to be enacted only with self-restraint but with acceptance of the restraint of others upon it" ("Introduction," *The Responsible Self*," 36). See also Richard B. Miller, "H. Richard Niebuhr's War Articles: A Transvaluation of Value," *Journal of Religion* 68 (1988): 242–62, which analyzes the relation between the pacifist and nonpacifist writings of H. Richard Niebuhr.

57. H. Richard Niebuhr, "The Grace of Doing Nothing," 219.

58. Ibid., 221.

59. Rienhold Niebuhr, "Must We Do Nothing?", *Christian Century* (March 30, 1932), in *Christian Century Reader*, 225

60. For instance, ibid., 224.

made the basis of a civilization," or that, falling short of a purely Christlike alternative, "it is better not to act at all than to act from motives which are less than pure," or to act with less than Christian methods.[61] Such standards immobilize social action. Moreover, he rather gratuitously adds, the hope of changing society by "purely ethical means" that do not entail the coercion of the privileged classes by the underprivileged or their champions "is an illusion which was spread chiefly among the comfortable classes of the past century."[62]

More to the point, perhaps, is Reinhold's critique of H. Richard's eschatology. "What makes my brother's eschatology impossible for me is that he identifies everything that is occurring in history . . . with the counsels of God," and then, by a "leap of faith," concludes that the same God who determines the course of history with "brutalities and forces" will "finally establish an ideal society in which pure love will reign."[63]

Implying gently that Reinhold may have missed at least some of his points, H. Richard begins his answer, published inconspicuously among the journal's letters to the editor, by aiming to define "as accurately as I can" the "exact locus of the issue between us," which does not, after all, "lie in the question of activity or inactivity."[64] The real issue is the justification of "the 'eschatological' faith," by which the younger Niebuhr affirms that "tragedy is only the prelude to fulfillment," since "the kingdom of God comes inevitably." For humans, the crucial question is not whether they can bring about the kingdom through loving activity or even through inactivity, but whether they will be able to see the kingdom and enter it, by cultivating "the only kind of life which will enable us to enter it, the life of repentance and forgiveness."[65]

For H. Richard, God is not beyond history, a transcendent ideal that judges without truly reconfiguring historical realities. God is "always in history" as "the structure of things," a structure that does result in "war and depression"—not by direct divine interference or punishment, but "when we bring it upon ourselves" by violating the structure inscribed by the "creative will" of God. "He is the rock against which we beat in vain, that which bruises and overwhelms us when we seek to impose our wishes, contrary to his, upon him."[66] H. Richard does not in the end really justify in apologetic terms his essentially optimistic faith.[67] His mode is more that of witness to the necessary specifics

61. Ibid., 222–23.

62. Ibid., 224.

63. Ibid., 225.

64. "The Only Way into the Kingdom of God: A Communication by H. Richard Niebuhr," *Christian Century,* April 6, 1932, in *Christian Century Reader,* 228.

65. Ibid., 229.

66. Ibid., 229.

67. Gustafson, closely familiar with Niebuhr personally as well as through his writings, offers a more experiential and psychological explanation of his teacher's faith in divine providence. " 'Whatever is, is good' was axiomatic in Niebuhr's thought, and this led to an appreciative, affirmative disposition toward the world as his first response to it. . . . And the One who made all things good has made himself known in his creation and in his redeeming work as One who is loving. We are valued by God, just as the rest of creation is; thus we are free to love the goodness of the world without being preoccupied with our own value" ("Introduction," *Responsible Self,* 30).

of discipleship for a community that perceives as its core God's gracious action. He concludes his letter in inclusive terms, with advice he thinks to hold for societies as well as individuals:

> Man's task is not that of building utopias, but that of eliminating weeds and tilling the soil so that the kingdom of God can grow. His method is not one of striving for perfection or of acting perfectly, but of clearing the road by repentance and forgiveness.[68]

Richard Miller makes the point that even when H. Richard Niebuhr later justifies military involvement in World War II, his understanding of God's sovereign action in history remains unchanged. War as judgment is a part of God's redemptive process, a conviction that Niebuhr advances with the symbol of the cross. The suffering of war falls on the innocent at least as much as on the guilty. Insofar as it is an imitation of Christ's vicarious suffering, war is a transformative event, demanding a response of trust in divine purpose. War cannot be evaluated in terms of the rightness of particular causes, an exercise that results only in self-righteous hubris both for pacifists and for war's advocates. Even war must be placed against the backdrop of God's immanent and overarching agency.[69]

H. Richard Niebuhr's early *Christian Century* essays on pacifism focus themes that are exemplified in other writings. Some of these writings, published reasonably soon after the debate with Reinhold, are particularly helpful in placing the pacifist response in theological perspective. Appearing five years later, *The Kingdom of God in America*,[70] envisions that symbol as the source of the revolutionary, creative, and prophetic strain that has always characterized Christianity and saved it from becoming simply the universalistic projection of one particular set of historical experiences. Niebuhr characterizes the kingdom of God in Calvinist and almost neoorthodox terms: God's kingship, human dependency; God's demand, human obedience; pure grace, human impotence.[71] His vision of the kingdom is set off from his brother's notably by the fact that, for H. Richard, the kingdom is vivid, absolute, and temporally immediate.[72] Especially in Protestant Christianity, exemplified by American Puritans and Quakers, "God's present rule" is a "living reality," both

68. "The Only Way into the Kingdom of God," 231.

69. Miller, "War Articles," 254. Miller also argues against the frequent thesis that this emphasis on repentance rather than on evaluation of right and wrong in war results for Niebuhr in a merely "dispositional" ethics. Although Niebuhr does not offer any clear set of directives, he does develop criteria for social ethics such as self-criticism, a preference for the innocent, and the importance of other-regard even in choosing means in war. Miller also surmises that, for Niebuhr, both just war theory and pacifism remain legitimate options for individual consciences in the Christian tradition.

70. H. Richard Niebuhr, *The Kingdom of God in America* (New York: Harper and Brothers, 1937).

71. Ibid., 18.

72. Ibid., 25.

in nature and in history. But, for these Christians, God's kingdom "was not an ideal dependent for its realization on human effort; men and their efforts were dependent upon it; loyalty to it and obedience to its laws were the conditions of their temporal and eternal welfare."[73] And again, "the way into the coming kingdom lay . . . through the kingdom of Christ; the function of the church was to prepare men for crisis and for promise by proclaiming to them the gospel of repentance and faith rather than by persuading them to undertake specific political activity."[74]

Following Jonathan Edwards's critique of partiality, Niebuhr suspects even love of neighbor of being self-love extended. Although true love of God is shown in active charity, others ought to be loved, not because they are persons like oneself, but because they are sacred in relation to God, the ultimate Being who is also humanity's true good.[75]

Even more interesting is a lecture, not published until 1988, delivered by H. Richard the year following the *Christian Century* series.[76] In a typically Calvinist and Edwardsian manner, Niebuhr observes that the "mind of Jesus" which remained undiscovered by the social gospel was a mind directed not toward human welfare and divine aid in achieving it, but toward "what God was doing and what man ought to do in the light of God's doing." God is no "moral ideal" but a "cosmic reality."[77] The Jesus of the gospels is not the Jesus of the social gospel with his "anthropocentric morality," nor is he a pacifist in order to realize some social ideal. And if one sees Jesus only in such a light, then he becomes irrelevant to the historical problem and is in one way or another relegated to the margins. In this paper, H. Richard allows himself one last rebuttal to his brother's construal of the problem of Christian action:

> Reinhold Niebuhr's perfectionist Jesus remains a pacifist out of obedience to the ideal, but since Niebuhr himself sees that perfectionism is no answer to the problem of human welfare and happiness, this perfectionism and pacifism are dismissed, save as qualifications of the social struggle and as the transhistorical reference which gives ultimate meaning to a divided life.[78]

The faith of Jesus truly recaptured is a faith in "the God of the creative process" who forgives, heals, and redeems. Both Jesus and the social gospel theologians had faith in the ultimately beneficent nature of the divinity and of the historical and cosmic processes. But "Jesus knew what the social gospel

73. Ibid., 51.
74. Ibid., 149.
75. Ibid., 114–17.
76. "The Social Gospel and the Mind of Jesus," lecture to the American Theological Society meeting in New York, April 23, 1933; in *Journal of Religious Ethics* 16 (1988): 115–27, edited and introduced by Diane Yeager.
77. Ibid., 118.
78. Ibid. He adds, "The God of Jesus is neither the kind father whose concern is the welfare of his people nor the transcendent ideal or source. He is the dynamic driving force immanent in the events of time; he is the judge, the destroyer" (p. 122).

intention, last resort, reasonable hope of success, proportionality, and just conduct. All of these criteria taken together, with the exception of the last one, establish the *jus ad bellum*, the right to go to war, while the last criterion focuses on the *jus in bello*, right conduct within war, and includes both intention and proportionality, which are also part of the *jus ad bellum*.[82]

James Johnson points out that a major shift occurred in the international political picture in the nineteenth century due to the amassing of large standing armies by the European nations and the development of new military technologies.[83] Concepts aligned with the historical just war tradition, such as last resort, proportionality, and noncombatant immunity, allowed subsequent Christian thought to oppose militarism and to renew its pacifist expression, especially in relation to nuclear weapons. However, as we have just seen from our discussion of Reinhold Niebuhr, opposition to war—even nuclear war—has hardly been univocal within recent Christianity. Whether war in the nuclear age is a qualitatively different prospect, bursting the categories of traditional just war thinking, has been hotly debated in the present century. While Protestant theologian Paul Ramsey has tried to justify nuclear deterrence within the criteria of the just war, the Roman Catholic "peace pastoral" expressed some ambivalence about the possibility of doing so. In 1963, the encyclical *Pacem in Terris*, authored by Pope John XXIII, had gone so far as to assert that just war in the nuclear age is "barely imaginable."

## Paul Ramsey

Paul Ramsey (1913–1988), a Methodist, was born in Mississippi, graduated from Millsaps College, and received his doctorate from Yale University. After teaching at Millsaps, Garrett Theological Seminary, and Yale, he joined the faculty of Princeton University in 1944, where he remained a professor of religion for nearly forty years. A prolific writer, Ramsey spent much of the last fifteen years of his life preparing an edition of the complete works of Jonathan Edwards. He was also energetic and versatile in his approach to the interdisciplinary aspects of ethics. Meeting the challenges of increasing field specialization, he developed expertise in military ethics and in bioethics by mastering technical levels of material in military technology and in medicine. Basically, Ramsey's instincts were conservative on just about every issue, with the possible exception of the use of technology to prolong dying life. He tended to want to preserve the U.S. political and the theological just war status quo. Another part of his conservatism, however, with genuinely transformative implications for the style in which Christian ethics was being done in the Niebuhrian era, was his passion to resituate theological ethics in general, and

82. Childress, *Moral Responsibility*, 64–65.

83. James Turner Johnson, "Just War," in *The Westminster Dictionary of Christian Ethics*, ed. James F. Childress and John Macquarrie (Philadelphia: Westminster Press, 1986), 329.

just war theory in particular, on biblical grounds, specifically the love command. The problem of the just war occupied most of his attention in the 1950s and '60s, whereas bioethics moved to the forefront of his scholarship in the '70s and '80s.

In one sense, Ramsey can be seen as a reactor against the dominance of Niebuhrian political realism on the Protestant ethical scene—not because of its realism about coercion, but because of its political approach to morality. In the first place, thinks Ramsey, the political calculation of good ends is not a sufficient base for a *Christian* ethic.[84] And in the second, the utilitarian and pragmatic mode of moral calculation that Reinhold Niebuhr represented in World War II had given way by the '50s to a soft love-situationism. Ramsey saw Protestant Christian ethics as floundering in a swamp of relativism,[85] and he diagnosed in theologians a "professional allergy to rules." Ramsey viewed these trends as inconsistent with Christian ethics' biblical base, of which Niebuhr's critique of the social gospel had partly lost sight. The latter may have been right that the social gospel preaching of the historical Jesus' love command was inadequate as a foundation for effective social responsibility; but Ramsey was not content to rest with Niebuhr's counterproposal of a tensive and perennially unspecified dialectic between love and justice. These concerns yield two problematics that pervade Ramsey's writings: the relation between the biblical norm of love or agape and natural justice; and the derivation and function of norms in ethics. Ramsey wanted to permit love to transform and even appropriate justice in a systematic and integral way; and he wanted to tie norms closely to the love command.

Ramsey's first book, *Basic Christian Ethics*, remains the most systematic exposition of his theological convictions. The purpose of the book is to elaborate a characteristically Protestant (Reformation) Christian ethics from a scriptural base.[86] The controlling concept in this ethics is covenant; in Christ, God initiates a covenant with human persons, who respond in obedient love. The norm of the covenant is agape, God's righteousness or steadfast saving love. Human love thus takes the form of a responsive and imitative love that answers the need of the neighbor.

Christian ethics is correlatively a deontological ethics, an ethics of the "right," of the present demand of love, rather than a teleological ethics of the "good" of some future goal to be attained. Agape as the norm of right action is not commensurate with the dictates of created reason but is known only in Jesus Christ. However, there are many indications in Ramsey's thought that, just as God's saving action is universal in scope, so knowledge of the

84. Paul Ramsey, *War and the Christian Conscience: How Shall Modern War Be Conducted Justly?* (Durham, N.C.: Duke Univ. Press, 1961), 5–7.

85. Paul Ramsey, *Deeds and Rules in Christian Ethics* (New York: Scribner's, 1967), 3; see also chap. 7, "The Case of Joseph Fletcher and Joseph Fletcher's Cases"; and Ramsey's *Basic Christian Ethics* (New York: Scribner's, 1951), 77.

86. Ramsey, *Basic Christian Ethics,* xiv.

ethical mandate revealed in Christ also extends beyond the Christian community. For instance, in *Deeds and Rules in Christian Ethics*, Ramsey calls his own ethics "mixed agapism." Reason and revelation can be companion sources, since God's covenant is established with all persons in Christ.[87] This covenant is also known through what might be called, with Luther, the "orders of creation." In a later work, Ramsey declares, "I hold with Karl Barth that covenant-fidelity is the inner meaning and purpose of our creation as human beings, while the whole of creation is the external basis and condition of the possibility of covenant."[88]

In *Basic Christian Ethics*, Ramsey also takes a stand on eschatology and the nature of the kingdom that is a necessary step toward his justification of war. Ramsey interprets Jesus to have had a "literal eschatological belief in the end of history." He judges that Christians today rightly no longer share this belief, and concludes that Jesus' ethical teaching must be reinterpreted with this difference in mind. Moreover, according to Ramsey, "Jesus himself did not think that the gospel of love would be sufficient by itself to resolve the totality of evil in many life-situations . . . ."[89] "The first step to an understanding of the validity of Jesus' strenuous teachings must involve putting a limitation upon the area of their intended application."[90] The critical message of Jesus is that we ought to attend wholeheartedly to the neighbor close at hand, the one whose clear and present need exerts a claim. But the qualification of this message in its actual implementation arises because, "in a non-apocalyptic world," "there is always more than one neighbor and indeed a whole cluster of claims and responsibilities to be considered."[91] The multiplication and eventual conflict of neighbor claims demand that these be adjudicated in some orderly fashion, and for Ramsey, that means further specifying the love principle in terms of consistent action-guiding rules.

In Ramsey's writings, the norm of love functions in a distinctive way, appropriating much of the function of a Roman Catholic natural law ethics without either its metaphysical or its teleological grounding. (Ramsey rejects an ethics of the natural law on the Reformation grounds that it is wrongly directed to the cultivation of virtue toward human fulfillment, rather than to present obedience to God's commands.[92]) Not only is the norm of love potentially universal, but, perhaps more importantly, it functions as a source of clear and stable directives for action at the concrete level. Ramsey's notions of fidelity to covenant, of the specificity of the claims of the neighbor, of the possibility that conflict and ambiguity will arise in human attempts to meet

87. Ramsey, *Deeds and Rules,* 29, 122.

88. Paul Ramsey, *The Patient as Person: Explorations in Medical Ethics* (New Haven: Yale Univ. Press, 1970), xii.

89. Ramsey, *Basic Christian Ethics,* 36.

90. Ibid., 39.

91. Ibid., 42.

92. Ibid., 116, 130, 216–19.

these claims, and of the need for moral consistency, give rise to his deep conviction that the norm of love cannot guide decisions in any vague or discontinuous way.

A phrase often used by Ramsey to express this conviction is "faith effective through in-principled love," proposed in an early article of the same title.[93] The phrase is used explicitly to denote love that works itself out concretely through principles, either by the inner demand of love itself, or by the transformation of justice-based rules by love. When love moves into and employs reason, justice, or natural law, the norms and principles of human moral wisdom are not derived deductively or metaphysically, as in neo-scholastic Catholicism, but inductively and phenomenologically. The law of nature is not known by reflecting on essential human nature abstracted from the contingencies of experience, but by love discerning in practice, and then generalizing, what lines of behavior are necessary to respect fellow human beings.

*War and the Christian Conscience* and *The Just War* present a similar perspective, in that love is conceived as not only using but also transforming norms of justice. Both books emphasize the role of love in forming the secular political doctrine of just or limited warfare. This is a doctrine accomplished by a "love-transformed justice," "love-informed reason," or "love-inspired justice."[94]

> The change-over to just-war doctrine and practice was not a "fall" from the original purity of Christian ethics; but . . . a change of tactics only. The basic strategy remained the same: responsible love and service of one's neighbors in the texture of the common life. . . . Christians simply came to see that the service of the real needs of all the men for whom Christ died required more than personal, witnessing action. It also required them to be involved in maintaining the organized social and political life in which all men live. Non-resisting love had sometimes to resist evil.[95]

Another proposition, which Ramsey sees as of "the utmost importance," is that it was love in particular which in the Western political tradition placed limits on the conduct of war.[96] He argues further that, stemming from Augustine, there is warrant in the just war tradition to see right and wrong as always mixed or at least ambiguous in the decision to go to war. Given the vicissitudes of history, neither side can ever be the object of a clear declaration of righteousness or evil. This gives a special reason to focus just war thinking

93. Paul Ramsey, "Faith Effective Through In-Principled Love," *Christianity and Crisis* 20 (1961): 77. As early as *Basic Christian Ethics,* Ramsey spoke of love as having "internal self-regulations" (p. 78).

94. Ramsey, *War and the Christian Conscience,* xxii; *The Just War: Force and Political Responsibility* (Lanham, Md.: University Press of America, 1983; first published 1968), 142, 151.

95. Ramsey, *War and the Christian Conscience,* xvii–xviii. See also *The Just War,* 142–45.

96. Ramsey, *War and the Christian Conscience,* xviii.

on the limitation of means to prosecute war, rather than on the rectitude of the purposes of regimes.[97] A special example of the work of love transforming justice in service of the limitation of war is the principle of double effect, used typically to prohibit direct attacks on noncombatants.[98]

In the earlier *War and the Christian Conscience*, Ramsey had rejected the use of any deterrence policies built on the possession of weapons that would be immoral ever to use.[99] In *The Just War*, he explicitly retracts that position.[100] By the mid-1960s, entrenched in the Cold War, he is willing to go along with the by-then-strengthened pragmatic political consensus that, as a nuclear power, the United States was entitled to build, store, and position nuclear weapons in order to maintain its balance of power with the Soviet Union. Using nuclear weapons against civilians violates the just limitation of war.[101] However, as is especially clear in the nuclear era, noncombatants cannot always be isolated from the military target, "roped off like ladies at a medieval tournament" (in Ramsey's unsettlingly cavalier expression).[102] Thus, while it is incumbent on the political leadership of the country to renounce the use of "morally repugnant means"—indiscriminate attacks—this does not preclude either a specifically military use of or the continued possession of nuclear weapons, which, because of the very ambiguity of their potential to be used against or to "indirectly" damage civilians, can be relied upon to produce the desired deterrent effect.[103]

Considered as a whole, Ramsey's just war theory is Augustinian in flavor, both because a kingdom ethic recedes in deference to the ambiguities of history, and because the acts of violence are legitimated primarily as requirements of love and only secondarily as requirements of justice in pursuit of the common good. The danger in this approach—also Augustinian—is confirmed in the words of Richard Miller, who warns that when war engaged to protect the innocent is presented as "an expression, not a compromise of agape, then qualifications become almost unnecessary." The effect of an argument like Ramsey's is to remove the thoroughly exceptional character of war, "to render war analogous with other moral acts, to domesticate war as

97. Ibid., 30–32. James Turner Johnson questions this interpretation of Augustine, and observes that, in any event, this position did not become "mainstream" until introduced by Victoria over a thousand years later ("Morality and Force in Statecraft: Paul Ramsey and the Just War Tradition," in *Love and Society,* 103.

98. Ramsey, *War and Christian Conscience,* 33, 47–48, 60–65.

99. Ibid., 270–72.

100. *The Just War,* ix.

101. Ibid., 145, 212.

102. Ibid., 145.

103. Ibid., 253. I can only agree here with Richard Miller that, on this point, Ramsey falters, "insofar as his proportionate deterrent relies upon prospective disproportionate use against civilians and combatants" (Richard B. Miller, *Interpretations of Conflict: Ethics, Pacifism, and the Just War Tradition* [Chicago: Univ. of Chicago Press, 1991], 164).

it were."[104] However, compared to Augustine, Ramsey is decisively more systematic (though not always thoroughly consistent) and rule-oriented. We find little here of the Augustinian maxim, "Love and do what you will."

A neoorthodox note is present in Ramsey's writing, insofar as he tends to assert God's sovereignty over against human designs; his language of deontological duties expresses in a more philosophical vocabulary much of what Barth captured with his divine imperatives. On both these points, Ramsey bears some resemblance to the way in which H. Richard Niebuhr appropriated the Barthian protest against the social gospel. But Ramsey shares in common with both the social gospel and neoorthodoxy (and less so with Niebuhr) the claim to root theological ethics today in solid biblical foundations.

To base one's ethics in the Bible can obviously mean different things, evident enough in the opposition of the Barthian reclamation of a revealed dogmatics and ethics to the activist kingdom ethics of a Rauschenbusch.[105] Certainly aware of modern historical work on biblical materials and their cultural settings, Ramsey does not attempt to derive specific rules from biblical texts; but he also does not rest content with the more general, conversionist appeal either to the revealed grace and claim of God (Barth), or to the life of Jesus (Rauschenbusch), as a comprehensive model for discipleship. Ramsey's method of establishing a biblical base for ethics is to select an overarching ideal or principle (covenant) that can be substantiated historically and textually, and then to seek a structured movement from ideal to conclusions using extrabiblical resources. Ramsey permits a natural sense of justice, by "love transformed," to be assimilated to what he sees as a strongly biblical method. For that matter, Ramsey's original selection of the covenant theme is guided by a sense of the dignity and inviolability of the human person, a perception owing much to Kant.

Ramsey's talk of neighbor love and its practical demands conveys some of the immediacy usually associated with a realized eschatology; but in this case the moral urgency derives more from the so-called deontological imperative than from the radical presence of the kingdom in history. Immediacy of obligation combined with deferral of kingdom life allows the element of conflict in social life to come through more strongly than that of transformation, and also helps motivate Ramsey's move, in dealing with practical problems, from agape as such to justice norms.

The following chapter will contrast the just war tradition, as developed here in the realism of Reinhold Niebuhr and the covenant theology of Ramsey, with the "natural law" version of just war thinking found in Roman Catholicism—at once less biblical and more optimistic about the human potential

104. Richard B. Miller, "Pacifism and Just War Tenets: How Do They Diverge?" *Theological Studies* 47 (1986): 469.

105. See James M. Gustafson, "The Place of Scripture in Christian Ethics: A Methodological Study," *Interpretation* 24 (1970): 430–55.

## JUST WAR: ROMAN CATHOLIC EXAMPLES

The modern social encyclical tradition began to develop at around the time of the social gospel, and it replied to some of the same phenomena of social inequality and unrest. As industrialization was increasing economic inequities, Enlightenment esteem for the freedom and dignity of the individual, and its confidence in rationality, combined with the Marxist critiques of capitalist exploitation to create an explosive situation in many European countries as well as in America. In 1891, Leo XIII published *Rerum Novarum (On the Condition of Labor)* in an attempt to preserve social harmony by adapting what remained an essentially medieval view of society, organic and hierarchical. *Rerum Novarum* was a reformist effort to respond to some of the workers' pressure, while still protecting private property and a qualified capitalism, thereby to prevent a mass defection to socialism.[3]

Just as this tradition responded to labor questions out of a characteristically Catholic framework, which was grounded in a conception of the natural law as directed toward the common good and was inclined toward conservatism, so too it handled the just war discussion. And just as later social encyclicals (from Pius XI's *Quadragesimo Anno* [1931] through John XXIII's *Mater et Magistra* [1961] and *Pacem in Terris* [1963], and Paul VI's *Populorum Progressio* [1967]) were to gradually expand the role of government in guaranteeing the mutual observation of rights and duties, and finally to enlarge the concern for the common good from the nation-state to the "world community" and "universal common good," so the teaching on war and peace has become gradually more cautious about championing the unfettered sovereignty of individual states and more interested in joining nations together in the common cause of peace under the leadership of a world government. With the refocusing of Catholic vision from the common good of the nation-state to the integrated good of interdependent states, the medieval legitimation of violence in terms of defending the political order from outside attack has been qualified. Building upon the Enlightenment's confidence in the dignity of the individual and the universal objectivity of reason, it has been more possible for both Protestant and Roman Catholic thinkers to see all cultures in terms of common humanity bound together by compassion as well as rational justice. The proclivity to view foreigners not only as outsiders, but as enemies to whom one does not apply the same requirements of justice, much less compassion or love, is converted in recent encyclicals into a view of all persons and groups as constituting one community of human persons.[4]

3. See John T. Pawlikowski, OSM, "Modern Catholic Teaching on the Economy: An Analysis and Evaluation," in Bruce Grelle and David A. Krueger, *Christianity and Capitalism* (Chicago: Center for the Scientific Study of Religion), 3–10; and David J. O'Brien, "A Century of Catholic Social Teaching: Contexts and Comments," in John A. Coleman, SJ, *One Hundred Years of Catholic Social Thought* (Maryknoll, N.Y.: Orbis, 1991), 13–24.

4. On this same point see Richard B. Miller, *Interpretations of Conflict* (Chicago: Univ. of Chicago Press, 1991), 64.

Bryan Hehir observes that the specific link between the just war tradition as formulated by the time of the seventeenth-century Spanish scholastics and its modern Catholic version is the teachings of Pope Pius XII in the 1940s and '50s;[5] John Courtney Murray analyzes the ways in which that tradition was specifically received and revised by Pius.[6] Like the social gospel writers and the Niebuhr brothers, Pius struggles with the new specter of nuclear war. He and subsequent popes decry the immense suffering and chaos that modern war brings in its wake, they sound increasingly clearer notes of caution and reserve about embarking on military solutions to political problems, or even defense against aggression. They also consider and eventually reinterpret the problem of the conscientious objector, moving gradually to the contemporary magisterium's recognition of pacifism as a valid path of Catholic Christian commitment. Two central problems for recent teaching have been what moral view to hold of deterrence, and how to reconcile the legitimacy of the pacifist response with the approbation of even modern war when and if it can be said reasonably to further the common good.

Pius himself follows the tradition in forbidding wars of aggression but goes further in disallowing to individual states the right to resort to arms in order to vindicate wrongs or redress violations of legal rights.[7] Having declared as lawful a war of last resort "for effective defence and with the hope of a favourable outcome against unjust attack," however, Pius also warned that "a Catholic citizen cannot invoke his own conscience in order to refuse to serve and fulfil those duties the law imposes." There would be no right of conscientious objection against a war rightfully declared.[8]

Although Pius XII called for international conventions that would renounce research on and use of nuclear weapons as well as establish general arms control,[9] John Courtney Murray interprets him as never having rejected in unqualified terms the actual use of nuclear weapons as "somehow in principle, evil."[10] Murray, while not taking issue with the pope, refers to the bombing of Hiroshima and Nagasaki as "atrocities" that presumably did not meet the criteria of proportionality and last resort (he does not mention discrimination as a principle applicable to the moral analysis of atomic war). He also calls the demand for the unconditional surrender of the foe a violation of right

5. Bryan Hehir, "The Just-War Ethic and Catholic Theology: Dynamics of Change and Continuity," in *War or Peace?,* ed. Thomas A. Shannon (Maryknoll, N.Y.: Orbis, 1982), 15–39.

6. Murray, "Theology and Modern War," 74–83.

7. See ibid., 75.

8. Pius XII, Christmas Radio Message, December 23, 1956, in *Peace and Disarmament: Documents of the World Council of Churches and the Roman Catholic Church,* presented by the Commission of the Churches on International Affairs and the Pontifical Commission "Justitia et Pax" (1982: n.p.), 137. The address is also included in *Pattern for Peace: Catholic Statements on International Order,* ed. Harry W. Flannery (Westminster Md.: Newman Press, 1962), text cited at p. 283.

9. "Nuclear Weapons and Armament Control," Christmas Message, December 24, 1955, in *Pattern for Peace,* 271.

10. Murray, "Theology and Modern War," 79.

intention, and laments the fact that no Catholic voices during the war brought just war theory to bear on such policies.

During the pontificates of John XXIII, Paul VI, and John Paul II, the visibility of pacifism within Catholicism has grown, and skepticism about any moral use of nuclear weapons has increased virtually to the point of repudiation.[11] John's *Pacem in Terris* (1963) faults the arms race for the climate of fear it produces, the mistrust among nations it perpetuates, and the grave economic injustices it wreaks on less developed nations. Because of "the terrible destructive force of modern arms, . . . it is hardly possible to imagine that in the atomic era war could be used as an instrument of justice."[12] "Justice, then, right reason and humanity urgently demand that the arms race should cease," that nuclear stockpiles should be dismantled through progressive disarmament, and that nuclear weapons eventually should be banned. The "true and solid peace of nations" can rest "on mutual trust alone," not on equality in war-making capacity, nor on fear.[13]

The explicit acceptance of pacifism as a Catholic alternative, however, had to await the Second Vatican Council. Laws should make "humane provisions for the case of those who refuse to bear arms, provided however that they accept some other form of service to the human community."[14] The same document moves unequivocally to exclude at least nuclear attacks on civilians, even while retaining a right to war in general. "Any act of war aimed indiscriminately at the destruction of entire cities or of extensive areas along with their population is a crime against God and man himself. It merits unequivocal and unhesitating condemnation."[15] The Council also calls for progressive disarmament under the supervision of an international authority with "effective power" to safeguard peace, but, like John, exhibits a Catholic optimism about human nature in avowing that true peace "must be born of mutual trust among nations."[16]

What about deterrence as an interim measure? Clearly, the evolving Catholic teaching tradition sees mutual lethal threat as an inadequate solution to the prospect of war. Nations are called to form a world community founded on justice and aiming beyond that to compassion and fellowship. Addressing the United Nations, Paul VI implored,

11. Hehir traces this development through the writings of these popes and the documents of Vatican II, in "The Just-War Ethic," 20–29.

12. *Pacem in Terris,* no. 127, in *Seven Great Encyclicals,* ed. William J. Gibbons, SJ (New York: Paulist Press, 1963), 127.

13. Ibid., nos. 112 and 113, respectively, at pp. 312 and 313.

14. *Pastoral Constitution on the Church in the Modern World,* no. 79, in *The Documents of Vatican II,* ed. Walter M. Abbott, SJ (New York: America Press, 1965), 292.

15. Ibid., no. 80, p. 294. Yet some Catholic theologians have continued to argue that prospective uses of nuclear weapons must be evaluated individually and cannot be ruled out in principle without specific information about their limitation or lack thereof. See John Langan, SJ, "The American Hierarchy and Nuclear Weapons," *Theological Studies* 43 (1982).

16. *Pastoral Constitution,* no. 82, 295–96.

> If you want to be brothers, let the weapons fall from your hands. You cannot love with weapons in your hands. Long before they mete out death and destruction, those terrible arms supplied by modern science foment bad feelings and cause nightmares, distrust, and dark designs. They call for enormous expenditures and hold up projects of human solidarity and great usefulness.[17]

Characteristically for his tradition, Pope Paul does not rest his case on specifically religious warrants and conversion experience. His arguments aim at broad cross-cultural agreement. Yet for him, an accurate depiction of the human situation does not rest on so-called political realism, with its pessimism about human potential. He has enough confidence in human nature, and even in the universally healing effects of the one redemption in Christ, to urge recognition of common humanity, generosity, solidarity, and brotherly love. But even though his appeal is global in thrust, it is clear that its persuasive power has remained limited. In the 1980s, the moral problem of continued nuclear deterrence as an interim means of averting open conflict was key in the just war discussion.

This problem is one the Vatican has never clearly resolved. As we saw in chapter 1, the U.S. bishops in the 1980s made an uneasy truce with mutual nuclear threat, while they virtually ruled out any actual use of the weapons. The central ambiguity in their pastoral letter, an ambiguity shared by other Catholic versions of moral toleration of deterrence, is created by the fact that deterrence loses effectiveness to the extent that use of its constitutive weapons capacity is disavowed. Or, conversely, deterrence policy is premised on an at least implicit threat to do that which it seeks to avoid as an irreducibly immoral violation of the immunity of noncombatants from direct attack.

David Hollenbach reaches three conclusions at the end of his study of the matter: (1) both pacifist and just war approaches should be represented within the church in order to serve the pursuit of both peace and justice; (2) no use of nuclear weapons is justified in any circumstances presently envisioned, and hence no planning for their actual use is justified; and (3) concrete deterrence policies must be evaluated individually in light of their effect on the balance of power that staves off war and on the prospects of eventual disarmament.[18] The paradox of the ostensibly moral threat to do the immoral is acknowledged rather than resolved. Hollenbach articulates fairly the prevailing Catholic consensus on the matter up through the end of the 1980s.[19]

17. Paul VI, Address to the General Assembly of the United Nations, October 4, 1965, no. 23, in *The Gospel of Peace and Justice: Catholic Social Teaching since Pope John,* ed. Joseph Gremillion (Maryknoll, N.Y.: Orbis, 1976), 384.

18. David Hollenbach, SJ, *Nuclear Ethics: A Christian Moral Argument* (New York: Paulist Press, 1983), 86.

19. For a view that deterrence is so morally bound to the immoral threat that it is an immoral policy, see Germaine Grisez, *Life and Death with Liberty and Justice for All: A Contribution to the Euthanasia Debate* (Notre Dame, Ind.: Univ. of Notre Dame Press, 1979). For a view more sympathetic to U.S. policy than Hollenbach's, see William V. O'Brien, "The Failure of Deterrence and the Conduct of War," in *The Nuclear Dilemma and the Just War Tradition,* ed. William V. O'Brien and John Langan, SJ (Lexington, Mass.: D. C. Heath and Company, 1986), 152–97.

John Langan comments aptly that Catholic teaching (*Gaudium et Spes*) replicates a "standard pattern of reactions" to the nuclear predicament: an acknowledgment of the right to defense along with warnings of the unconscionable horrors of modern war, and finally "a final uneasy acceptance of deterrence," making for "a kind of averting of the eyes from what is being endorsed."[20] More sympathetically noting the ambiguities in Catholic teaching, as embodied in the U.S. bishops' pastoral, Hollenbach credits the authors as "good practitioners of Augustinian moral theory," who at least seek to "redeem a broken polis" by seizing the opportunities to augment peace, order, and justice that history may offer at the moment.[21] The '90s, of course, have brought dramatic changes both in East-West relations and in the nuclear scenario. The question of deterrence as it was posed during the decades of U.S.-Soviet tension is being rephrased, although the issue of the nuclear threat worldwide has hardly disappeared.

The pacifist challenge is met uneasily within this recent Catholic just war tradition. While the bishops' peace pastoral welcomes pacifism as a counterpoint to just war thinking, Hollenbach, Bryan Hehir and Kenneth Himes raise the question of the consistency of the two attitudes toward war and peace.[22] Although he is essentially in agreement with the bishops, Hollenbach warns, "this way of thinking has a tone and a lack of analytic rigor that results from refusing to face the conflicts that can and often do exist between justice and peace."[23] An important factor in properly defining the question is understanding what is meant by pacifism. Are both its critics and its nonpacifist allies understanding it appropriately when they juxtapose it to the just war solution?

As Hehir sees it, in pacifism, the presumption against war of the just war tradition becomes an absolute rule rather than a prima facie duty. Against the possible conversion of the Catholic tradition to this absolute, he objects that, even in *The Pastoral Constitution on the Church in the Modern World*, the document defending conscientious objection, "Catholic moral theology retained the conviction that war is possible, may be necessary in the name of justice, and, if necessary, must be a rule-governed activity pursued within a fabric of moral restraints."[24] Just war thinking and pacifist thinking are two essentially different responses to the prospect of violent force. And, because "moral positions must be submitted to the tests of consistency and coherence,"

20. John Langan, SJ, "Between Religion and Politics: The Morality of Deterrence," in *The Nuclear Dilemma,* 138.

21. David Hollenbach, SJ, "Ethics in Distress: Can There Be Just Wars in the Nuclear Age?", in *The Nuclear Dilemma,* 27.

22. From the pacifist side, Stanley Hauerwas raises a similar question about the viability of an authentic pluralism in church teaching (*Against the Nations: War and Survival in a Liberal Society* [Minneapolis: Winston Press, 1985], 188–92).

23. David Hollenbach, SJ, "The Role of the Churches in the American Search for Peace," in *The American Search for Peace: Moral Reasoning, Religious Hope, and National Security,* ed. George Weigel and John P. Langan, SJ (Washington, D.C.: Georgetown Univ. Press, 1991), 249.

24. Hehir, "The Just War Ethic," 23.

he is led to ask, "In the new state of the question, do we have moral complexity or simply contradiction in the two positions?"[25]

Picking up where Hehir left off, Himes explicitly inquires whether the allowance made by *The Challenge of Peace*[26] for both pacifism and just war as individual vocational choices (and even as characterizing subcultures within the one religious community) can be translated into a coherent overarching theory. Himes, like Hehir, doubts it. He also observes that for pacifism, the presumption against war "makes war always and everywhere illegitimate," rather than simply placing a burden of proof on those who would override the presumption.[27] Merely having roots in the Catholic tradition, as many conflicting positions do, is no guarantee of complementarity. Although he grants to the just war position the stronger support of the church, Himes concludes that there is genuine moral ambiguity in the problem of war, and suggests that allowing pluralism on the matter in theory as well as in fact may be the most adequate present alternative.

Just war theorists often tend to grapple with pacifism by posing it as a matter of an absolute rule against violence. To phrase the matter in this way is congenial to the rule-exception premises of the just war theory itself, but is such a rule-based approach the surest or the most universal substructure of pacifism? The absolute rule version of pacifism may often be assumed by critiques of it in the Roman Catholic tradition and elsewhere—and this assumption about it may also underlie its inclusion as an uneasily aligned option within the natural law strand of just war thinking.

It is questionable, however, both whether pacifism as sanctioned and appropriated by recent magisterial teaching is essentially different in its premises and method of argument than just war theory; and whether pacifism as described and quasi-appropriated by proponents of the latter theory really gets to the heart of the ancient pacifist tradition in Christianity.

Building on a distinction used by John Courtney Murray,[28] the pacifism of *Pacem in Terris* and onward is relative rather than absolute pacifism; it disallows morally the option of war, not because killing is in principle always wrong, but because nuclear war constitutes insufficiently limitable killing. Moreover, as a sort of supporting argument, the war experiences of this century have taught us that violence and terror cannot build truly stable and humane international relationships. This variety of Roman Catholic pacifism is an evolution out of and even past just war theory, but it is still based on an assessment of justice in relation to the common good, and is articulated in terms of criteria or rules. It finds its coherence with the just war tradition

25. Ibid., 24

26. ¶121. See chap. 1, note 3, above.

27. Kenneth R. Himes, "Pacifism and the Just War Tradition," in *One Hundred Years of Catholic Social Thought*, 340.

28. John Courtney Murray, SJ, *Morality and Modern Warfare* (New York: Council on Religion and International Affairs, 1959), 70.

as a statement of caution and skepticism about whether just war criteria can be met in the nuclear age, not of exclusion of violence as such from the life of a Christian.[29]

So, in the first place, the "no" to war of Roman Catholic social teaching is a negative answer to the question whether the criteria of the still-central just war tradition can be applied to war in the nuclear era and result in a permission. Pacifism in this mode still presupposes a natural law or justice-based approach to morality, and assumes that moral obligations can and should be best articulated in rules about permitted and excluded varieties of specific conduct.

In the second place, pacifism in general can hardly be tied definitively to this mode of moral reasoning. The formulation of an absolute rule is not necessarily the core concern of pacifism in its biblical, kingdom of God, and usually Protestant strand, nor in Roman Catholic strands that also make central the urgency of the kingdom present. In at least some historically important forms of the pacifist witness, religious conversion and life in Christ are the root of which the commitment to nonviolence is a branch, and not necessarily one that would readily rely on the formulation of absolute rule as a support. George Fox says neither, "Human life is an absolute value," nor "Christians hold as absolute the presumption against violence," but "We live by 'that life and power that take away the occasion of all wars.' "

Hehir and, especially, Himes give indications that they appreciate that the pacifist message may originate in a distinctive understanding of discipleship. Most to the point, Himes takes up the pastoral letter's allusion to the grounding of the dual option in the twofold character of the kingdom as both present and future.[30] The letter's authors hope to "reflect something of the broad nature of human experience of the kingdom."[31] After having set up the question in terms of absolute rules, Hehir in the end brings the question around to ecclesiological considerations, articulated in terms of Troeltsch's distinction between the church and the sect. Hehir respects the latter as a countercultural posture, but he is clearly more willing to defend the former as an expression of Christian social responsibility better interrelating faith and reason, grace and nature. And it is precisely what he takes to be the assumption of some Catholic pacifists (like Gordon Zahn) that pacifism might become a nonminority position even within Christianity that Hehir finds troubling and inconsistent with just war assumptions.[32]

29. This is not to say that all Roman Catholic pacifist individuals fit this just-war-derived model of relative pacifism. See Ronald G. Musto, *The Catholic Peace Tradition* (Maryknoll, N.Y.: Orbis, 1986), for a variety of examples of Catholic pacifism.

30. *Challenge of Peace*, ¶62.

31. Himes, "Pacifism and the Just War Tradition," 340.

32. Hehir, "The Just War Ethic," 33. See also an exchange that took place after this manuscript was substantially complete: J. Bryan Hehir, "Just War Theory in a Post-Cold War World," and Lisa Sowle Cahill, "Theological Contexts of Just War Theory and Pacifism: A Response to J. Bryan Hehir," *Journal of Religious Ethics* 20 (1992). A major concern of Hehir is that current Catholic (papal) teaching is veering anomolously close to absolute pacifism.

The real potential for inconsistency of pacifism with just war tradition lies precisely in its distinctive view of the kingdom and of the role of the Christian community vis-à-vis the culture—not in the endorsement by the magisterium, universal or local, of a possible pacifist outcome of just war-based analysis. But it is only incompletely appreciated by just war thinkers, particularly within Catholicism, that genuine biblical pacifism does not revolve around the absolutization of any human values or rules, but around a converted life in Christ that subsumes and often changes every "natural" pattern of behavior. The incoherence of pacifism and just war thinking lies, perhaps not exclusively but certainly most characteristically, in their disagreement about how present and accessible in human life the kingdom, by the grace of Christ, really is.

## ROMAN CATHOLIC PACIFISTS

The writings of two notable Catholics, Dorothy Day and Thomas Merton, illustrate a more deeply pacifist turn within Roman Catholicism, a turn that has been amply followed out by Gordon Zahn, James Douglass, and Phillip Berrigan. All of these have in common with much Protestant pacifist thought a presentation of nonviolence as part of a total life of discipleship, growing out of deep religious commitment and community rather than out of an ethical analysis of values and norms. The commitment to nonviolence may indeed reach the level of a "nonnegotiable," as it did with Day. When the commitment is challenged in relation to a specific conflict of loyalties, it may be reaffirmed in language closely resembling that of exceptionless moral rules. It is important to note, however, that the unwavering stand is not primarily a rule-governed activity, but a conversion governed one. The spiritual dimension of pacifism is particularly evident in Merton's quasi-mystical identification of all human beings as part of one redeemed reality, a unity that he expresses, typically enough for a Catholic, in terms of compassion for fellow humanity.

### *Dorothy Day (1897–1980)*

Catholic pacifists are highly likely to stress common humanity as a source of nonviolent attitudes, consistent with their tradition of reason and natural law. Yet they also see Jesus' teaching as central, often alluding to the Sermon on the Mount and to the kingdom he inaugurated. The life and work of Dorothy Day are, in fact, centered around compassionate identification with outcasts and "failures" on society's fringes. Founder, with the French peasant and activist Peter Maurin, of the Catholic Worker movement, Day embodied many of the ideals of American social radicalism of the first half of the twentieth century.

The daughter of a newspaper sportswriter, she and her three siblings grew up in New York, San Francisco, and Chicago. Although the Day family occasionally faced financial difficulties, it generally provided a loving and protective middle-class environment, where reading of literary classics and philosophy was encouraged. From childhood, Dorothy loved books, determined to become a writer, and was sensitive to the fact that many neighborhood families were considerably less comfortable than hers. Just before World War I, she ended two years of study at the University of Illinois and went to New York City. There, her incipient commitment to social action against poverty was galvanized by contact with a young and countercultural intellectual community centered in Greenwich Village. Describing this milieu, Mel Piehl writes of a "new radicalism" that rejected the bourgeois, took an experiential approach to life and art, identified with the working classes and immigrants, and was opposed to corporate capitalism.[33] Day found a practically oriented expression for her talents and her ideals in journalism, writing for papers with a socialist, activist, and radical bent. Yet she spent her young adulthood in a prolonged anguish of personal searching. For many years, direction and identity seemed to elude her. Unstable romantic liaisons, including an abortion and a brief marriage, culminated in her relationship with Forster Batterham, an avowed socialist and atheist, with whom she nonetheless experienced a deep bond. After the birth of their daughter, Tamar, Day finally took the step of seeking baptism for her child and herself; her religious conversion proved too great an affront to Batterham's own dearly held convictions, and the relationship ended traumatically for both.

For the remainder of her long life, Day devoted her considerable energies to marking practical paths in which Catholicism could develop a social critique and better the situation of the underclass. As a convert she was largely unfamiliar with papal social teaching. Responding to the same social issues that prompted the Protestant social gospel, Day and her colleagues cultivated a traditional Catholic piety—including, for instance, Marian devotions—in service of leftist ideals and solutions. A primary vehicle for these programs was *The Catholic Worker*, a paper which she and Maurin began in 1933. It advocated social change by publishing stories on, for example, migrant workers, labor organization, schools, housing, food relief, child care, race relations, militarism, and the draft. Day and Maurin founded soup kitchens called Houses of Hospitality to serve the unemployed and established a series of farming communes in the hope that they could unite religiously commited co-workers in communities of mutual love, worship, and labor and offer some solution to the crises of urban life for the disadvantaged guests whom they would welcome. Since the farms never turned away would-be residents, they never succeeded in achieving economic viability.

Peter Maurin brought the influence of European Catholicism and its intellectual traditions into the Catholic Worker movement, and his ideas, though often abstractly expressed, motivated much of its work. Maurin held a special

33. Mel Piehl, *Breaking Bread: The Catholic Worker and the Origin of Catholic Radicalism in America* (Philadelphia: Temple Univ. Press, 1982), 9.

appeal for Day, not so much for his theoretical interests, but because she saw in him a gospel directness and purity of purpose. Impractical, tempermental, and even autocratic though he may have been, his love of the poor and hatred of violence had a sincere and obvious religious foundation. It was typical of Day in turn, who admitted that she had little talent for rigorous intellectual analysis, that she found her inspiration in a person rather than in a body of writings or set of ideas. Maurin, raised in a Catholic family of twenty-three children, had joined the Saint Jean-Baptiste de la Salle brotherhood. The La Salle brothers renounced the distinction of the priesthood and other recognitions within the church, devoting themselves to educating the children of the poor. Maurin also became engaged with the Sillon movement, a Catholic spiritual renewal effort heeding *Rerum Novarum*'s call for social justice and the sharing of wealth with the poor. It was committed to pacifism on the strength of Jesus' example and message; Maurin left his native country for Canada rather than comply with the French draft.[34] Capturing the way in which the presence and yet absence of redeemed life in Christian community contributed to Maurin's personal energy and magnetism, Day said later of him that he was "lonely . . . in the sense that he missed being near God all the time. But he had a vision of God, and so he wasn't really lonely at all. He was—I think it is true of many of us—lonely only because of what he saw, saw ahead, the moment of that meeting, that reconciliation between the human world and the divine one."[35]

In recounting her impressions of Maurin and her respect for his leadership, in her explanations of her conversion and in her own evocations of the Catholic Worker mission, Day drives home her personal sense of the nearness of the gospel and of Catholicism as a life of perfection in service of others to which all are called. Though she was conservative in theological and moral outlook, inclined to accept Catholic teaching unquestioningly, she had little use for the worldliness and clericalism of the institutional church. In her autobiography, *The Long Loneliness*, she wryly quotes a remark that "the Church is the Cross on which Christ was crucified."[36]

In writing of Maurin's death, Day reveals her vision of him as a truly humble man, "stripped" of the world and of the "old man," one who "was impersonal in his love in that he loved all, saw all others around him as God saw them, saw Christ in them."[37] For Maurin, to love God with one's whole heart, mind, and strength, and to express that love by means of "social responsibility in a chaotic world," was "not just a counsel."[38] Pacifique Roy, a Josephite priest

34. Robert Coles, *Dorothy Day: A Radical Devotion* (Reading, Mass.: Addison-Wesley, 1987), 12.

35. As interviewed by Coles, *Dorothy Day,* 63.

36. *The Long Loneliness: The Autobiography of Dorothy Day* (New York: Harper & Row, 1981; originally published 1952), 150.

37. Ibid., 274.

38. Ibid., 281.

who visited a Catholic Worker house in New York, similarly captivated Day. Roy's preaching of the Sermon on the Mount held his listeners "spellbound," as he told them "to aim at perfection," to "be guided by the folly of the Cross," and as he showed them that they "were like workers for a Utopia already living in their Utopia."[39]

Day quotes the Sermon at length to explain the Catholic Worker policy of never evicting troublemaking guests. Workers were "trying to follow the dear Lord's teachings," including the sayings "Give to him that asks of you and from him that would borrow, turn not away," and "love your enemies, do good to them that hate you. . . ."[40] In this, too, they followed Maurin's example, according to Day, for "he took the Gospel counsel literally," and would give away his own coat to the needy, then take another pauper to a friend to beg an additional one.[41]

A cutting instance of gospel radicalism in Day's life was the separation from Batterham in order to follow what she regarded as the unyielding demand of God. "To become a Catholic meant for me to give up a mate with whom I was much in love. It got to the point where it was the simple question of whether I chose God or man."[42] Although she took great solace in her love for her infant daughter, she still compares her desertion of her "married" life with Batterham to Abraham's sacrifice of Isaac. "You do these things blindly," she declares, "not because it is your natural inclination—you are going against nature when you do them—but because you wish to live in conformity with the will of God." She then adds, "Love is a commandment. . . . If we love God with our whole hearts, how much heart have we left? . . . We must live this life now. Death changes nothing. If we do not learn to enjoy God now we never will. If we do not learn to praise and thank Him and rejoice in Him now, we never will."[43]

Day was likewise singleminded in her rejection of any form of violence, and especially of war. She wrote in 1952, "We had been pacifist in class war, race war, in the Ethiopian war, in the Spanish Civil War, all through World War II, as we are now during the Korean War. We had spoken in terms of the Sermon on the Mount.[44] To the often-heard query as to what she would do to protect a loved one from harm, she replied that an "armed maniac" might be restrained but not killed, for "perfect love casts out fear and love overcomes hatred. All this sounds trite but experience is not trite."[45] Against taking sides in the Spanish Civil War, Day had maintained, "Our side should be a side that follows the teachings of Jesus. We are Christians, which means

39. Ibid., 246–47; cf. 251.

40. Ibid., 261.

41. Ibid., 179.

42. Ibid., 140; cf. 145: "I did not want to give up human love when it was at its dearest and tenderest."

43. Ibid., 256–7, cf. 236.

44. Ibid., 264.

45. Ibid., 270.

we take our Lord's words and His example as the most important message in the entire world."[46]

Although her own religious language on the subject tends to be biblical and even eschatological, Day also cites at considerable length the writing of Robert Ludlow, an editor of *The Catholic Worker,* as the theory behind the movement's pacifism. The pacifist position as Ludlow clarifies it has a strong affinity with the Catholic and Erasmian appeal to reason and humanity, as confirmed by the revelation in Christ and the tradition of the early church. Not only are nonviolent resolutions always "more reasonable" than violent ones, and thus more in accord with human nature, but also, "The increasing horror and immorality of modern war which, because of the means used, necessitate the slaying of the innocent, should serve to recall this latent pacifist tradition so that the Sermon on the Mount will be seen to confirm and sanction non-violent procedure which is already sanctioned by reason.'"[47]

Day's insistence that *The Catholic Worker* stick to a pacifist stance in the face of American patriotism before and during the Second World War caused a sizable rift in the movement itself, reducing the financial support on which it depended, and even prompting the closing of some of the Houses of Hospitality in which the leadership refused to yield. Mel Piehl reports that in "1939 and 1940 the thirty or so Worker Houses were torn by debate over pacifism and the draft, specifically over the radical antiwar propaganda appearing in the New York *Catholic Worker.*" Day's 1940 open letter to all Catholic Workers had a dramatic and divisive impact, leading some within the movement to accuse her of authoritarianism in attempting to close discussion and impose her viewpoint on all. Although she denied that she required orthodoxy on the subject, she persisted in her plan to distribute the paper with her letter. "By the end of 1942 only sixteen Houses remained in operation. By January 1945, just ten were left."[48]

Even though from this point on pacifism was a clear mark of the movement, as Piehl notes, neither Day nor other writers who wrote in support of her position made pacifism preeminent among the social concerns of the movement; "pacifism was no more the whole of the 'Catholic worker' idea than soup lines or unionization had been in the thirties."[49] Day herself suggested later that the practice of nonviolence grew integrally out of the movement's commitment to try to respond as Jesus would to the immediate situation. It was hardly a matter of moral absolutes, which, once abstractly justified and stated, exerted an extrinsic yet adamantine claim on particular decisions. "We haven't figured out what we should do down to the punctuation marks. In fact, we haven't written a lot of the sentences. We are responding to a life, to Jesus and how He chose to live; we believe that choice says something,

46. As interviewed by Coles, *Dorothy Day,* 79.
47. As quoted in Day, *The Long Loneliness,* 269–70.
48. Piehl, *Breaking Bread,* 197.
49. Ibid., 198.

even now, to us who live so many centuries later . . . it is in our everyday lives that God judges us, not in the positions we take on issues."[50] For Dorothy Day, the Christian life is found in a community of love whose essence is service of the poor and needy. It may require personal sacrifice, even of one's most dearly held bonds. Yet it is an *imitatio Christi* in which humanity's own deepest fulfillment is found.

### *Thomas Merton (1915–68)*

Thomas Merton was, like Day, converted to Catholicism in young adulthood, but he gave his religiosity the ostensibly opposite expression of monastic withdrawal from the world into a Trappist monastery. Born in France of parents from America and New Zealand, Merton spent his childhood and youth in a perpetually nomadic existence.[51] His parents were artists who met while studying in Paris and later returned to New York state to experiment with self-reliant labor (farming) complemented by aesthetic and spiritual expression (painting). Ruth Merton died of stomach cancer when Thomas was six; tragically, his father too was to die early, in 1931 after a two-year battle with a brain tumor. Although the Merton family had not been particularly religious, Owen Merton had been a pacifist in World War I, and had an inchoate religious sensibility expressed through his art rather than through organized religion. His illness may have deepened and focused his religious faith, or so his son was later to remember.

Thomas Merton attended Cambridge and Columbia universities. He left the former institution after one year, having managed a satisfactory academic performance, but having also spent a considerable amount of his energy in what he and his friends were later to agree was debauchery. The year's nadir and conclusion was the birth of Merton's illegitimate son to a girl of "lower class," with whose family Merton's guardian settled a lawsuit out of court. Merton looked back on this episode (and other relationships with women) with a good deal of remorse; the son and his mother died in air raids in London during World War II.

It was after entering graduate studies in English that Merton became seriously interested in Catholicism, studying Aquinas and Maritain for his thesis and reading Hopkins and Joyce. He was baptized in 1938, and worked for a time at Friendship House in Harlem. Its founder, Baroness Catherine de Hueck, was a Russian refugee inspired by the Catholic Worker movement. Living in working-class poverty, she endeavored to serve the impoverished black population. Merton, fearing that the war and the draft would cut off any opportunity to follow the vocation to which he was increasingly attracted,

50. As interviewed by Coles, *Dorothy Day,* 101.

51. This biographical sketch of Merton is primarily dependent on Monica Furlong, *Merton: A Biography* (San Francisco: Harper and Row, 1980).

finally determined to enter Gethsemani Abbey in Kentucky shortly after the Japanese bombed Pearl Harbor.

Life at Gethsemani was austere but not without camaraderie and humor for Merton, despite an ongoing personality conflict with his abbot. Merton chafed under the monastery's authority, demands, and controls, many of which not only seemed pointless but interfered with the solitude necessary for contemplation and with his ever-prolific writing. Merton was encouraged to write, producing his phenomenally successful autobiography in 1948,[52] but was often censored by his superiors, particularly to avoid political controversy. For many years he served as novice master. The role's demands for teaching and spiritual direction were burdensome to Merton, despite his rapport and popularity with the young monks.

Eventually, in the early '60s, Merton was permitted to move for periods of time to a hermitage (originally a meeting center) in the woods on monastery property, and by the end of his life that modest cinder-block building was his home. His isolation was broken by his ceaseless correspondence and by a stream of international visitors. In 1968, with a change of superiors and the advent of Vatican II, Merton was permitted to undertake a final pilgrimage: a tour of Asia, during which he delivered a paper in Calcutta and pursued his interest in Asian religions, above all by meeting with the Dalai Lama in Tibet. While attending a conference on monastic renewal in Bangkok in December 1968, he died in his guest room, accidentally electrocuted at age 53.

Merton's interests had shifted during his years of monastic life. At first more concerned with spirituality and a transcendence of worldly concerns, Merton's interest in social issues grew as the cultural turbulence of the late 1950s and 1960s penetrated the abbey. He began to read contemporary social commentary and politics, works of literature, philosophy, and psychology, and to receive and to correspond with prominent Catholic figures, including Day.

A major focus of his writings in the 1960s was the problem of peace in a nuclear age. Much more familiar than Day with the intellectual traditions backing Catholic social teaching, Merton was impressed by the hegemony of the just war tradition and was reluctant to exclude completely the use of violence to repel injustice. His ambivalence is expressed in his statement; "If a pacifist is one who believes that all war is always morally wrong and always has been wrong, then I am not a pacifist. Nevertheless I see war as an avoidable tragedy."[53] Merton was aware not only of the horrors of Auschwitz, but also of the liberation theology beginning to arise out of the faith of the poor in Latin America, a theology that had to deal at least indirectly with the prospect

52. Thomas Merton, *The Seven Storey Mountain* (New York: Harcourt Brace, 1948).

53. Thomas Merton, "Peace and Protest," in Thomas Merton, *The Nonviolent Alternative,* rev. ed. of *Thomas Merton on Peace,* ed. Gordon C. Zahn (New York: Farrar, Straus, Giroux, 1980; originally published 1971), 67.

"destroys communion." On nuclear war specifically, Merton avoided the law-based approach. He thinks it beside the point to proclaim "absolutely and infallibly" that it would be a mortal sin to hold an opinion in favor of the nuclear bomb's use. "There is no special point in condemning one weapon in order to give casuistical minds an opportunity to prove their skill in evasion by coming up with another, 'licit' way of attaining the same destructive end."[64]

At one point, Merton seemed to accept the adequacy historically of Augustine's justification of war as an act of love, on the grounds that war in the Constantinian era could not have been avoided, but only moderated by love's influence.[65] However, the eventually developed set of refined criteria for adjudicating just cause and means in war yielded an illusory sense of moral precision and righteousness, and led to egregious offenses. Merton referred to Augustine also as "the remote forefather of the Crusades and the Inquisition."[66]

In 1962, Merton wrote to the Catholic Worker community in New York that the central problem for the church's approach to peace is "spiritual renewal." The renewal required is not otherworldly, but must "be expressed in the historical context." Historical crises must be understood spiritually, but they must also be evaluated "in terms of man's growth and the advancement of truth in man's world: in other words, the establishment of the 'kingdom of God.' "[67]

The renewal of the human attitude to neighbor and enemy, resulting in the realization of the kingdom, is in an important way dependent on a principle that Merton claimed to find in both Christianity and Buddhism. That grounding principle is "a true compassion for others," a "sincere intention of seeing others as ourselves and treating others as we would want to be treated ourselves." Violence, indeed, depends on the premise that the enemy is not only different, but evil and deserving of destruction. "There must be a new force, the power of love, the power of understanding and human compassion, the strength of selflessness and cooperation, and the creative dynamism of *the will to live and to build, and the will to forgive. The will for reconciliation.*"[68] The capacity to love is, for Merton, the most distinctive quality of humanity, and it is grounded in our created nature as "image of God." But this power is also linked to the Sermon on the Mount, and thereby to the specifically Christian vocation to redeem the world's brokenness in very practical terms, a vocation that Merton assumes the kingdom to imply.[69]

64. Thomas Merton, "Peace: A Religious Responsibility," in *Nonviolent Alternative,* 121.

65. Merton, *Seeds of Destruction,* 146.

66. Ibid., 147. See Ronald E. Powaski, *Thomas Merton on Nuclear Weapons* (Chicago: Loyola Univ. Press, 1988), 1–18, for an account of Merton's view of the just war tradition.

67. A letter of April 9, 1962, as quoted by James H. Forest, "Thomas Merton's Struggle with Peacemaking," in *Thomas Merton: Prophet in the Belly of a Paradox,* ed. Gerald Twomey (New York: Paulist Press, 1978).

68. Thomas Merton, "Preface to Vietnamese Translation of No Man Is an Island," in *Nonviolent Alternative,* 64–65.

69. Merton, *Disputed Questions,* 98–99.

It is characteristic of Day and Merton as Catholic pacifists that they have an eminent commitment to social change, and that they tend to see the pacifist response to conflict as confirming humanity's deepest values and truest rationality. But they also have a strong view of the presence of the kingdom of God that stands somewhat in tension with these Roman Catholic commitments. Day, for instance, knew from personal experience that to follow Christ and God's will can require one to surmount one's natural inclinations. Merton suggested that pacifism goes against the grain of what comes "naturally" to sinful humanity with its drive to objectify other persons.[70] Moreover, neither author is really rule-oriented, as most moral thinking in the recent Catholic tradition has been. Pacifism, not a typically Catholic stance, flows from conversion to Christ and response to neighbor, from personal relationships with an integral communal aspect.

## SOME PROTESTANT EXAMPLES

The emphases on community and on a realized eschatology are carried through and thematized even more explicitly in contemporary non-Catholic representatives. In authors drawing from the Reformation heritage, the vision of pacifism as humanity's true fulfillment is muted, if not absent; accentuated instead are obedience and fidelity to God's will revealed in Christ. If patient obedience in recognition of God's sovereign providence is emphasized, the hope of social change is remote, and in its stead is the symbol of the Cross. Those who challenge the powers and sinful structures of the world will suffer. Love and sacrifice are construed in terms of witness, rather than of social activism. Hence, pacifists such as John Howard Yoder and Stanley Hauerwas are not infrequently painted as sectarians advocating steadfast withdrawal from a corrupted world. While it is true that they see the Christian community in a real sense as having a vocation "against" the world, it is not wholly accurate to see them as retreating from the possibility of Christian social responsibility. It is more true to say that fidelity rather than effectiveness is the primary (not exclusive) criterion of the Christian life.

### *John Howard Yoder*

John Howard Yoder, a Mennonite, is undoubtedly the most renowned Christian pacifist currently writing in the United States. He brings an unusual expertise in biblical exegesis to his field of social ethics. He was born in Ohio, received a doctorate from the University of Basel, and served Mennonite relief efforts in France after World War II. In addition to having held professorships at the University of Notre Dame and the Associated Mennonite Biblical

70. Thomas Merton, "Blessed Are the Meek: The Christian Roots of Nonviolence," in *Nonviolent Alternative,* 217.

dissent some ideas that may well seem impracticable or unrealistic in the present circumstances of the wider community.[86] Yoder even provides a scheme of analogical languages by which one might take Christian values and translate them into rough equivalencies in the vocabulary of secular leadership and power.[87] *When War Is Unjust* is a more sustained effort to enter into dialogue with historical institutions and powers that can be called into greater conformity with justice, even if not with Christian ideals. The subtitle describes the project: *Being Honest in Just-War Thinking*.[88]

## *Stanley Hauerwas*

Stanley Hauerwas, an intellectual and onetime institutional colleague of John Howard Yoder, develops the communal emphasis in Christian social ethics in more philosophical terms. Hauerwas borrows additionally from Thomistic notions of virtue to contribute to a notion of character as providing consistency to moral agency within the historical particularity of Christian community. A controlling concept for Hauerwas is that of narrative, permitting him to interpret Christian history as a story founded in the life of Jesus, a narrative within which character is formed and discipleship community reengendered.

Hauerwas describes himself as a Southern Methodist (from Texas) who has taught and worshiped regularly with, and even been supported financially by, Roman Catholics; "who believes that the most nearly faithful form of Christian witness is best exemplified by the often unjustly ignored people called anabaptists or Mennonites."[89] This last was a conviction to which Hauerwas came primarily through his contact with Yoder when they both held faculty positions at Notre Dame. (Hauerwas at this writing holds a professorship at Duke University.) Among his intellectual models, Hauerwas also lists classical Christian authors such as Aristotle, Aquinas, Augustine, Calvin, Wesley, and Edwards; modern theologians, including the Niebuhrs, Barth, Ramsey, Yoder, and Gustafson; and the philosophers Plato, John Dewey, R. G. Collingwood, Ludwig Wittgenstein, and Alasdair Macintyre. Yet despite his use of these sources, Hauerwas criticizes theologians such as Rauschenbusch, the Niebuhrs, Ramsey, and Gustafston for having compromised the authentically theological nature of Christian ethics in order to gain greater currency in the public and policy arenas, "for having largely sought to show that the modes of argument and conclusions reached by philosophical ethicists are no different from those reached by ethicists with more explicit religious presuppositions."[90]

86. Yoder, *The Priestly Kingdom,* 96.

87. Ibid., 160–66.

88. John Howard Yoder, *When War Is Unjust: Being Honest in Just-War Thinking* (Minneapolis: Augsburg Publishing House, 1984).

89. Stanley Hauerwas, *A Community of Character: Toward a Constructive Christian Social Ethic* (Notre Dame, Ind.: Univ. of Notre Dame Press, 1981), 6.

90. Stanley Hauerwas, *Against the Nations: War and Survival in a Liberal Society* (Minneapolis: Winston Press, 1985), 39.

Although at many points, Hauerwas's position is substantively similar to that of Yoder,[91] it provides a useful additional illustration of the way community functions theoretically as well as practically in Christian pacifism. His work also demonstrates again how conversion and discipleship articulated within a concept of community can ground a social ethics with a mandate against violence, which, for all its specificity, does not assume the distinct form of a rule absolutizing the value of life as such.

Although Hauerwas does not develop biblical resources in the same exegetically detailed manner as Yoder, he sees biblical symbols, especially cross and kingdom, as foundational. When Christians regard Scripture as an authority, they "mean to indicate that they find there the traditions through which their community most nearly comes to knowing and being faithful to the truth." However, "Scripture is not meant to be a problem solver" in the dilemma-ethics sense. "It rather describes the process whereby the community we call the church is initiated by certain texts into . . . biblical traditions," with their particular patterns of argument and controversy (not settled moral codes).[92]

The sine qua non of the biblical traditions, of course, is the story of Jesus, who preached the kingdom and made it present, not only in his lifetime. The kingdom is present in Jesus' community to the extent that that community is true to his story, "a story which gives us the means to live without fear of one another." Jesus' story *is* in fact a social ethic, because of the sort of community that it creates.[93] Hauerwas, like other pacifists, begins from the premise that Jesus does not merely preach "impossible ethical ideals," but "actually proclaims and embodies a way of life that God has made present here and now," a life of "forgiveness and peace."[94]

Although Christians may certainly be committed to making nations more just, they harbor a deep distrust of violence as a means by which to do so. However, Christians aim to overcome the disunity created by nations, cultural systems, and other limited imperialistic commitments. "As Christians we are committed to the view that justice is possible between peoples because trust is finally a deeper reality in our lives than distrust." Christian hope is not "an unrealistic, idealistic, or utopian strategy," but a confidence that the world is ultimately under divine, not human, rule.[95]

The Christian fights injustice, but not with violent means—"any resort to violence betrays one's relation to God."[96] As for Yoder, faithfulness is prized

91. For an early critique of Yoder by Hauerwas, see "The Nonresistant Church: The Theological Ethics of John Howard Yoder," in *Community of Character,* 197–221. The references are to essays from the 1960s, in which a latent dualism between faith and justice was more pronounced than in later writings.

92. Hauerwas, *Community of Character,* 63.

93. Ibid., 37.

94. Stanley Hauerwas, *The Peaceable Kingdom: A Primer in Christian Ethics* (Notre Dame, Ind.: Univ. of Notre Dame Press, 1983), 83, 85.

95. Hauerwas, *Community of Character,* 119.

96. Hauerwas, *Against the Nations: War and Survival in a Liberal Society* (Minneapolis: Winston Press, 1985), 135.

on issues of inclusivity, solidarity, equality, compassion, forgiveness, and mercy.

The concluding reflections of the final chapter will include an assessment of the grounds of just war thinking itself, especially in relation to the Christian context in which it has been refined. It is important to confront the relative advantages and inconsistencies, from a Christian point of view, of accepting war as an offshoot of the love command or as a form of natural justice.

# 11 THE FRAGILITY OF THE GOSPEL

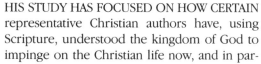

## *Concluding Reflections*

THIS STUDY HAS FOCUSED ON HOW CERTAIN representative Christian authors have, using Scripture, understood the kingdom of God to impinge on the Christian life now, and in particular how they deal with what they agree with virtual unanimity to be the ideal of peace and nonviolence presented in the words and deeds of Jesus. Many authors, especially (but not exclusively) those writing after modern historical research encouraged a renewal of interest in early Christian eschatology, organize their views about nonviolence, killing, and social responsibility specifically around the biblical image of the kingdom of God. "Kingdom" is an eschatological symbol that combines both a present potential to show forth God's own mercy and righteousness, and an expectation that it is only through a decisive divine intervention in the future eschaton or end time that kingdom life will be fully realized.

The Sermon on the Mount of the Gospel of Matthew (chaps. 5–7) has served as a moral compass for both pacifist and just war thinkers. Most authors who justify killing and war do not take quick resort to the divinely commanded battles of the Old Testament of Christianity. Instead, they press the question of how the New Testament ideal of love both of needy neighbors and of the enemy (Matt 5:38-48) is to be applied in history, given conflicting duties to the guilty, the innocent, and the political order.

Chapter 1 introduced these issues by way of two recent pastoral letters on war, peace, and nuclear deterrence. Chapter 2 reviewed recent scholarly work on the New Testament significance of the kingdom symbol. The work of several writers on the Bible and ethics, such as Norman Perrin, G. R. Beasley-Murray, Wolfgang Schrage, and Richard Hiers, together suggests that in its New Testament context, the symbol "kingdom of God" implies a transformed life that is initiated even now through Jesus as the Christ. Moreover, even if the kingdom is ultimately transcendent of history, its future dimension must

noted by Christian ethicists, Martha Nussbaum puts forward a thesis about "the fragility of goodness" with reference to classical Greek philosophy and drama.[4] Moral goodness is like a tender plant requiring the proper conditions for its nourishment, and the availability of the right environment is in no small part due to chance. Moral virtue is not, as on the Platonic model, equally available to all through transcendence of the shadowy world of history. Aristotle was more right when he portrayed goodness as a matter of practice and decided that the attainment of virtue and of friendship required a certain number of preconditions, among them education, leisure, the polis, and even a certain race, sex, and class. So with the attainment of the gospel. Whether Christians have truly heard the gospel, seen the kingdom, and faithfully embodied it in practice has been in no small part dependent on the opportunities and temptations offered by their circumstances. In particular, Christians need vital communities of faith and life that can nourish personal conversion and social commitment; their eyes must also be opened to the nearness of the kingdom, to its urgency and vitality.

Appreciation of eschatological nearness has tended to flourish under persecution, as with the early church and the Reformation radicals; and when certain forces or currents of thought combine to revitalize the accustomed phrases of the Bible so that they are seen in a wholly new light and with an unaccustomed urgency. This happened for some, such as Menno and even Luther, with the rediscovery of Scripture in the sixteenth century; and for others, like the social gospel and contemporary "kingdom" pacifists, with the various rediscoveries of the "historical Jesus" that historical criticism made possible. As far as creation of community is concerned, that is also no doubt heightened by persecution. Since the modern age of religious tolerance, many pacifists have found community in religiously motivated service to society's outcasts and in dedicated work to change the conditions of social life that perpetrate economic injustice and the ever more immense threat of war's destruction.

Yet one may hardly remark approvingly on the congeniality of pacifism with a practical and committed way of life without noting the fact that holy war ideologies are likewise anchored in concrete, converted, and disciplined communities. What sets pacifist communitarianism apart from holy war fanaticism, enabling the former to bear out the biblical ideal of discipleship that the latter certainly betrays?

From a New Testament standpoint, it is striking that holy war advocacy and pacifism construe and depend on wholly different relationships between persecution and cross-bearing. Christian holy war advocates have virtually always been themselves the objects of persecution or duress, real or perceived. Some pacifists (first- and second-century Christians, Anabaptists, and Quakers,

4. Martha C. Nussbaum, *The Fragility of Goodness: Luck and Ethics in Greek Tragedy and Philosophy* (New York: Cambridge Univ. Press, 1986).

for example) are in fact and historically also persecuted. All pacifists appropriate and accept suffering or its prospect voluntarily in the form of cross: as service, sacrifice, and witness to the new age. The substance of the witness is that disciples can and do live in the new life in Christ, no matter what social resistances they may meet. Holy war advocates, on the other hand, experience persecution yet cannot accept it with Jesus' prayer at Gethsemane: "Father, if you are willing, remove this cup from me; yet, not my will but yours be done" (Luke 22:42). The holy war response, to the contrary, is active and violent resistance. Although there indeed are apocalyptic strands in the New Testament that voice the sufferer's expectation of vindication by God and the extermination of enemies, no New Testament speaker urges that vengeance be taken into one's own hands, on one's own behalf (Mark 13, Revelation 20, 1 Thess. 2:14-16).

Indispensable, as we have seen, to the task of understanding pacifism is the realization that it is above all not a theory but a communal practice in imitation of Christ's servanthood and cross. In a more general sense, just war theory too is set in a practice—which some would affirm as a justice practice, and others reject as a Constantinian one. And at least some pacifists eventually analyze and theologize their practical commitments. Nonetheless, it is more true of Christian pacifism than of just war thinking that it is embedded in a concrete, shared, and converted way of life. Just war theory is not communal in any specific sense (other than that it emerges from Western cultural and moral traditions), precisely because its purpose is to unite different and even antagonistic religious, moral, and cultural communities around a set of excluding or negative and minimal criteria of mutual association in exceptional circumstances. The presupposition of these limiting criteria is positive—peace is a value and is to be sought—but while the just war theory deters infractions against peace, its so functioning does not depend on agreement about a positive, substantive view of peace or justice or even war.

Another distinction between just war theory and pacifism lies in their relative dependence on rules. When pacifist practice moves to theoretical expression, it is not exclusively or primarily via criteria or rules, not even an absolute injunction not to kill (though it is hard to make a global generalization that rules about violence are and always have been avoided).[5] Christian pacifism is nourished primarily in spiritual fellowship, prayer, and communal rededication to social action; just war theory is refined through more analytical means, by increasingly stringent and self-critical application of its criteria, increasingly nuanced to changing historical and technological contexts of war.

5. Richard B. Miller comments that "Christian pacifists develop their views by appealing not only to negative duties (e.g., nonmaleficence) but also to positive duties, theories of virtue, social ethos, the nature of violence, the beneficial outcomes of nonviolence, and the fundamental religious beliefs according to which ethical claims gain added force and intelligibility" ("Pacifism and Just War Tenets: How Do They Diverge?" *Theological Studies* 47 [1986], 468).

to have permeated thoroughly the texture of actual moral existence does not result in narrow behavioral definitions of who is to be considered a disciple, or in clear boundaries between disciples and outsiders, or between the Christian's "old" and "new" selves.

A comparable tension between the near kingdom and the living community is glimpsed in other areas, such as slavery, the redistribution of wealth to the needy, and the inclusion of women as equal disciples. In all these areas, as in that of violence, a commanding vision of inclusiveness and solidarity is at once powerfully radical and tenuous in its transformation of ingrained patterns of life. For instance, Jesus' attitude toward women is iconoclastic for his time, and Paul addresses women leaders in the early churches, consistently with Galatians 3:28. Yet it is no doubt unrealistic to think that a couple to whom Paul writes (Prisca and Aquila, Rom. 16:3) experienced a nonpatriarchal metamorphosis of all their personal and social relations, even though their joint church leadership was unusual and radical. Paul himself recognizes women's role in public worship, even while he urges on them traditional forms of respectable feminine demeanor (1 Cor. 11:5). Similarly, Christians living in communities shaped by gospel inclusivity still possessed both slaves and wealth.

Moreover, in the New Testament, change never occurs via intentional adherence to a superior moral system, but by conversion to more compassionate and inclusive attitudes. It is not possible to "get to" the kingdom by a system of prescribed behavior, as the New Testament recognizes in its preference for parable, story, image, and exhortation over moral argument and in its ambivalence toward the law.

Just war theory differs from pacifism not only insofar as it is precisely that—an ethical system—but because it also is not addressed to Christian pacifism's question of what the kingdom is or entails. Just war theory speaks to relations of citizens and of states in the political world. If we miss the incommensurability of level, audience, and purpose between just war theory and pacifism, we misunderstand both and conflate the frameworks in which they need to be understood.

It is precisely this lack of conceptual fit between just war thinking and pacifism that drops out of sight when war is depicted as a work of love. Just war is not only more appropriately but more safely engaged, not as an enterprise of the love command, but as an undertaking of justice. Just war thinking recognizes the natural dignity and value of all human persons as creating a prima facie duty not to kill, but it also seeks ways to resolve conflict situations in order to preserve the public order and common good. The Thomist over the Augustinian paradigm has this to recommend it from a biblical and Christian point of view: not that it more explicitly takes into account the core command of the New Testament, but that it less pretends to do so. (The first-order justice considerations in pursuing and limiting war can certainly be highlighted and reinforced by Christian considerations, such as recognition of God as Creator of all and of Christ as Redeemer of all. Yet these will retain a secondary character in the just war framework.)

The final issue is whether, in its dialogue and working partnership with the culture and its values, Christian moral thought—particularly about justifying war—has "sold out" some definitive quality of discipleship, something without which Christian commitment cannot survive or can do so only in a sadly reduced state. Although early Christians certainly marked themselves off from their culture in certain ways, they did not see the cultivation of a unique moral identity as an overriding concern. When cultural practice was consistent with the gospel, they adopted it, and even—for better or worse—adapted their own communal forms to social institutions. There was no strict division between the sect and the culture.[8] Christianity was neither an elitist nor a sectarian movement, as the Essenes had been within Judaism. The first believers were, as now, trying to live in two worlds, which sometimes coincided and sometimes conflicted.[9] Yet the sine qua non of moral discipleship is inclusive forgiveness and compassionate service, and these are grounded in converted community life. Nonviolence flowers from this life, and it is hard to say that it is in relation to it a dispensable component, for an unwillingness to harm seems virtually required by the essential Christian virtues.

Do the virtues of compassion and mercy survive the just war project? Although it may be true that just war thinking begins with a presumption against war, the focus on the exception grew from Augustine to Aquinas and onward, so that what might have originally begun out of an inquiry as to the practical meaning of discipleship became distorted. Needed today is a way to move away from the focus on the atypical and back to the foundational Christian moral sensibility—unity with and in Christ—while still allowing the realization that the foundational gospel commitment is lived socially and historically.[10] Treating the right of self-defense, even when exercised on behalf of an innocent victim, as the point of departure has a way of insidiously shifting the foundation of the discussion to a different view of the moral life than that embodied in the gospel. The foundation of moral reflection becomes, not a discipleship of love and the cross, but self-assertion and the *limitation* of the obligations to include, to love, to forgive, to serve.

## BIBLICAL COMMUNITIES AND DISCIPLESHIP TODAY

A project that may be helpful in reestablishing the gospel as an integral base of Christian thought about violence is a trend toward seeing the Bible itself

8. Wayne Meeks, *The Moral World of the First Christians* (Philadelphia: Westminster, 1986), 106.

9. Ibid., 161.

10. Even in the New Testament churches, "negotiating the inevitable tension between radical renewal which challenges the given realities of the world and accommodation to generally accepted views of good behavior was clearly a problem." Overarching criteria of acceptability and universal answers are not objectives warranted by the New Testament model. "Resolution of particular instances depended upon the discernment, persuasive or prophetic power of individual Christian teachers and communities" (Perkins, "Ethics, New Testament").

as a product of early experiments in discipleship, ventures that it both reflects and historically enabled. A normative interest in biblical authority for the church and its moral practice could then find expression in the question, Can the Scriptures somehow enable our own discipleship communities to resemble the prototypical ones, especially by means of an analogous challenge to the status quo? Efforts to relate the Bible to ethics via the notion of community formation have gathered significant momentum in the past two decades.[11] We would be likely to add now that Scripture and other sources, such as tradition, experience, the empirical sciences, and philosophy, are not even fully distinguishable from one another. Especially when the emphasis is on communal formation and practice, the ethicist or biblical critic will recognize that all these shaping factors are already at work when explicit reference to any one is made.

A significant number of biblical scholars employ such tools as sociology, social history, and cultural anthropology to better understand how the New Testament narratives interacted with their original environment and functioned in the creation of communities that were not only of religious significance, but of integral social, political, and economic import. Christian communities always give meaning and content to discipleship within specific social situations. Of vast importance in shaping a more praxis-based approach to Christian ethics has been the emergence of the liberation theologies, whose orientation toward concrete sociopolitical outcomes is deeply ethical.[12]

Lively current discussions of biblical authority (including moral authority) as located in community reflect tacitly the postmodern context of theological inquiry. Over against the modern, Enlightenment confidence in the power of critical reason to unmask hidden interest in favor of objective, universal knowledge (a standpoint reflected in the first wave of historical criticism), postmodern thought does not necessarily give up truth claims. But it "is more likely to see truth served by divesting oneself of the conviction that we possess

11. See James M. Gustafson's "The Place of Scripture in Christian Ethics: A Methodological Study," *Interpretation* 24 (1970): 430–55. Reprinted in James M. Gustafson, *Theology and Christian Ethics* (Pilgrim Press: Philadelphia, 1974), 121–45. Even as his essay reveals that the problem then tended to be construed in terms of how the Bible could furnish the ethicist with definite moral rules, principles, or ideals, it moves the discussion toward a more communal and practical understanding both of biblical authority and of the interworking of biblical and other sources in forming the Christian moral perspective. See also Pheme Perkins, "Scripture in Theology," in *Faithful Witness: Foundations of Theology for Today's Church,* ed. Leo J. O'Donovan and T. Howland Sanks (New York: Crossroad, 1989), 122.

12. The Peruvian Gustavo Gutiérrez coined the phrase "theology of liberation" in 1968, publishing his view of all theology as "critical reflection on historical praxis" in 1971 (*Teología de la liberación* (Lima, 1971); trans. as *A Theology of Liberation: History, Politics and Salvation* (Maryknoll, N.Y.: Orbis, 1973). See also David Tracy, "The Uneasy Alliance Reconceived: Catholic Theological Method, Modernity, and Postmodernity," *Theological Studies* 50 (1989): 569; and Matthew L. Lamb, "The Dialectics of Theory and Praxis within Paradigm Analysis," in *Paradigm Change in Theology: A Symposium for the Future,* ed. Hans Kung and David Tracy (New York: Crossroad, 1989), 63–109.

unshakeable foundations on which to adjudicate claims to truth,"[13] and is committed to seeking the disclosure of reality in language, discourse, and dialogue. Hence the crucial importance of community as affording continuity and as testing dialogue in action. It is within the church as faith community that the Scriptures assume authority; the church is the community whose language and dialogue are shaped by the scriptural witness.[14]

Wayne A. Meeks shows how hermeneutical and historical issues are inseparable from ethical ones and calls for "a conversation between social historians of early Christianity and Christian ethicists."[15] In *The Moral World of the First Christians*, Meeks explains that the New Testament literature functioned in a process of resocialization, in which new identitites and new social relationships are established, even though members of the Christian community may live simultaneously in other communities with other values.[16] A "hermeneutics of social embodiment" neither patterns contemporary community on the historically described world of the first audience, nor on the internal dynamics of a literary product or narrative structure conceived ahistorically. Instead, it investigates the patterns of interaction between biblical narratives and their generating environment, then seeks appropriate recapitulations of such patterns in the contemporary church.

Meeks accepts that not all social interactions indicated by texts historically understood are ones we necessarily want to replicate. Not only may our own situation be different in morally relevant ways, but the New Testament communities may have accommodated to their culture in ways from which time has given us more critical distance. Hence, the notion of analogy (a word Meeks does not use) may be helpful.

Meeks and others suggest that what should be analogous are communities themselves, and that historical and sociological study can help provide criteria of adequacy for analogous communities and action by revealing the impact the earliest Christian communities had in their sociopolitical contexts. Both the first Christian communities and latter-day ones are transformations and resocializations that sometimes challenge, sometimes reorder, but also sometimes incorporate the values and structures in which their members participate; the shape and reality of life in Christian community is constantly responsive to its actual circumstances.

Several exegetical studies use sociological and historical tools to illumine the originating environment of biblical materials, and so disclose the interaction both of narrative and community and of community and society. These

13. David E. Klem, *Hermeneutical Inquiry,* vol. 1: *The Interpretation of Texts* (Atlanta: Scholars Press, 1986), 21.

14. David H. Kelsey, *The Uses of Scripture in Recent Theology* (Philadelphia: Fortress, 1975); Darrell Jodock, *The Church's Bible: Its Contemporary Authority* (Minneapolis: Fortress, 1989), 74–75.

15. Wayne A. Meeks, "A Hermeneutics of Social Embodiment," *Harvard Theological Review* 79 (1986): 184.

16. Wayne A. Meeks, *The Moral World of the First Christians* (Philadelphia: Westminster Press, 1986), 126.

studies are motivated especially by an interest in economic and class justice, but they frequently address as a related issue the repudiation of violence as a means of social change. Far from exhibiting an arcane interest in past meaning, this scholarship makes direct recommendations about the normative character of the radical social configurations embodied by the New Testament communities refracted through the Bible. Historical research thus becomes a necessary first step in the constructive ethical task, and the concrete social strategies of biblical narratives become components of their normative status. Many of these authors reflect a Marxist concern with production, consumption, and control of the means of production as basic to social relationships, particularly exploitative relations between poor and rich. In setting a specific context for such relations at the time of Jesus or of the genesis of the New Testament, they draw on history, sociology, and cultural anthropology.

A common presupposition is that ancient Palestine exhibited an "embedded economy," that is, one in which the economy is not a separate sector but is enmeshed in religious, political, and cultural institutions to a much greater degree than in modern societies.[17] Moreover, in traditional peasant societies, social goods (both material and nonmaterial) are perceived to be limited, so that the welfare of all persons is thoroughly interdependent, and any improvement in the situation of one is thought to occur at the expense of another. Patron-client relations characterized by hierarchy, asymmetry, inequality, power, and status largely determine the way in which resources are channeled.[18] Obvious consequences for the subsistence-level economy of the peasant village are high levels of anxiety, subservience, resentment, envy, and competition, as well as in-group loyalty centered on the family.

New Testament commentators such as Richard Horsley, Halvor Moxnes, Michael Crosby, and Ched Myers see historical research as crucial for discovering the ethical relevance of the Bible today, and all rely on the hypothesis of an ancient "embedded" economy. In several books on the socially revolutionary nature of the Jewish Palestinian movement focused on Jesus, Horsley, for instance, uses social history and sociology to examine "the salvation embodied in Jesus . . . in its historical context of concrete political, economic, religious relationships."[19] In his view, the communities of the Jesus movement, for which "kingdom of God" functioned as a symbol, renewed the social

17. See, for instance, Halvor Moxnes, *The Economy of the Kingdom: Social Conflict and Economic Relations in Luke's Gospel* (Philadelphia: Fortress, 1988), 28–30. He and others draw centrally on Moses I. Finley, *The Ancient Economy* (Berkeley: Univ. of California Press, 1973). On this theme as well as those of reciprocity and redistribution, also note Richard A. Horsley, *Jesus and the Spiral of Violence: Popular Resistance in Roman Palestine* (San Francisco: Harper and Row, 1987), 152–53, Horsley, *The Liberation of Christmas: The Infancy Narratives in Social Context* (New York: Crossroad, 1989), 68–70; Horsley, *Sociology and the Jesus Movement* (New York: Crossroad, 1989), 88–92; Ched Myers, *Binding the Strong Man: A Political Reading of Mark's Story of Jesus* (Maryknoll, N.Y.: Orbis, 1988), 47–53; and Michael H. Crosby, *House of Disciples: Church, Economics, and Justice in Matthew* (Maryknoll, N.Y.: Orbis, 1988), 102–4.

18. Moxnes, *Economy of the Kingdom,* 36–47.

19. Horsley, *Liberation of Christmas,* xii.

order, especially through local communities as new "families" that were nonpatriarchal, but "tightknit and disciplined." A special feature was the concrete cooperation and care of these members of communities for one another, expressed in the saying, "love your enemies," which Horsley refers not to external political enemies but to renewed reciprocal generosity among households.[20] In *The Liberation of Christmas*, Horsley explicitly draws a modern analogy to the exploitative relation of North America to Latin America, highlighting religiously inspired "base communities" as a powerful source of political and economic change.[21]

Ched Myers reinforces the emerging consensus about the inclusive implications of Christian community by focusing on the problem of violence. He argues that Mark's Jesus confronts the powers via militant nonviolence (1:21–3:35), instructs in revolutionary patience (4:1-36), presents an alternative eschatological community of compassion and inclusivity (4:36–8:9), and calls the disciple to servanthood and the way of the cross (9:30–10:52). Myers calls Mark's ideology "an *analogue* for our modern practice of revolutionary nonviolence."[22] Nonviolence begins in the family and household, by means of a nonpatriarchal and nonhierarchical community. Grass-roots Christian communities constitute a "revolutionary strategy" against power and domination and establish a new social, economic, and political order. The baffling "silent ending" of Mark is interpreted as a solicitation of the reader's discipleship commitment; the challenge of discipleship can only be resolved in practice, not in a text.[23] The Gospels are subversive ideologies, conducting a "war of myths" with the dominant ideologies. Hence a political reading seeks "a distinct relationship" between the Gospel and its setting, specifically one that challenges whatever may be the reigning social and economic hierarchies maintained by violence.[24] Social science contributes, either by looking for social indicators within texts, or offering historical information about the likely social worlds grounding texts.

Several authors—for example, Yoder, Hauerwas, Myers, Richard Cassidy, and (less decisively) Horsley)—emphasize pacifism (but not nonresistance) as a crucial aspect of Christian communities analogous to the communities of Jesus and the Gospel writers. But they do not approach it prescriptively, as an absolute rule derived from the injunction to "love your enemies," or even from Jesus' death on the cross. There is a consensus that moral norms are justified not as transcriptions of biblical rules, as entailments of crucial events, or even as references to key narrative themes; but as expressions of

20. Ibid., 92, 122–23, 125, respectively.
21. Ibid., 27–43.
22. Crosby, *House of Disciples,* 22–23, 41, 86, 47, respectively.
23. Ibid., 398–401.
24. Richard J. Cassidy, an author with high interest in nonviolence, seeks information about social circumstances to support his claim that the Lukan audience was called first to "allegiance" and then to "witness" by challenging Roman rule and rejecting violence (*Society and Politics in the Acts of the Apostles* [Maryknoll, N.Y.: Orbis, 1987].)

and inseparability of present and future aspects in the teaching of Jesus that make extrapolation of his kingdom preaching so endlessly controversial and richly provocative.

Even without issuing a final judgment on the theological credentials of an expected "event at the end of history," we may conclude that, at a minimum, kingdom futurity as divine transcendence and sustenance is required by New Testament eschatology as a prototype for the faith texture of discipleship. The kingdom is both present or immanent in our experience, and transcendent in that it is graciously enabled by the saving inauguration of a new divine-human interaction, a mutually responsive relationship profoundly beyond human creation or control. The question of violence, then, turns not on whether a new life is only partly possible now, because the kingdom is moving in a linear progression toward a future greater fulfillment. Pacifism as a mode of Christian discipleship depends on whether, in presently living out of the kingdom-as-reality, we see, trust, and lay hold of a judging but sustaining power that enables us to respond to the "other"—stranger, friend, or enemy—with the compassionate, enfolding love that is God's. If Perrin, Beasley-Murray, and others are right that the Lord's Prayer captures kingdom futurity, we see the tensive mutuality of future and present in the petitions, "Your kingdom come. Your will be done, on earth as it is in heaven" (Matt. 6:10) and "forgive us our debts, as we also have forgiven our debtors" (Matt. 6:12; cf. 14-15). The immediate presence of the kingdom to us, combined with its "out of reach" dependence on God's sovereign and gracious act, produces the eschatological tension. It also produces the prospect of judgment on those who either despair of transformation now or pretend to it via a purely humanitarian moral project.

The ultimate question, then, becomes the credibility of this biblical future expectation as enabling present Christian action by grounding it in a realm of existence, meaning, and redemption that is beyond humanity and history as such. This transcendent grounding may culminate in an event at the end of or beyond history (as New Testament expressions of faith seem to presuppose) or not (as some contemporary theologians feel forced to conclude[28]). But it inevitably is the "future" power in the "present" that sustains compassion, forgiveness, and even nonviolence as the edge of God's healing action amid the ambiguities, evils, and despair of history. "If Christ has not been raised, your faith is futile and you are still in your sins" (1 Cor. 15:17). So also futile, the pacifist might add, would be our slender hope that the kingdom already is present among us, even where only "two or three" are gathered in Christ's name (Matt. 18:20) and aim to shape their action after his example.

28. In *Ethics from a Theocentric Perspective,* 2 vols. (Chicago: Univ. of Chicago Press, 1981, 1984), James M. Gustafson evidently has taken this radical but honest option.

# INDEXES

## MODERN AUTHORS

# SUBJECTS

Stories for Kids
on phone

(301-) 372-1733

↑
Free call for all DC Metro
exchanges - new story
every day